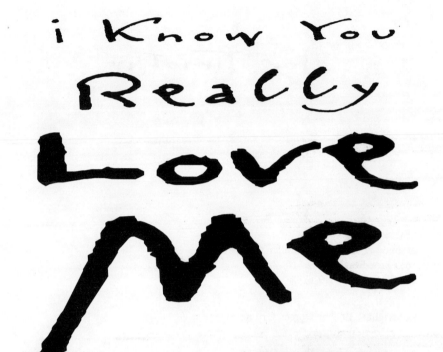

i Know You Really Love Me

A PSYCHIATRIST'S

JOURNAL OF

EROTOMANIA,

STALKING, AND

OBSESSIVE LOVE

DOREEN ORION

MACMILLAN • USA

For Timothy

MACMILLAN
A Simon & Schuster Macmillan Company
1633 Broadway
New York, NY 10019-6785

BOOK DESIGN BY KEVIN HANEK
JACKET DESIGN BY MICHAEL J. FREELAND

Library of Congress Cataloging-in-Publication Data available

ISBN 0-02-861665-0

Manufactured in the United States of America
10 9 8 7 6 5 4 3 2 1

Contents

Acknowledgments

I AM DEEPLY INDEBTED TO THE MANY PSYCHIATRISTS, PSYCHOLO-GISTS, researchers, and writers in the fields of erotomania and obsessional pursuit whose excellent work I have relied on for help in my own case and as the basis for formulating the ideas and opinions expressed in this book. I wish to particularly thank the many professionals who so generously shared their thoughts with me on a more personal level through interviews: Drs. Robert Fein, Bonita Hammell, Reid Meloy, Stephen Signer, Pat Tjaden, and Michael Zona; District Attorney Bob Gallagher, deputy district attorneys Howard Kelner, Rhonda Saunders, and Kerry Wells; Los Angeles police detectives Walter de Cuir and Doug Raymond; administrator Ronnie Harmon, and Congressman Ed Royce. I would also like to thank Gavin de Becker, for the invaluable information he provided, and Professor Paul Mullen in Victoria, Australia, for his helpful correspondence.

My special gratitude goes to the many victims I interviewed. Although they must remain anonymous, all were willing to share their stories in the sole hope that they might be of help to others. One who can be named, Evonne von Heussen-Countryman, is already well known in her native Great Britain due to her activism in the development of that country's antistalking legislation. I also wish to thank her for the additional information she so generously provided.

This book would have greatly suffered without Carol Olsen and the staff of Denison Library at the University of Colorado Health Sciences Center, who collected most of the research materials I used. Liz Wohlken, policy specialist at the National Victim Center was also extremely helpful in steering me in the right direction for additional information. A special note of gratitude to Dan Gelinas of Automated Retail Systems for his unfortunately oft-needed technical support and understanding whenever my computer got the better of me. Linda Fangman provided clerical support I could always depend on. So did Olga Moya and Michelle Tupper at Macmillan.

Thanks also to attorney Maggie Drucker at Simon & Schuster for her expert (and prompt) legal help with the manuscript. I also wish to thank Matthew Saver for so generously giving his considerable legal expertise in other matters connected with this book.

I wish to pay a special tribute to my most wonderful agents, Jane Jordan Browne and her associate, Danielle Egan-Miller, at Multimedia Product Development, Inc., in Chicago. Without their tireless assistance and unwaveringly honest encouragement, this book would never have been possible. I also wish to thank my editor at Macmillan, Mary Ann Lynch, for her tremendous skill in helping me—as she heard Peggy Noonan say—find the book in my manuscript. Thanks also to the rest of the Macmillan team: Susan Schwartzman, senior publicist, production editor Francesca Drago, Cheryl Mamaril, senior production manager, and Brian Phair, Beth Jordan, Richard Hollick, and publisher Natalie Chapman, whose combined dedication helped keep the book on schedule.

I also thank my friends and family for their vigilant contribution of magazine and newspaper articles on stalking. Kitty Donich's mentoring especially meant a lot to me. Special appreciation to my uncle, George Feldsher, and to my parents, Gertrude and Henry Orion, for their aid and enthusiasm. In particular, I wish to extend my loving gratitude to my cousin, Doug Roemer, whose active, ardent encouragement gave me the confidence to begin in the first place.

Finally, my love and appreciation goes to my husband, Timothy Justice, for his devoted support and incomparable companionship.

Foreword

I AM A PSYCHIATRIST WHO HAS BEEN HAVING A LONG-TERM LOVE affair with a former patient—in her mind, that is. She is an erotomanic. Erotomania is the delusional belief that one is loved by another, and it is the most bizarre mental disorder associated with stalking. Although most erotomanics today are women and most other stalkers are men, throughout the text I have alternated genders in referring to both stalkers and victims.

The following is a true story. A few minor details and dates have been changed in the interest of protecting the identities of victims, stalkers, patients, and sources. The use of a full name indicates that the name has not been altered except in the case of the erotomanic who stalked me. Her name has been fictionalized.

"Love is a madness, *furor amoris*."

—CICERO

Chapter One

SOMEONE TO
WATCH OVER ME

"DR. TROTTLE," I SAID IN A trembling voice as I began the phone call. "Remember your patient Fran Nightingale? The one I discharged from the hospital a few weeks ago? She just ambushed me in the parking lot. Do you have any idea what's going on?"

"I was afraid this would happen," he replied.

Thus began the eight-year (and counting) ordeal of my being harassed, stalked, and hauled through the legal system, courtesy of Fran and her obsession with me. Simply by responding to a nighttime call to hospitalize an outpatient who I later learned had already been under Dr. Trottle's care, I had unknowingly purchased a one-way ticket on the erotomania express.

It had been a typical weeknight in September 1989. My fiancé, Tim, and I were at home, just finishing dinner, when the phone rang.

"Damn!" Tim exclaimed. He was on call at the psychiatric hospital at which we both practiced and had already accepted two admissions whom he would see the next day.

"Maybe it's not the hospital," I suggested. But of course, it was. I knew, as I silently handed him the phone, that he neither needed nor wanted the extra work. Tim had been in private practice for two years and already had a more-than-full roster of just his regulars scheduled for the next day. He listened as the nurse told him about yet another new patient, then gave her some instructions, and told her he would see the person in the morning. Hanging up the phone, he looked at me, expectantly. I already knew what was coming.

"Honey," he began in his best I-need-your-help-and-I-know-you'll-do-it-since-you-went-into-this-profession-to-help-people-in-the-first-place voice. "Will you take an admission for me?"

I didn't hesitate to say yes. I was in love. And besides, I had just graduated from residency and had started my own practice two months before. Unlike Tim, I could use the extra work.

Ironically, if I had taken all his other patients that night, leaving Fran to him, the next eight years of our lives probably would have been blissfully uneventful, or at least free of an erotomanic's stalking me.

When I walked into the interview room on the locked ward the next day, the new patient, a woman, was sitting in a chair, looking out the window.

"Hello, I'm Dr. Doreen Orion. I'll be the psychiatrist working with you." As I introduced myself, the woman turned and looked blankly at me. I couldn't tell if she really saw me at all. Finally she said hello in a slow, measured voice, as if every syllable were an effort. Apparently she had been heavily sedated. She was of medium height and build, with brown, shoulder-length hair badly in need of combing. Her chart listed her age as thirty-eight and her name as Fran Nightingale. Her face was ordinary in its features except for its being rather puffy, as if she had slept too much. Probably an effect of the medication, I thought. She wore a hospital gown, standard procedure for newly admitted patients considered a suicide risk—such attire makes them easier to spot if they run away. Overall, there was nothing particularly remarkable about her.

"Can you tell me what brought you here?" I asked. In responding, Fran spoke slowly in a monotone, taking some time to tell her story, a not unusual one of schizophrenic breakdown. As she spoke, her movements, like her speech, remained subdued. She kept her arms stiffly folded, resting in her lap. Her feet were flat on the floor, knees together. She seemed to be wearing an invisible straight jacket.

She told me that she could not work regularly, because of her illness, but that she could and did play the flute in several amateur musical groups. I guessed that this instrument was particularly important to her, because through it, she could maintain meaningful connections with others. Fran explained that when she woke up the morning before and could not find her flute, she quickly lost control. Neighbors heard her loud screaming and banging and called the police. Fran was throwing herself against the walls. Although the officers quickly located the flute in the front seat of her car, by then, she was "too far gone." Afraid to leave her alone, they took her to the emergency room of a local hospital, where the physician concurred with the officers' assessment that she would likely harm herself. Fran, thereby, readily agreed to be admitted to a psychiatric facility. Her chart showed that this was not her first time.

During that initial encounter I found it hard to believe that the drab, unanimated woman sitting before me was capable of the intensity she described. I tried to imagine her screaming or even just raising her voice, but I could not. Fran must have sensed my inability to visualize, to connect with her story, because after she was finished she said, "I think they gave me too much medicine in the emergency room." It was as much a statement of fact as it was an explanation of her demeanor. I asked her if she was experiencing any side effects—stiffness, a thick tongue, or blurred vision. When she said she was, I went to the nurses' station to get a pill to take away her discomfort. On my return, I gave it to her and she took it immediately, telling me that she was familiar with its effect, and attempting a smile of thanks. It looked as if her face would crumble with the effort. I asked her permission to call her regular psychiatrist and told her that we would meet again the next day when she should be feeling much better. At that, Fran seemed to look at me for the first time and said, "Thank you."

Fran had been seeing Dr. Trottle on an outpatient basis for several years. I knew him fairly well. Dr. Trottle was considered an elder in the psychiatric community because he had been practicing in Tucson for many years and was affiliated with the town's only residency program as a supervisor and a teacher. I had even gone on rounds with him once or twice during my training. Now close to retirement, Dr. Trottle had also, for some years, been the medical director of a psychiatric hospital that competed with the one at which Tim and I practiced. I had never worked with Dr. Trottle on a case before, and I hoped this would be a pleasant experience: Although well respected for his clinical skills, he had a reputation for being pompous. I called Dr. Trottle later that day, hoping for the best.

"Dr. Trottle, this is Doreen Orion. I'm a psychiatrist at Tucson Psychiatric Institute. I don't know if you remember me. I just graduated from the residency program."

"Oh, yes, Doreen, of course. How are you?" he asked warmly.

"Fine, thanks. I'm calling because a patient of yours, Fran Nightingale, was admitted here last night. I need to get some more information about her."

"Admitted there? Why was she admitted there?"

"Well, she lost her flute and—"

"No, no." He cut me off. "I mean why was she admitted *there* and not here?"

"I have no idea." I had assumed that our facility was probably just closer for the police and that Fran had been too confused to tell anyone that she already had a psychiatrist who practiced at another one. Clearly Dr. Trottle was not pleased. The warmth left his voice, and his tone became cold and business-like as he briefly informed me that he had been treating Fran for schizophrenia for several years. He confirmed the medications she had told me she was taking, then abruptly ended the call.

That night I remember telling Tim that Trottle had seemed more concerned about where Fran had been admitted than why she had been admitted. Tim told me that Trottle's hospital was not doing very well. I understood that as medical director, Trottle was partly responsible for ensuring that his hospital had enough patients, but I was still naive enough to be shocked at his insensitivity. More important, I did not suspect that this new patient was soon to become a burden that would not only hinder my professional and personal life but also pose a grave threat to my very existence.

The next morning, the day after her admission, Fran was looking much better. She had washed her hair. The puffiness was gone from her face, which now seemed drawn and deeply lined, making her appear well into her forties. In what was to be one of the last instances of empathy I would feel for her, I remarked to myself that she bore the demeanor of one who had suffered a lot during her life. Someone must have brought her some clothes, I noticed, because she was now wearing an old pair of jeans and a white T-shirt, although she still wore her hospital slippers. I made a mental note to decide if I could let her wear her own shoes or if she should be kept in the slippers so she would not try to escape. Fran smiled when I entered. I took that as a good sign: Although by now the medicine was wearing off, she was still able to tolerate, even welcome, human contact. I asked her how she was feeling.

"I don't feel the medicine as much," Fran confirmed. "But I still don't feel safe."

"Are you still wanting to hurt yourself?" I asked, gently.

"I don't know," Fran answered, truthfully, it seemed.

Fran was clearly more animated than she had been the day before. Her entire body appeared to be more relaxed as well. The medication I had prescribed to take away the stiffness had obviously worked. Still, anyone seeing her for the first time would have described her as "odd." Her speech, though no longer slowed by the effects of the medication, was drawn out and exaggerated in a way that could be only partly explained by her Midwestern drawl. Her hand movements were also exaggerated, as if she were constantly misjudging the space around her. I recalled Dr. Trottle's saying he was treating Fran for schizophrenia. Schizophrenia is an illness of distorted reality. The way Fran presented herself, her posture, her hand movements, even her speech, seemed to reflect altered perceptions she was experiencing in her mind. Although she looked at me when I spoke, she frequently looked away when she answered my questions, as if this sudden intimacy with a stranger threatened her fragile equilibrium.

Fran told me that she had been living alone in an apartment for some years. When she was well enough, she was employed part-time as an insurance agent. This arrangement was perfect because it allowed her to work on commission, at her own pace. The flexibility was important to her since even everyday stress that most people could tolerate sometimes proved too much for Fran. Schizophrenics seem to have fewer reserves with which to deal with ordinary difficulties, and for Fran, a minor inconvenience could cascade into catastrophe. When she became too ill, she simply did not work, and her parents, both retired and living in town, helped her. They must have been through a lot with their daughter; Fran's chart revealed two suicide attempts and half a dozen hospitalizations since her first "break" more than ten years before. Most of those inpatient stays took place under circumstances similar to the one in which we met.

A few nights before her current admission to the hospital, Fran said, she had gone out for her usual evening walk. She had wandered through the small park in her neighborhood many times before and was not really paying attention to where she was going. It had grown quite dark when she suddenly came upon a middle-aged man, just off the path. Their eyes met and, then, through the dimness, she realized that he was masturbating. Panicked, she fled back to her apartment. At this point in her narration, Fran's ability to relate her story began to fail. It was as if she were randomly putting a puzzle together without considering which pieces actually fit; everything she said was related, but I had to concentrate intently to sort out exactly how and to discover the underlying logic.

As her story tumbled out in confusion, I was able to piece together that she had been raped several years earlier. Coming upon the stranger masturbating in the dark would have been disturbing for anyone, especially a woman who had been raped, but the incident was heightened even more by Fran's distorted sense of reality. She, like many other schizophrenics, viewed the world through a prism of paranoia that dispersed its dark images onto everyone and everything in its path. A dog's barking in the distance became a personal harbinger of danger. A broken street light was a sign of something sinister.

After the encounter in the park, Fran said, she stayed in her apartment for days, crying and barely eating, her already tenuous grasp of reality slowly slipping farther away. The morning before her breakdown, she had had a brief, lucid moment, and decided that playing her flute might bring her some relief. Not finding the instrument was too much for her to bear, and the incident that had brought the police to her apartment ensued. The more Fran told me about her difficult last few days, the looser her connection to the present became. She was soon crying freely, talking loudly between sobs about "everyone" always trying to hurt her. I offered her some tissues, assuring her that we would continue to talk about what had happened and try to find a way to help her deal with such painful situations.

Early the next day, I received Fran's laboratory results. Every patient admitted to a psychiatric hospital gets a complete physical exam by an internist as well as routine, screening laboratory work. Test results showed nothing abnormal, but something was amiss. Fran's urine tested positive for marijuana. I would have to confront her with this finding. When I walked into her room, I asked her how she was feeling.

"A little better," she said.

"Good," I replied, and sat down. "Fran, you've been smoking marijuana."

"I know—but I don't very much. Just when I can't sleep."

I told her what I was sure she had been told many times before: Marijuana would make her symptoms much worse, interfere with the clarity of her thoughts, and work against the medications she was taking. She said she understood all that, but she didn't know what else to do when she couldn't sleep. I promised to adjust her medications to help her sleep better at night. I was pleased that I might be able to help this troubled woman, to make a difference in her life. This was, after all, the reason I had gotten into psychiatry in the first place.

Ironically, I had come to Tucson at about the same time as Fran, several years earlier. I had just graduated from medical school at George Washington University and, full of enthusiasm, moved from Washington, D.C., to Tucson, Arizona, to begin my four-year residency in psychiatry. I had always wanted to be a psychiatrist, and can even recall answering the perennial question, "What do you want to be when you grow up?" with "A psychiatrist," when I was in the fourth grade. I don't think at that time I really had any conception of what psychiatrists did, other than having a vague idea that they helped people. No one in my family was a doctor or therapist, or had ever been to see a therapist (that they would admit to, anyway). Yet, psychiatry was what drew me. After majoring in psychology and nutrition as an undergraduate at Cornell University, I entered medical school knowing exactly what kind of doctor I wanted to be. Nothing but psychiatry appealed to me. I was intrigued by the unique prospect of helping people feel better than they ever had through the power of talk therapy as well as with medications.

As soon as I began my residency and finally had some responsibility and autonomy with patients, I knew I had made the right decision. Although I was working eighty-hour weeks, I was totally absorbed in what I was doing. I felt honored that strangers would entrust me with their most private thoughts in the belief that I could help them. This excitement carried me through my training and into the initial years of my private practice. Things seemed to be going right for me. I even met

Tim during my residency. He was two years ahead of me, and the enthusiasm we shared for our work intensified our personal relationship as well. I never doubted that I had made the right decision, and I could not imagine doing anything else for the rest of my life. I was still caught up in that exhilaration when I met Fran.

From the beginning of her 16-day hospitalization, I adjusted her medications, trying to give her some relief from the paranoia that led her to alienate herself from those she most needed to get well. She believed that the other patients wanted to harm her, and she refused to attend group therapy. Even though her mother visited almost every evening, Fran suspected the staff of trying to prevent these visits and accused the nurses of intercepting her mother's calls and letters.

I never met Fran's family, but the social worker on the unit told me that her mother was an elderly woman who seemed worn out and weary in having to deal with yet another one of her daughter's frequent breakdowns. Her father, I was told, had a more impatient air, as if he couldn't quite believe that Fran wasn't somehow contributing to her own problems. On hearing this, I thought how sad it was that he did not understand that Fran was not to blame for her mental illness. How could Fran possibly be responsible for believing that the other patients wanted to harm her? No one would choose to have such terrifying thoughts. Delusions were not volitional, I knew, regardless of what her father's reproach suggested, and as with most delusional patients, it was pointless to try to talk Fran out of what she honestly believed to be true. It was mainly a matter of time, of waiting for the medications to work.

Although I was in the early stage of my career, I had already seen many patients with a wide variety of delusions, both in my four years of psychiatric training and in my two months of private practice. Delusions, like the ones Fran was experiencing, are unshakable beliefs that are nevertheless untrue. Clinically speaking, a delusion is either considered "bizarre," that is, it involves believing in something that could never in reality happen, or "nonbizarre." Some examples of nonbizarre delusions include thinking strangers are out to get you or that you are on a special mission for the FBI; both of which have been known to happen. Examples of bizarre delusions are thinking that Peter Jennings is sending you personal messages through the evening news, or believing that look-alike space aliens have replaced family members or that other people are inserting even more incredible thoughts into your head.

The key, however, to understanding either type of delusion—bizarre or nonbizarre—is the word *unshakable.* Trying to talk someone out of something he or she totally and completely believes is as futile as telling Superman he can't fly. One person's delusion is often another's reality. Ask Christopher Columbus or Galileo. In fact, if someone can be talked out of his or her false belief, such as suspecting that a spouse is having an affair, then that belief is probably not a delusion. It is generally impossible to talk people out of their delusions, but I, like many new psychiatrists, had to learn this basic fact the hard way.

A not-too-unusual delusion among schizophrenics is the belief that they are Jesus Christ. Even as a first-year resident, I had seen several such patients. My supervisor tried to explain that it was no use attempting to talk these patients out of their Messianic delusions. But being young and inexperienced, I thought that with a little patience and understanding, I could help them see the light (or not see it, depending on your point of view). Finally one particular "divine" encounter helped me understand how naive I had been in thinking this way.

The police had picked up a disheveled, dehydrated young man who apparently had been wandering out in the Arizona desert for days and had brought him to the hospital where I was doing my rotation during my internship. Although convinced he was Jesus Christ, he accepted my offer of some food and a place to rest (which just happened to be on the psychiatric ward). While going over the routine paperwork to admit him from the emergency room, I asked without thinking, "Do you have insurance?" He replied with saintly conviction, "Ma'am, I'm Jesus Christ." I wrote down Blue Cross.

So if you can't talk patients out of their delusions, what do you do with them? Antipsychotic medications, like the ones I prescribed for Fran, are really the only viable alternatives, yet psychiatrists generally agree that delusions are among the most difficult symptoms to treat, even with the most intensive therapy and strongest medicine. I am certain there are many "subclinical" cases: people who have delusions that they don't act on or that don't significantly interfere with their lives, allowing them to function fairly well without treatment. While these are still unfortunate cases, because undoubtedly a lot of psychic energy is wasted on the delusions, what I find most tragic is when acting on the delusion ruins the life of the person experiencing it. One of the most dramatic examples of this that I ever saw occurred early in my residency. A middle-aged man and his wife wove a web of delusions out of their love that made perfect sense to them but resulted in a tragic act that would ensnare the husband for the rest of his life. This particular type of delusion, called *folie à deux*, or shared delusional disorder, is extremely rare, but it finally convinced me of the devastating power of delusional beliefs, especially where "love" is concerned.

Albert C. became known to the psychiatry service quite by accident when I was interning at a local hospital. The head of our department, Dr. Feldsher, had been called to the surgical intensive care unit to consult on a patient. As soon as he walked through the door, he was surrounded by the nurses, clamoring for the chance to tell him how pleased they were that someone was finally going to see Albert. Dr. Feldsher protested in bewilderment, saying he had not been called to see Albert at all, but was coming to see someone else. Now it was the nurses' turn to be bewildered, but they filled him in on Albert's case, anyway.

About a week before, Albert had walked into the emergency room, slipped unnoticed into a bathroom, and cut off his penis with a razor blade. He then flushed it down the toilet to ensure that it could never be reattached. As he stumbled out of the bathroom clutching blood-soaked paper towels to his groin, he grabbed the first white-coated person he saw, who, unfortunately for them both, happened to be a medical student. He handed the startled student a note written earlier that day. It said simply, "I just cut my penis off. I need medical attention." At that point, the medical student did, as well.

Remarkably, though, no one, including the surgeons, who later did a masterful job of repairing the wound and refashioning Albert's urethra, ever thought to ask for a psychiatric consultation. Surgeons tend to be rather goal-oriented: If it's not there, build it. If it's not supposed to be there, cut it out. Sometimes minor details, such as finding the cause of the problem, get lost in the surgical shuffle. The nurses hoped that in Dr. Feldsher they had found a sympathetic listener, and their efforts were duly rewarded. On hearing the story, Dr. Feldsher immediately called the main surgeon and asked his permission to see Albert who happened to have recovered sufficiently to be transferred to the psych ward the next day on Dr. Feldsher's recommendation. That's where I first met him.

Albert was forty-five and married. He was balding, short, plain, and wore glasses. Yet he somehow conveyed the impression of substantial physical power, and I recall being a little frightened of him. Since then, I have learned to pay attention to my reactions to patients and to use my feelings to better understand them, but at that time, I did not probe the source of my discomfort. If I had, I might have discovered that my fear was, in fact, a response to the rage simmering under Albert's calm exterior. It was easy to be fooled, because Albert was extremely coopera-tive, going along with whatever we asked of him during his month-long stay. He did, however, seem genuinely bewildered by our interest in him. Albert felt that what he had done had been perfectly logical under the circumstances.

Several months earlier, his wife, Sarah, began suspecting he was having an affair. She was convinced that every night while she slept, Albert left their trailer to rendezvous with his lover. They discussed his supposed infidelity endlessly, month after month. Albert tried every means of persuasion to convince Sarah of his love and monogamous devotion, but he could never prove to her that she was wrong. On the contrary, she finally proved to him that she was right.

Here is how she did it. With meticulous precision, Sarah started putting peanut butter and cat hair in the toes of Albert's shoes when he went to bed at night. Discovering that this mysterious melange had moved each morning became Sarah's "proof" of her husband's nocturnal romantic excursions. Finally, she wore him down. He came to believe that he must be doing whatever his beloved wife said he was, even if he could not remember it. He desperately searched for an answer, but how could he stop what he had no memory of? Sarah was the most important thing in the world to him. They had only been married a few years, and he had no children, no other family, and no friends. He would not risk losing her. His only solution was to ensure that he had no reason to have an affair, so he cut off his own penis. One might call this a bizarre solu-tion to a nonbizarre delusion.

While Albert was in the hospital, Sarah's demeanor toward him totally changed. She became supportive and solicitous, lovingly car-ing for him each and every day. This only served to strengthen Albert's conviction that he had done the right thing. He had saved his marriage. Sarah had never suspected what her husband was going to do, but once he had accomplished the awful act, she clearly appreciated his sacrifice, agreeing, with him, that it was a reasonable solution to their problem. It became apparent over the next few weeks that Albert, while having done a really crazy thing, was not crazy. He was just extremely dependent on Sarah. *She* was crazy. His absolute subordinance to her had driven him to accept her delusions as true. For Albert's sake, as well as her own, we urged Sarah to take medication, but she refused.

I must admit, when I first heard his story, I had a hard time believing he had actually done it. He couldn't really have cut off the whole thing, could he? I soon found out because being low woman on the totem pole, I got to do his physical exam. Actually my medical student was even lower and normally would have had the honors to himself, but I just didn't have the heart to make him go into that exam room alone. When it came time for his physical, I asked Albert if we could see his, ah, wound, fervently hoping he'd say no. But as he had with everything else we requested, he answered a hearty, "Sure, doc," pulling down his pants as if he were proud of his accomplishment. Yep, he'd done it all right. Clean off.

I tried not to dwell on that part of the exam, other than to perform the routine inspection of what was left of his male genitalia. In spite of myself, I was strangely compelled by the appearance of the feminine on this obviously male body. My medical student did not share my fascination, however, and could barely bring himself to glance at Albert's handiwork. I think he went into radiology or some other specialty where he would never have to so much as look at a living patient again.

After Albert was discharged, the couple enjoyed a few calm weeks until Sarah again began claiming that he was cheating on her. He became frantic. What did she think he was cheating on her with, he wondered. We became rather frantic as well, pondering which body part might be sacrificed next in the name of marital harmony. I pictured Albert as a faceless head propped up in a wheelchair; ears, nose, limbs, and the rest of him relinquished to the cause. Finally they both agreed to take medication. I wish I could say they lived happily and delusion-free ever after, but as is often the case, the medication did not fundamentally alter Sarah's delusions. Still, Sarah seemed to be less preoccupied with her suspicions, no longer sharing them with Albert. Her diminished accusations, along with the medication he was taking, allowed Albert to think more clearly and extract himself from the delusional web he had helped to weave. Now he just wanted to kill her.

I have always wondered if we really did Albert a favor. Would he have been better off staying with Sarah, believing he had done the right thing? Who else would now have him? Eventually, the couple divorced and with the blessing—and urging—of his psychiatrist, Albert moved away to avoid the temptation of murdering his former wife. Sarah continued in treatment but remained fairly delusional. I would often later think of this case in relation to Fran and her delusions. Albert and Sarah's *folie à deux* taught me the uniquely awesome, twisted power of delusions involving love, because if such delusions could compel someone to mutilate himself in the way Albert did (when the delusion did not even originate with him), merely confronting someone on the implausibility of his or her amorous assertions is doomed to fail. As Fran would later teach me, erotomanic delusions are just as powerful, just as impossible to talk someone out of.

During her inpatient stay, I did not learn that in addition to her easily recognizable paranoid delusions, over the years Fran had had many delusions that near-strangers, always women, were in love with her. I did not find out this information until several weeks after she was discharged from my care. In all the time we had spent together during her hospitalization and among the many areas of her life that we had covered, I never thought to ask, "Ever stalk anyone?" The question just was not part of the normal psychiatric interview that I was taught in my training.

Fran, of course, never volunteered the information. She did tell me, however, that she was a lesbian and had suffered several failed relationships with various women in which she always seemed to be the one who was dumped, in situations that fed her paranoia and usually precipitated another hospitalization. If she could have told me the truth about these "relationships" (that initially until she started stalking them, the other women probably barely knew of her existence, let alone were in love with her), I would have discovered an alarming history.

But Fran shared other, less disturbing delusions. She dreamed of making it in the entertainment industry with her music and poetry and believed that certain people in Hollywood were interested in her work and were trying to contact her. I, probably in part due to my last name, which also happens to be the name of a motion picture company, Orion Pictures, would eventually figure into those delusions as well. But for now, while Fran was in the hospital, I continued her treatment, oblivious to the potential danger of any obsession that might include me.

Despite the medication changes I made, Fran regressed and became almost childlike early in her stay, writing me angry, paranoid notes about the very changes to which she had agreed. These notes were extremely disjointed and almost impossible to understand, making me wonder if I were treating her correctly. Even more disconcerting to a new psychiatrist, when Fran became frustrated, she would let me and everyone else on the unit know by suddenly screaming and making bizarre facial expres-sions while holding her head or beating her chest. I was called several times by the nurses because Fran was yelling uncontrollably, throwing whatever she could get her hands on at whomever, patient or staff member, happened to be in the way. In a couple of these instances, she wouldn't or couldn't stop, and I had to put her in a seclusion room. There, she would bang on the door, screaming for hours. Although I knew that it would be at least a few days before the new medicines would take effect, I started to second-guess myself. Was I missing something? I was also a little embarrassed by Fran's behavior. Would the nursing staff or even my other patients begin to doubt my capabilities, just as I had started to?

One day toward the end of her first week in the hospital, I happened to be on the locked unit. I had just finished a session with another patient and was writing in his chart at the nurses' station. Suddenly I heard Fran scream "I can't! I can't!" I looked up and recognized a woman from the hospital's business office, beating a hasty retreat from Fran's room. On her way out the unit door, the woman passed where I was sitting. She turned and mouthed "I'm sorry" to me, rushing to safety with the alacrity of a passenger evacuating a sinking ship. The situation was not difficult to understand: The clerk had come to see Fran about her portion of the bill, and Fran, while still in the throes of psychosis, but well aware of her limited financial resources, must have developed some paranoid scenario for what might happen next. Perhaps she thought we would throw her out on the street or that we would repossess her car, or even her flute. I hurried to Fran's room and found her standing in the corner, screaming, alternately holding her head and pulling her hair.

"Fran, what's going on?" Her screams became shriller. "Fran," I said again in a slightly louder, and I hoped, authoritative voice. "You need to stop screaming and tell me what happened." To my astonishment, she did, immediately.

"I can't pay. I can't. I need to be here, but I can't pay!" she cried, still pulling her hair.

"Fran," I said firmly. "The hospital is very good about working out payment plans, but if you can demonstrate that you are financially unable to pay your bill, they will forgive your part of it and accept insurance only." She stopped her hands in midpull.

"They will?" she asked, hesitantly.

"Yes, they will. And you should know that my fee is separate from that of the hospital's, but if they accept insurance only, so will I."

"You will?" she asked, seeming not to believe me. When I nodded, she thanked me and said she was going to call her mother to tell her. Adjusting rates was something I and a lot of psychiatrists I knew routinely did for patients who did not have the financial means to pay their bills. Doing so was nothing personal. I had adjusted my rates for patients I enjoyed working with as well as for those with whom I had had a more difficult course. Fran apparently interpreted my offer otherwise. At the time, the speed with which Fran's demeanor changed in response to such a small gesture puzzled me. While I left her room immensely relieved that I had managed to stop this latest instance of her bizarre behavior, I wasn't exactly sure what I had done. I had never seen a patient just snap out of psychosis before.

After this episode, I found myself wondering how much of Fran's conduct was truly psychotic and, therefore, not under her control versus how much was simply a function of her personality and an inadequate way of relating to others. The latter would be more easily influenced by external factors, and unlike many psychotic patients, Fran seemed able to quickly alter some of her more outrageous actions in response to firm limit setting. I felt certain, given her history, that Fran did indeed suffer from an underlying disorder of her thinking, such as schizophrenia, but more and more, I was finding that some of her behaviors seemed to be awfully strange ways to get attention, designed to do nothing more than elicit sympathy. It appeared that as the medicines took effect and her psychosis somewhat abated, she was becoming better able to control her peculiar reactions.

For example, a few days after the incident with the clerk, Fran and I were discussing some routine problem she was having with her roommate. I was trying to get her to understand the role she might be playing in their difficulties. Suddenly she slid off her chair onto the floor, flapping her arms and legs and moaning loudly. She looked like a wounded bird, but I didn't feel any pity for her. I felt manipulated. I decided to trust my instincts.

"Fran," I said in a firm voice, remembering her response from a few days before. "If you want our session to continue, you'll have to sit up and communicate appropriately." Just as abruptly as she had left her chair, she now returned to it. I started wondering if Fran's father had been more astute about his daughter's psychiatric problems than I had been.

By the beginning of her second week in the hospital, the medications and structure on the unit seemed to be working, and Fran began to feel better. She could handle stress with more ease and she no longer believed that the staff was sabotaging her treatment. She even started playing her flute and the unit piano for me during our sessions. The songs, all original compositions, can only be described as extremely primitive expressions of her feelings about global issues, containing lyrics such as: "We have to be aware, for the earth will soon be bare." Still I gave her positive feedback for her compositions, viewing them as a constructive means of getting attention. She gave me copies of some of her songs, which I placed in her chart.

Fran continued her gradual improvement. Toward the end of her second week on the ward, she no longer screamed or pulled her hair. She started going to the group therapy, which consisted of interacting with her peers on the unit, in sessions that focused on a variety of issues, from assertiveness training to setting reasonable goals. The notes left in her chart by the various group therapists indicated that Fran was participating appropriately, exhibiting none of the paranoia I had seen earlier in her stay. Soon, I transferred her from the locked unit to a less restrictive ward, where she seemed to do well. After a few more days in the hospital, during which she received several four-hour passes with her family that Fran described as going smoothly, I became satisfied that she was stable and no longer a danger to herself or others. Sixteen days after she was admitted, I discharged her. She already had an appointment with Dr. Trottle for the next week, and I assumed that would be the last I would hear from her.

Looking back now, I can see hints of Fran's developing devotion to me during her stay. But at the time, I hadn't even an inkling of what lay ahead. The Saturday before her release, for example, I made my usual rounds at the hospital. I, like every other psychiatrist there, tended to dress less formally on the weekends. That particular Saturday I recall wearing a casual blouse and skirt that came just above my knees. Since it was still over one hundred degrees in Tucson, I was not wearing stockings. As Fran and I sat facing each other, talking in her room, she suddenly pointed to a scar on my left knee and asked, "What happened?"

The stereotype of patients asking psychiatrists questions only to be answered with another question is generally true. Usually it is more important to hear what the patient's fantasies are about the psychiatrist's personal life, rather than close off such a discussion with a direct answer. I have found that I learn much about my patients and they about themselves by exploring such fantasies, but with patients like Fran, there are other concerns. Her fantasy life had already overripened into delusions. I didn't want to encourage that trend. So instead of asking her the standard, "What do you think happened?" I simply answered her question honestly and directly. I had been in a bicycle accident several years earlier. Fran shyly looked up at me and said, "Ooh, that must have hurt really bad." At the time, her effort to connect with me had seemed painfully juvenile, but I took it as a sign, along with her diminishing delusions, that she was getting better and trying to relate to me in a healthier way. In hindsight, I see that it was an effort to be coy, but she was flirting with me in such an awkward, immature manner that my inexperience caused me to completely miss her true intent.

The day after her discharge, Fran returned to the hospital and delivered a letter for me to the receptionist. It was written in the same childlike scrawl and disjointed style I recognized from her inpatient stay. It said: "I was surprised, flattered, by your interest, since I know you and Dr. J. are an item. Hope we can pursue, but if don't respond, I'll understand" and included her phone number. I was stunned. How could she think I was interested in her? Had she mistaken my offer to forgive her portion of her bill as something more than routine kindness? I was angry at myself that I had not picked up on Fran's amorous interest while she had been in the hospital, but I really wasn't worried. I took her at her word that if I did not respond, she would drop the matter. Still, it bothered me that she had somehow managed to find out that Tim and I were "an item." Maybe she just overhead some of the staff talking, I told myself. By the time I got home that day and showed Tim the letter, any nagging doubts I had about Fran's further intentions had been calmed.

"What are you going to do?" he asked.

"Well, nothing." I shrugged. "She said she'd understand if I didn't call her." Oh, to be young and innocent again. Within a few days, another letter followed: "This entitles bearer, Dr. Doreen Orion, to free concert by sender, Fran Nightingale, length depending on ability to play." She followed up the next day by calling my office, twice, leaving a number where I could reach her. When I still did not respond, she sent me an extremely hostile, disorganized "play" she had written that seemed to be about a doctor who mistreated his patients. It contained angry, accusatory lines that told of "unforgivable behavior" and "molesting" people's minds with "psychological rape," and ended with "I hate your fucking guts" repeated over and over. With every contact, I was becoming more troubled, but I wasn't really afraid yet. Fran hadn't directly threatened me, I reasoned. If I continued not responding to her, I thought she would make good on her original promise and just go away.

Three weeks later, I had just finished seeing my last inpatient in the hospital and was on my way to my office, when I remembered that I had left my appointment book in my car. I would certainly be needing it that afternoon to schedule patients for the coming weeks. The covered parking lot was between the hospital and my office, set back from a busy thoroughfare. It was the beginning of November, my favorite time of year in Tucson: still warm enough to be out without a jacket, with the oppressive heat of the summer at last just an unpleasant memory. I was hoping that my appointment book was, indeed, in my car, and that I had not left it at home. I had done so once before, resulting in some embarrassing moments as I blankly looked out into the waiting room, trying to discern who my new patients were. Just in case the book was still sitting on my dining room table, I attempted to reconstruct my schedule for the coming afternoon from memory and was not having much luck.

Absorbed in these thoughts, I was not paying attention as I walked to my car. I could afford to be preoccupied; it was the middle of the day and I was vaguely aware that the entire lot was still. I opened the door and sat sideways in the driver's seat with my legs dangling to the ground, intently rummaging through the piles of papers and work-related items scattered about the "auxiliary closet" that doubled as my transportation. Where was the book? It was black, and even in midafternoon, the covered parking made seeing within almost impossible. It must have slipped out of my bag this morning, I hoped. Maybe it had fallen behind my seat.

Using the steering wheel as a handle, I pulled myself out of the car and onto my feet—coming face-to-face with Fran. I gasped involuntarily, but quickly stifled any further response. I needed to assess the situation calmly, not just react to it. I had been faced with potentially dangerous patients many times before, I reminded myself, and had never gotten hurt—yet. I saw that Fran was standing between me and the open door, effectively blocking any escape. She looked almost as disheveled as she had the first day I had met her. She wore a T-shirt that was only half tucked into her jeans. Her eyes had a glazed stare that frightened me. How long had she been watching me? She didn't look rational, but I didn't know if I could continue to force myself to think rationally, either, as I felt the adrenaline surging in my brain, seeming to wash away more of my psychiatric training with every accelerating pulse.

I glanced around, hoping to find someone who could help me. The parking lot was empty. I had never felt so vulnerable. Reflexively, I took a small step backward, closer to the car so that I was forced to lean against it awkwardly. But at least we were not standing quite so close. Until Fran took a step toward me.

"What do you want, Fran?" I asked, trying to control the fear in my voice, and hoping to stop her with my words.

"I've taken a lot of Navane. I don't know what to do," she said as she fished an empty bottle out of her pocket. That explained the glazed look. While she was absorbed in her task, I noticed that the step she had taken meant she was no longer blocking the space between her and the car door. I reasoned that with all that Navane, a major tranquilizer, slowing her down, I could probably outmaneuver her. I sidestepped quickly around her, shut the door and locked it. Fran stood holding the empty bottle, as if it were an offering to me.

As I started to walk away, I was more concerned for myself than for her. Fran was probably experiencing some muscle stiffness, some drowsiness and dullness of thinking, but she was not in any danger. Even ingesting a full bottle of Navane would not kill her. The worst that could happen was that she would become terribly uncomfortable, if she did not fall asleep first. Through my terror, I saw this overdose as a desperate ploy to get my attention, to finally get me to respond to her. And I knew, as memories of Sarah upping the ante on Albert flashed through my mind, that if I responded, there was no telling what Fran would do in the future.

"Fran," I said as I continued to walk away from her. "You need to call your psychiatrist. I am not your psychiatrist anymore. Do not contact me again." Not wanting to encourage her, I did not look back. But the entire walk to my office was spent in fear, straining to hear her footsteps behind me, not knowing if she would do anything to me or to my car while my back was turned. My thoughts were racing. She knew which car I drove and she already knew where I worked. She had obviously been waiting for me. For how long, I wondered. And was this the first time?

It was not until I reached my office, closed the door, and sat down that I realized I was trembling. I called Dr. Trottle immediately. That's when he said those words I'll never forget: "I was afraid this would happen." Now I understood what those who called him pompous meant. He proceeded to tell me the part of Fran's history that he had somehow neglected to mention when I first called. Dr. Trottle's initial meeting with Fran had been three years before, in 1986, when she had been assigned to him as an inpatient, just as she had recently been assigned to me. At that time, she had been hospitalized under court order for violating a restraining order.

"She was suffering from erotomania," Dr. Trottle intoned.

"Erotomania?" I pronounced the unfamiliar word for what would be the first of thousands of times to come. "What's that?" I asked. I soon wished I hadn't, because Dr. Trottle told me that Fran had believed a married law student was really a lesbian and in love with her. Fran would show up on this poor woman's front porch, guitar in hand, and serenade her with original love songs. When gentle explanations and then forceful insistence did not stop Fran's ardent pursuit, the woman obtained a restraining order. When this only led to Fran's jumping up and down in frustration on the hapless student's car, she was involuntarily hospitalized under Dr. Trottle's care. He soon discovered that this was neither the first nor the second time she had had such delusions. Nor was it even the third. Apparently Fran had become obsessed with and stalked five or six other women, all professionals of some kind. At least two of these victims had taken out restraining orders against her.

I started feeling smothered, as I had the one time I had tried to scuba dive, a few months before on a vacation in Hawaii. It was an introductory dive that included no classroom preparation, and little other instruction beforehand. I was a bit apprehensive even suiting up, and once in the water, holding onto the anchor line that was supposed to guide us into the deep, I felt none of its steadying force. Instead, all I could envision was plunging into some cold, dark, terrible unknown. As I felt the water closing over my head and the pressure building all around me, I thought that if I went any deeper, I would surely suffocate. Panicked, I returned to the boat. I felt that way again, talking to Dr. Trottle. I couldn't listen anymore. I couldn't take any more in, as if going any further into the depths of Fran's erotomanic delusions would consume me. I thought I might faint from the tingling, stifling heat closing in around me in my air-conditioned office. I had to get off the phone. I did not want to be vulnerable with the very one who had made me so.

I was unable to speak for several moments, when Dr. Trottle said, "Don't worry. I'll handle it." I hung up the phone without another word.

I sat in my office for some time, staring at nothing in particular. I could still feel the fear suffocating me. But as I replayed our conversation over and over in my mind, I gradually became aware that I could breathe again, because instead of fear, I was now burning with anger. Why hadn't Dr. Trottle warned me? Obviously, our conversation when Fran was first admitted to the hospital would have been the most opportune time to enlighten me. Surely he knew there were several male psychiatrists practicing at Tucson Psychiatric Institute that I could have asked to take over the case. And just what did he mean, he would handle it? Could I look forward to the same insensitivity he had shown when I had first called him?

I became lost in thoughts of what he had allowed to happen to me, focusing more on what he had done than on what Fran might do. It was easier to feel rage at him than fear of her. When my receptionist buzzed me, I nearly jumped out of my chair. So much for not feeling fear. My next patient was waiting and I had two more after that. How could I possibly focus on them or on anything except what I had just learned? I was resigned to not doing my best therapy that afternoon, knowing that my patients and I would somehow get through. But how would I get through the coming days and weeks? How, indeed, would I get home that night?

Chapter Two

WHEN LOVE IS JUST A DELUSION

WHEN I SAID GOOD-BYE TO MY LAST
patient that day, I was relieved to
see that it was just before five. I
knew that Tim was supervising a clinic in another town, so I ran down
the hall to the hospital's business office. I asked a male friend who
worked there to walk me to the parking lot. He was about to leave anyway but gave me a quizzical look because it would not be dark for hours.

"I've had a rough day," was all I could manage to tell him. Walking
to my car, my eyes darted everywhere. No Fran.

"Are you all right?" he asked, clearly puzzled by my behavior.

"I'll give you a ride to your car," I offered, avoiding the question and
wanting the company for as long as possible. Another quizzical look. His
car was only a few aisles down, but sensing my desperation, if not the
reason behind it, my friend agreed. I glanced as nonchalantly as I could
into the back of my car as we got in. When I dropped him off a minute
later, I made sure the doors were locked. Although it was a lovely, temperate Tucson evening, I rolled up the windows and began the half-hour
drive home, gazing into the rearview mirror all the way.

I had no idea what kind of car Fran drove. The few times I thought
a particular vehicle had stayed behind me for too long, I pulled over to
let it pass. As soon as I got home, I ran to the dictionary. Erotomania was
not listed. I paced for two agonizing hours until Tim arrived. He had
barely gotten through the door and hadn't even put down his briefcase
before I practically pounced on him.

"What's erotomania?" I demanded.

"Don't I even get a hello?" he asked with mock hurt. I gave him a look that said, "Don't mess with me," a look still possessed of the lingering rage from my conversation with Dr. Trottle. Tim quickly answered, a bit perturbed, "I don't know."

"*Webster's* doesn't either," I said dejectedly. Tim heard the despair in my voice.

"What's going on?" he asked, suddenly concerned.

"I think we have a problem," I said, and like a child in need of comfort, he led me toward the couch, sat down, and pulled me onto his lap as I recounted my day.

"Oh, sweetheart," he said, trying to soothe me. "You'll be okay. We'll figure out something." He held me for a few moments, stroking my back, when a thought came to him. Hesitantly, he ventured, "Erotomania. Isn't that what the guy who killed that actress had?"

"Oh God," I gasped, "I think you're right." I remembered the case instantly. It had gotten a lot of local press because Robert Bardo, the teen who had murdered actress Rebecca Schaeffer just a few months before, had lived in Tucson. Tim and I were quickly able to piece together the story. We recalled that the twenty-one-year-old actress, star of the television sitcom, "My Sister Sam," had been shot and killed by the nineteen-year-old Bardo that last July. He had been stalking her on and off for over two years, writing her dozens of letters and attempting to call her at her studio numerous times. After traveling to Los Angeles on one of his several visits to be near her, he showed up on the studio lot with a giant teddy bear and became incensed when a security guard turned him away. He believed this rebuff meant Schaeffer was becoming arrogant.

But, we remembered, it was apparently only after seeing her onscreen in bed with an actor in the movie *Scenes from a Class Struggle in Beverly Hills* that Bardo began planning her murder. He paid a private detective to find Schaeffer's address (which he did through motor vehicle records), got his brother to buy him a .357 Magnum, and took a bus from his home in Tucson to Hollywood. There, he quickly located her apartment, walked to the door with the gun in a bag, and rang the buzzer. As the intercom had been broken for weeks, Schaeffer came down and opened the door for him herself. They talked for a few minutes. She apparently chalked up the visit to his being an overzealous fan, telling him, "Take care, take care" as she closed the door. A little while later, he was back, and she opened the door for him one last time.

"I forgot to give you this," he said, as he took the gun out of the bag, and fatally shot her in the chest. After his arrest, police found a note in his attic with the words, "Rebecca S. 1967–1989."

As we recalled the terrible story, I became even more frightened of Fran. Is that what erotomanics did? I knew that Tim was concerned as well, although he was trying not to show it, for my sake. Ever since we had first dated, two years previously, I had marveled at how Tim had always seemed to know exactly the right words to comfort me in any and all situations. I could always count on him to make me feel better, to give just the right advice. But what could he say about Fran?

"Do you want me to talk to Trottle?" he asked.

"What good will that do?"

"Probably nothing, but it would make me feel better to yell at him," he said, trying to get me to smile.

I managed only a weak acknowledgment of his humor.

"Let's wait for now. He's still treating Fran, and I don't want to anger him. I may have to depend on him in the future."

"Okay," Tim agreed, and, still trying to cheer me up, added, "I can always beat him up later."

When he saw I still hadn't smiled, he changed his tone.

"Don't worry, we'll figure this out. She'll leave you alone."

I looked into his beautiful blue eyes—eyes I trusted more than anyone else's.

"How do you know?" I asked through the tears that had finally come.

For once Tim didn't have an answer that could comfort me.

I couldn't sleep at all that night. Lying in bed, I went over and over my conversation with Dr. Trottle and my encounter with Fran. I kept asking myself what I was going to do. What could I do? When I came up with no answers, I started focusing on what Fran might do, instead. That only got me to think more about Rebecca Schaeffer.

"This is ridiculous," I thought as I flopped on my side one more time. "There have to be some answers, somewhere." Then I suddenly realized that I just might not have to look much farther than my own home. I quietly got out of bed so as not to disturb Tim, who I noted ruefully, was snoring away. One of the things I liked least about him was his ability to sleep through anything, especially while I was lying wide awake. I went into our den where we kept our psychiatry texts and found my copy of the psychiatrist's bible, the *Diagnostic and Statistical Manual of Mental Disorders, 3rd. ed., rev.,* also known as the *DSM-III-R.* Every therapist owns one of these behemoths, a five hundred-plus-page categorization of every known psychiatric diagnosis. Revised about every seven years, this edition, the *DSM-III-R* was only two years old. Why had I not thought of this before?

Since I had never heard of erotomania in my training, I assumed it wasn't a real diagnosis. Maybe it was an older term, perhaps no longer in use. First I checked the previous edition, the *DSM-III,* which we still had a copy of. Erotomania was not listed. Dejected and not holding out much hope, I looked in the more current *DSM-III-R* and, to my surprise, found it listed in the index under "erotomanic type, delusional disorder." I could feel my heart pounding faster. Now I was getting somewhere, because that meant that erotomania, as a formal diagnosis, was only two years old. No wonder I was unfamiliar with it. I flipped quickly to the designated page and read that erotomania was classified as one of five distinct "delusional disorders." I certainly had treated patients with delusional disorders before but not one I knew to identify with erotomania.

Delusional disorders are aptly named for their prominent delusion, which may be one of five primary types, four of which I had witnessed firsthand: grandiose, jealous, persecutory, and somatic. But now I read of a fifth type of delusional disorder: erotomanic. I ran through the catalog of patients I remembered in each of the other four categories, to clarify my thinking. In the grandiose category I recalled treating a man during my residency who was convinced that he was the president of a small African nation. He had carried himself quite presidentially. In the jealous category I had seen spouses convinced of the infidelity of their mates, despite overwhelming evidence to the contrary. Sarah and Albert's case immediately leapt to mind. Tim had recently treated a man who suffered from a persecutory-type delusion: He was convinced his boss was going to fire him because the boss had not greeted him in the elevator.

Somatic delusions can have particularly disturbing consequences. Plastic surgeons, perhaps even more than psychiatrists, come across these patients, who falsely believe part of their body is misshapen or ugly and demand surgery to correct a nonexistent problem. I once saw a patient, in fact, who, after an exhaustive search, actually found a surgeon to perform a nose job on his very nice nose. But because his conviction stemmed from a delusion, he was still convinced of the hideousness of his nose even after the operation.

About erotomania specifically, the disorder I was most eager to understand, the *DSM* was less forthcoming, offering only a handful of sentences in all. It defined erotomania as the delusion of being loved by another and said that the person about whom this conviction is held, or the object, is usually of higher status. "So," I thought, with growing excitement, "Fran really does think I love her. That should be easy to fix. I'll just tell her that. . . . " But then I remembered. Fran didn't just think that I loved her, she was deluded that I did. She even knew about Tim and it didn't seem to make any difference. Dejected, I finished reading what little remained in the brief section on erotomania. The *DSM* said that what all five delusional disorders have in common is that the delusions are nonbizarre and that the individual's behavior, other than that directly attributable to the particular delusion, appears to be fairly normal.

As I read, I could feel the same suffocating fear I had experienced just a few hours before spreading throughout my body. It was as if I were reading the patterns of my life that had yet to unfold: "Efforts to contact the object of the delusion through telephone calls, letters, gifts, visits, and even surveillance and stalking are common. . . . The prevalence of erotic delusions is such as to be a significant source of harassment to public figures."[1]

"This isn't fair," I whined out loud, "I'm not a public figure. I can't afford a body guard." I reread the entire entry, hoping to glean more from it. But instead of feeling bolstered by this new knowledge, I could only come up with more questions. I now knew that erotomania existed as a known disorder, but I still had to learn what to do about it and how to extricate myself from Fran's delusional embrace.

I had to get to the library to find what else had been written on erotomania. But it took several days to make the time, since I had patients both in the hospital and others scattered throughout the week for office visits, and my first obligation was to them. Waiting was agony, but I was thankful during that time to hear no more from Fran. I started to wonder, with the false hope of desperation, if this meant she was through with me, and I almost considered forgetting about my library trip altogether.

Regular visits to the library were already part of my life. I had always loved to read, loved to learn about different cultures, different histories, and different experiences. I suppose that interest is part of what drew me to psychiatry. Most therapists would acknowledge the voyeuristic aspects of our work. Good therapists use what they learn to help their patients. But Fran was no longer my patient, and now I needed to help myself. If I gave into my unrealistic hope and allowed myself, out of fear, to believe that Fran had gone away, I would be helpless if—no, when, the other part of my brain chimed in—she resurfaced. I needed to don my professional persona and visit the medical school library to research an interesting, esoteric illness. Never mind that the topic had been foisted on me or that it deeply involved me as an individual. I convinced myself that as a physician, I needed to know more.

Thus it was that I felt confident and strong when I walked into the medical school library. I was on familiar turf, taking action, not simply waiting idly by for Fran's next crazed contact. Surely, if I just *did* something, *anything,* I could control what was happening to me. I began in the card catalog. There were no books on erotomania. Next I tried a MEDLINE search, a computerized hunt through all the articles published in nearly every medical and psychiatric journal throughout the world, scanning for the word *erotomania.* There wasn't much. Fewer than three dozen articles in all the psychiatric literature, in every language, over the past twenty years. The library didn't even have some of the journals the articles were published in, and several it did have were just brief case histories without any analysis. Still, this was considerably more than the scant two paragraphs of information I had found in the *DSM.* I set about locating the articles in the library's voluminous archives and sat down with my meager find.

Almost every study seemed to note how rare erotomania was. I knew from my medical training that each specialty has its oddities, its so-called zebras. On their rare occurrence, they are invariably trotted out for all the medical students and residents to marvel over, relishing the opportunity to amaze their friends and families with stories of what they've seen and heard. In the medical world, many of these stories are dark, others are humorous, still others are almost impossible to believe:

the bulimic who binged on Chinese food, rupturing her stomach, so hours later, the nurses were still removing moo goo gai pan from the operating room; the woman admitted for stomach pains, not even realizing she was pregnant until her baby's delivery shortly thereafter; the alcoholic who, with every admission, tops his previous record blood alcohol level and is on his feet the next day, heading for the bar. In psychiatry, erotomania was apparently considered the mother of all zebras: One author called it, in reverent, almost rapturous tones, "perhaps the most elegant and esoteric clinical bauble of this kind."[2]

While all the authorities agreed with the *DSM* that erotomania was the delusional belief of being loved by another, most felt that despite its name, erotomania really had little to do with sex; it was the romantic, almost spiritual union with an idealized true love that most erotomanics seem to crave. On reading this, I could not help feeling just a little relieved. For the last few weeks, I had tried to push away the thought of Fran's having sexual fantasies of me. I had seen in the hospital how disturbed she was and the thought of just what those erotic delusions might be was too unsettling. Now I could rest a little easier.

I quickly realized that Fran perfectly fit the profile of a typical erotomanic: Unmarried and socially immature, a "loner" unable to establish or sustain close relationships with others. Erotomanics rarely date and have had few if any sexual relationships. The delusional attachment to some unattainable and therefore "safe" other seems to be the only way these severely inhibited people can allow themselves to experience intimacy of any kind. What erotomanics cannot attain in reality is achieved through fantasy, and it is for this reason that the delusion seems to be so difficult to relinquish: Even an imaginary love is better than no love at all.

Having scant sense of fulfillment in his own identity, the erotomanic strives for satisfaction through another, yearning to merge with someone who is almost always perceived to be of a higher class or social status. Many people I had worked with in psychotherapy discussed feeling as if something was missing from their lives. For an erotomanic like Fran, it seemed to be more than just a piece of a life that was missing; it was as if her very soul was vacant and needed to be filled not only with the love of another, but also with the idealized fantasy of what that love could be. Mere reality could never fill such a void. More than just desperation, an erotomanic crosses into the realm of delusions when the distinction between self and other becomes confused. According to the studies, it was not unusual for the erotomanic to "hear" the soothing voice of her object, or believe that her object was sending her cryptic messages through others. So what Fran might experience as a psychic connection with me, was, in fact, a psychotic disconnection with reality.

All I was reading seemed so close to home, so close to my own invaded world. The studies even explained the very first letter I had received from Fran, the one in which she said she was surprised by my interest in her: The erotomanic believes that feelings originating in herself are reciprocated in kind by the chosen other, so that the concept "other" loses its meaning, devoid of the very characteristics that make it so. In fact, the boundary between self and other is blurred to the point of irrelevancy.

When one study mentioned that these delusions are particularly tenacious, often lasting years and ending only when another love object was found, I frantically skimmed the rest of the articles for what I hoped would be conflicting information. I was to be disappointed. Not only did all the authors draw the same conclusion, but several of them described specific cases in which erotomanic delusions lasted five, ten, even twenty years. The words were beginning to blur on the page. I took a deep breath and continued reading. Maybe I would find something that could make me feel better, not that I really knew what I was looking for. Once again I found myself asking, how could this be happening to me?

I soon learned how, because unlike a person who is hopelessly and passionately in love with another, there is much more at stake in erotomaniacal ardor: survival. Fran could not live without me, just as she formerly could not have lived without any one of her previous objects. One paper described an erotomanic who put these sentiments well in a letter to her "lover," the married sales manager of a large department store who once had the misfortune of smiling in her general direction and was then compelled to leave the country to escape her unrelenting pursuit: "My dearest, beloved. . . I cannot live without you. You are God of God. . . . Your high learning and important status are your two most admirable qualities. Your wise breeding will make a perfect lady out of me and in you is all I need to find security in my life."[3] This relentless suitor/stalker was dependent on her object for life itself.

Most authors seemed to agree that when an erotomanic was employed, it was usually at a job that offered little opportunity for advancement or respect, one that would be considered menial by most. Yet this was not to be construed that erotomanics were unintelligent— quite the contrary. They tended to be older, smarter, and better educated than other mentally ill law breakers, and most had at least a high school education if not a bachelor's degree.[4] Unfortunately this did not seem to bode well for their victims, because it followed that erotomanics had more resources, intellectual if not financial, to effectively hunt their prey.

I left the library feeling exhausted, helpless, and completely defeated. Conspicuously absent in any of the articles was any mention of a cure for the disorder or even an effective treatment. All the studies seemed to agree that erotomanics often required "enforced separation" from their objects, as in legal interventions such as restraining orders or jail. When I got home, I shared with Tim what I had learned. He wasn't as concerned as I was, although it upset him that I was so shaken. In the past we had both received inappropriate letters and telephone calls from patients. It was one of the job hazards of psychiatry. Somehow I knew this was different, but I could not convince him. We discussed whether or not I should get a restraining order. Tim thought that given what Fran had done, a restraining order was overkill. I thought that given what she might do, it was a good idea.

In the end we both agreed that such a move was risky. Hadn't Fran tried to destroy the car of the last woman who had obtained one against her? What more might she do this time? Besides, she wasn't coming to the house as she had with her previous object. We hoped that meant her obsession with me was not as strong as it had been with this other woman and that she really would cease on her own. Yet none of the articles had mentioned a single case in which a patient with erotomanic delusions had simply stopped.

Fran continued to phone my office and to send letters. A poem to "Medicine Wuman" in which we would cross bridges and catch moonbeams together was typical. After every contact I could not sleep for days. I constantly looked in my rearview mirror when I drove and behind me when I walked, and even searched the house when I got home at night. I no longer looked forward to going to work in the morning because although Fran had not accosted me again, I knew she came to the hospital periodically to deliver letters to the receptionist for me. At times she was even somehow able to bypass the receptionist and to place her letters, poems, and cards directly in my hospital mailbox. I felt compelled to look over my shoulder when I walked down the halls. I still grasped at the hope that Fran would just give up, but by the time five months had passed and there was no sign of her letting go, any hold that hope had on me had grown more tenuous.

True, she would enter what I called her "dormant" phases now and then, when several weeks would go by and I would receive no contact from her. During those times I would inevitably get my hopes up yet again, especially when her absences were preceded by notes containing tortured but tantalizing hints that she just might stop, as when she offered to "bail out" if I continued my silence. At other times she appeared to be mocking me, as when she signed a letter with a string of derogatory adjectives about herself, including, "stupid," "dumb," "disrespectful," "revengeful," "incompetent," and "loved to be put down," saying that since she was all those things, I should just continue to ignore her. From her disjointed prose, I could not tell if she was angry at me or if she thought I was angry at her. Perhaps it was both. As I learned in my library research, in their delusional blurring of boundaries, erotomanics often perceive themselves as both pursued and persecuted by their victims.

More often, however, Fran's letters would reflect the psychic connection she felt we shared. Once, I received a greeting card that had a picture of Bugs Bunny asking, "What's up, doc?" with a note that said she had been going through some of her aunt's things and found this particular blank card. She wondered if it was a sign. In it she also wrote that the *I Ching* told her I was involved in another relationship, which was fine with her, because even though she wanted to be with me, she had been alone most of her life. She ended by apologizing for any "disturbance" she might have caused, saying she was "hoping my love would win."

I allowed myself to hope again that my unresponsiveness had won, until I received her next inevitable note. At times it was quite eerie, and I almost questioned my own sanity as I wondered if she really could read my mind and was plotting precisely just how much she could get away with. For during the times that one letter rapidly followed the next and the intrusion seemed too much to bear, I would swear to myself that any subsequent contact would prove her last and vow to get a restraining order. Then, all the letters and phone calls would uncannily cease, and I would become calm and complacent until, inexplicably, the onslaught, whether notes on my car, letters in my work mailbox, or telephone calls to my office, would resume as before. Soon nearly a half-year of this agonizing cat-and-mouse game had passed.

For the previous two years on Valentine's Day, ever since Tim and I had been dating, I always found a present awaiting me at work. So I was not surprised that particular February 14 in 1990, the first Valentine's Day since I had met Fran, at the big smile the hospital receptionist gave me. I followed her knowing nod to the bouquet of flowers with the pink, inflatable, four-foot-long Crayola crayon sitting on end amid the blossoms. I smiled, too, thinking warm thoughts of Tim as I scanned the picture on the front of the card filled with red hearts that said, "I love you" and "Be mine." On opening it, the warmth heated to a boil as I immediately recognized the disjointed style that I had come to know so well. Of course, they were from Fran. She missed me, she said. Fuming, I gave everything to the receptionist, including the big pink crayon that now seemed a crude, farcical, phallic caricature, and strode angrily to my office. There, I was startled by another big smile, this time from the office manager, and with trepidation I walked to my desk where yet another bouquet awaited me. It was with anything but warmth that I opened this card, but I was greatly relieved when I saw that it really was from Tim. Still, Fran had ruined what should have been a pleasant personal moment during my workday.

During that time I continued to keep Dr. Trottle informed of Fran's amorous activities in the vain hope that he would somehow be able to stop her. A few weeks later, Fran put a note directly into my box at the hospital, apologizing for her Valentine's Day gifts and ending it with the word "Bimbo." Who was she calling a bimbo? I assumed she was referring to herself, but why the sudden apology? She had never deemed it necessary before. Could this mean Dr. Trottle had finally gotten through to her? Once more, I dared to hope; but a mere few weeks later, I received Fran's angriest missive to date. She accused both me and Dr. Trottle of being homophobic, noting that he had informed her that I could lose my medical license if I became involved with a former patient. She wrote that I had managed to "dull" any "romantic stupidity" she might have had, assuring me she knew her "place" and would remember I was "gentrified." Containing her characteristic garbled messages, the letter closed with the assertion that she wanted to find a new psychiatrist, and she asked that I recommend one if I could "tolerate a moment's communication" with her, that is, "if you still believe me to be so out of control that I can't keep my pants on much less head to my shoulder [sic]." She ended by saying she hoped I would respond, even though she realized I had better things to do than to deal with a "hopeless case" like her.

For Dr. Trottle to make such a blunder in implying that it was the possibility of losing my license that kept me from becoming involved with Fran (thereby allowing her to read between the lines that without such an obstacle I would have chosen involvement), he must have been feeling as helpless about the situation as I was. By planting that seed in Fran's already myth-impaired mind, he was only contributing to the blossoming of her delusions.

By now Fran's actions had eroded any empathy I had once felt for her. At times I made the mistake of confusing what she was doing with who she was, and I almost hated her. Dealing with these feelings was not easy. How could I despise a former patient? I had spent years in training, learning to treat persons with mental illnesses with sympathy and understanding. I had always liked to think of myself as a compassionate physician, but now I had no compassion left for Fran, and I found this difficult to reconcile with my professional persona. Even so, I did not care what happened to her. I just wanted her out of my life.

My ambivalence only grew as I realized how my experience with Fran was affecting how I dealt with my patients. It was changing me as a therapist, chipping away at the reserves of empathy for others in my care. I had also become more suspicious, not necessarily a bad thing, because therapists never want to take everything their patients say at face value. They may be fooling themselves and, consequently, the therapist. Still, I sometimes felt less compassionate in my sessions, especially toward patients who were experiencing unrequited love. There were times I just wanted to say, "Look, he doesn't love you. Deal with it and move on." I knew a somewhat less harsh approach was called for and was at least able to resist giving voice to these dismissive thoughts.

I was also becoming more guarded about my personal life and rarely shared any information about myself with patients. Not that I ever really did that much anyway, but every now and then I felt a twinge of nervousness when a patient asked me a personal question, something I had never felt in the past. Before meeting Fran, I had accepted nearly all comers into my private practice and even had my receptionist set up new appointments for me.

After my experience with Fran began, I started speaking to all potential outpatients myself over the telephone, first, before ever seeing them in my office, and became much more cautious about taking any-one who was not referred by someone I knew. For a time, if a patient showed a hint of difficulty in keeping in touch with reality or of being an overly dependent personality, more often than not, I referred them elsewhere. I realized this was overkill and that as a relatively new private practitioner trying to build a practice, I was losing a lot of potential business, but I was cautious not only for my own sake; I knew that I would be too wary and distant to be effective with such patients. My office staff was also learning to be suspicious on my behalf: Once, think-ing she recognized Fran's voice, my receptionist told a legitimate patient of mine that I would not be returning her call.

One particular incident with a male patient whom I had seen in psychotherapy for more than a year illustrated to me just how paranoid I had become. We had begun to work together during my residency and continued the therapy when I started my own practice. We had an excel-lent rapport, and I enjoyed working with him. We frequently used humor in our sessions to make a point. One day, toward the end of a session he did not want to end, he said, "I may come over to your house tonight." Now normally a remark like that would have been wonderful grist for the psychoanalytic mill. But for one terrified second I froze and could think of no response. All I *could* think of was a barrage of ques-tions: "He wouldn't really do that, would he? He's not the type, is he?" Of course, the idea of his stalking me was ludicrous. But my experiences with Fran had made me always wary, always vigilant.

In another instance, I was definitely not as vigilant as I should have been. In that case, my experience with Fran clouded my judgment, obscuring the vista of erotomania developing before my eyes. Beth M. was an attractive, middle-aged Jewish woman, a well-known feminist attorney in the state who was an associate at a prestigious law firm and taught a class at the local law school. She had two grown children, had published quite a few papers in legal journals, and was working on a book. Certainly not the typical person one would think could develop erotomania.

I met Beth about the same time I met Fran. Beth had been admitted to the same psychiatric hospital for severe depression. She had requested a female physician, and I agreed to work with her. Beth was sitting in her room on the open unit of the hospital when I introduced myself. Although she had been feeling suicidal, she had never made an attempt, had brought herself in, and clearly wanted help. Therefore, unlike Fran, Beth did not require the restrictions of a locked unit. She was tall, almost six feet, but well proportioned and carried herself with an old-world, European elegance that belied her modern dress of designer jeans and T-shirt. She was quite attractive, with pronounced cheekbones, a large mouth, and wide-set, expressive blue eyes. She wore her long auburn hair high on her head in a stylish knot.

"How are you today?" I began.

"I'm not sure what I'm doing here," she replied.

"Why don't you tell me what led up to your coming in?" Beth began to relate a very confusing story about the last couple of years of her life, starting with the breakup of her brief marriage. Although quite self-assured and confident in her professional life, Beth was surprisingly naive, almost adolescent, when it came to relationships. Her husband had warned her before their marriage that he was bisexual, but Beth had not considered all the ramifications of this revelation and professed now not to have understood at the time exactly what he had meant. She certainly learned quickly the day she caught her husband in bed—with another man.

She had become progressively more depressed since the divorce, exacerbated by the fact that she had few friends or family for support. She went on leave from her law practice the next year, and it seemed that the loss of structure and purpose her job provided had contributed to her growing sense of isolation and depression. She had even left the city for another one nearby, hoping the change would do her good. But it only served to further isolate her, severing any remaining source of sustenance.

While we were discussing the recent upheavals in her life, Beth seemed to have a difficult time focusing. She skipped quickly from one topic to another, asking numerous questions along the way, but frequently not stopping to hear the answers. It was not difficult to deduce that her thinking was quite disorganized, and when I asked her how long she had been having difficulty concentrating, she replied that it had been getting progressively worse since her divorce. In fact, she admitted that the real reason for her leaving was that she could no longer be productive in her practice. She could not read and comprehend more than a few sentences at a time, and she could hardly write at all. This had become especially evident to her when, just before leaving the firm, she had presented a paper at a national conference and could barely focus on what she had been saying, and in her own words had "made an ass of myself."

Beth had been placed on a number of different psychiatric medications as an outpatient but had not been able to tolerate the side effects of any one of them. The same thing occurred now in the hospital, but it seemed that the side effects she was complaining about, like other difficulties in her life, were experienced in a very unfocused way. For example, she would tell me that a certain medication made her feel "funny. . . not anxious, really, but sort of on edge, sometimes, like I'm not myself." I encouraged her to stick with it, assuring her that every medicine had side effects and that I hoped once her body adjusted, they would go away. She recognized that the alternative was to continue on as she had over the last couple of years, increasingly unproductive and unhappy and in danger of losing her job, not to mention her life. She stuck with the medicine, remaining in the hospital for about two weeks until her mood improved to the point where she no longer considered suicide an option and to where a certain clarity of thinking was restored.

When I discharged her, Beth asked if she could continue working with me on an outpatient basis and I readily agreed. As her thoughts had become more organized, we were able to do some good work in psychotherapy, looking at how patterns in her life had developed from childhood, drawing her into ever-repeating bad choices in her adult relationships with friends, co-workers, and lovers. She was extremely intelligent and insightful, and I enjoyed working with her. I must admit that I also found myself identifying with her quite a bit: We shared an ethnic heritage as well as certain family dynamics, although clearly, if such things can be quantified, hers was a much heavier cross to bear. Still, whenever I sat with her, I had a sense of "There but for the grace of God go I."

Beth's mother was a Holocaust survivor. Her father's family managed to send him from Europe to the United States only months before the Nazis invaded their homeland, but the rest of his family, his parents, grandparents, and everyone else perished. Beth's mother was the only one in her family to survive the concentration camps, but not without suffering a terrible disfigurement of her entire right arm and hand. Like me, Beth was an only child, but because my mother was American and my father an Austrian Jew whose family managed to flee to Palestine during the war, I was spared the unspeakable tales of death and survival that were woven into the fabric of Beth's daily life, and most important, the guilt and overwhelming sense of hopelessness that being raised on such memories can instill.

Like victims who live through traumas in which others have died, children of Holocaust survivors may experience "survivor's guilt." Beth was no exception. She remembered always feeling a sense of responsibility to her parents to avoid making their lives any worse than they already had been. She became a model student and dreamed of a career that would make them proud, that might take away some of their suffering, as if anything could. It was no coincidence that she had chosen a profession that would allow her to alleviate the suffering of others caused by discrimination and injustice. Yet she was told by her parents that from a very young age, she pointed to her mother's scars, an act that compelled her mother to undergo multiple corrective surgeries that left her with great residual pain. Even more for the young Beth to try to make up to them.

Her parents' Holocaust experiences left their marks in other ways as well. Her father became chronically depressed and physically ill with a variety of complaints, rarely leaving the house. There seemed to be an unspoken competition between her parents for Beth's pity and, therefore, her love. Her mother had clearly suffered more during the war and would thus have seemed to have been ahead in the race for their daughter's attention, but her father upped the ante with his chronic, mysterious ailments and, from Beth's descriptions, was overprotective to the point of paranoia. Beth was not allowed to participate in any physical activities for fear that she might get hurt, and as a result stood out in school as different, the kiss of death for a child anywhere, further sewing the seeds for her chronic sense of isolation and alienation as an adult.

Interestingly, Beth's erotomania may have been germinating in her youth. She remembered that when she was seven or eight, she developed an intense crush on an older, popular boy in the neighborhood, following him around wherever he went, becoming such an embarrassment that he finally told her he hated her. She did not stop, even then, until he moved away. "It was as if I had to be near him, even if he didn't want me. Just being near him made me feel good, even though I knew he couldn't stand me," she recalled. Beth clearly recognized that the boy did not return her affection but still could not help her sophomoric stalking of the taxed teen. There was no delusion in this obsession; that would unfold later, in her adulthood.

As we continued to work together, Beth and I set two goals: By spring Beth would resume her teaching and at least be available to her law firm for consultation on a limited basis. We had several months until that time, and these seemed attainable ends. But soon a distinct pattern developed: Whenever Beth accomplished something toward her goals, such as calling her office to hear about current cases or preparing a teaching plan, she would inevitably backslide into her previous, severe depression, helplessness, and disorganized, almost paranoid thinking. Just before my two-week vacation, Beth sunk particularly low, and I even considered hospitalizing her again.

"What do you think is going on, Beth? You were doing so well."

"I don't know. I felt so good when I went to the law library to do a little research, but then I went home and just got more and more depressed all night. That's when I called you." Beth had also been using my emergency number with increasing frequency.

"What if it has something to do with doing well?"

"What do you mean?" she asked, sitting up, intrigued.

"What does it mean if you do well? If you accomplish your goal?" Beth paused for a moment, considering. Finally she shrugged, giving up.

"I don't know," she said.

"What would happen in your family if you did well?" I pressed. I was learning that it was much easier for Beth, still struggling with traces of psychosis, to answer more structured questions.

"My parents would tell me not to get my hopes up too high. I remember the time when it looked very good that I would get a scholarship to a big-deal summer study program in high school. It was in California—it sounded like heaven. All that was left was for me to take the exam. Every one of my teachers thought I would make it and encouraged me, but my father said, 'I don't know if I can handle the stress' and got sick again. He was afraid that even if I passed the test, I wouldn't be able to handle being away from them all summer. I felt like I was hurting him."

"How did you do on the exam?"

"I failed. It was a lot harder than I thought."

"I think that's what you told yourself. I think you sabotaged that exam to save your father." Beth looked stunned, then was silent for a while.

"I never understood why Barry passed that test and not me. He was never as smart as I was," she said finally and was silent again.

"What happened after you failed the test?"

"I got real sick, I couldn't eat. Looking back, I think I was depressed."

"What did your parents do?"

"They doted on me. I didn't have to go to school for two weeks. I didn't leave my room and barely left my bed. It was as if they were rewarding me for not going. I think they were the ones afraid of not making it without me."

It did sound like she had been depressed. No wonder; her life to that point had been geared toward making her parents happy. When she finally had a chance to do something that might make herself happy, she once again had to sacrifice her wishes for theirs or risk losing everything. Still, there was some payoff in failure.

"How did it feel, to have your parents doting on you?" Her voice lowered and she spoke more slowly. I had to strain to hear her.

"Actually. . . it was nice. . . in a way. I felt so loved and cared for. . . . " Her voice finally trailed off.

"When else had you felt that way with them?"

Beth thought for a moment and then said quietly, "I can't remember ever feeling like that with them. It's strange, but as depressed as I was, in some ways, that was the best time of my life."

She looked up at me with tears in her eyes, and her pain resonated through me. I could feel a wet, sweet heaviness rise in my throat and swallowed hard, hoping Beth would not sense it and feel compelled to stifle her own sorrow to save me, too. I pressed on.

"What's the feeling?" I asked gently, although I already knew.

"I guess I'm sad because to feel loved, I had to be sick," she said wiping her eyes.

"And if you're doing well, like you were anticipating with that test and that scholarship?"

"It's kind of like a Holocaust mentality. That you shouldn't do too well because something terrible is always lurking around the corner."

"And if you do too well, the people you need may not be there for you." I paused. "How do you feel about my going on vacation?"

"Scared," Beth responded immediately.

"Do you feel as if I'm abandoning you?"

"Sort of... yes," she said, looking up at me again as if asking permission to feel this way.

"Beth," I said slowly, gently, looking right at her, "I am going away for two weeks. I *will* be back." Normally such a direct, obvious statement would not be warranted, but Beth was not yet back to normal. She looked at me, considering what I had said. Then she nodded her head as if finally accepting my statement as fact.

"Okay," she said.

Her phone calls between sessions ceased. Getting well would also mean moving back to the city her firm was in, possibly losing me in the process, but Beth said she was willing to commute to see me once a week and continued to make slow progress.

Beth did well while I was away and was even able to resume teaching and some part-time work with her firm that January, but she continued to navigate the rocky road between sanity and psychosis, stumbling frequently along the way. Her class, unfortunately, was small and involved a lot of discussion. If her students had not done all the reading she had assigned, she felt they were conspiring against her. As she struggled with tasks that used to be routine, she became quite angry with me, even blaming me for her diminished capacities. Although I had never shared any personal information with her, she saw me as a successful Jewish professional, who although almost ten years her junior, did not seem to have the same struggles with self-confidence and relationships that she did. She was angry at her dependency on me, just as she had been with her parents and began to act out her anger and "prove" her independence by missing sessions and skipping her medicines, maneuvers that only made her situation more precarious.

I felt as if I was walking a fine line. Here was a woman who had the potential to sink deeper into psychosis. If she did so again and could not fulfill her teaching duties or the demands of her law practice, it might very well mean the end of her career. Yet although we had to work through the demons responsible for her inner turmoil, to do so too aggressively while she was in such a fragile state could do much more harm than good. Then she began to tell me about the senior partner at her law firm.

He was a married man whose frequently absent wife was a head-hunter for a large international firm. He had apparently developed an interest in Beth, and they began to have lunch together and occasionally dinner. At first his interest was sparked because of his understandable and well-placed concern for a prominent member of his firm who had obviously been having a difficult time and was neither publishing nor lawyering as she used to.

This professional interest soon seemed to turn more personal, however, as he and Beth began to realize that they had in common a certain feeling of abandonment and betrayal by those who professed to love them. He told Beth that his wife was rarely at home and that even when she was, she seemed preoccupied and not interested in him. While I warned her about affairs with married men, I felt indignant that the senior partner would abuse his power in this way over my highly vulnerable patient. Beth acknowledged that if he actually propositioned her, she would not even try to resist. This truth about herself and her own vulnerabilities frightened Beth, and she would frequently cry out in anguish, "How can I call myself a feminist? How could I do this to another woman?" In her mind, it was almost as if she had already started an affair with him.

The misguided attentions of this lonely father figure were clearly not helping Beth stay on the sanity track. After a few weeks, the senior partner's wife returned, and the lunches and phone calls ceased with an abruptness that only accentuated Beth's continuing isolation and loneliness. She could not stop thinking about him, made up excuses to go to his office, called him with inane questions, and ate lunch at the restaurant they had gone to in the hopes of seeing him again. She neglected her work; she could only think of him. This was more than just a brief, adolescent regression in a previously competent woman. Beth's judgment was growing more impaired, and her behavior was becoming more bizarre. Another doctor at the hospital who knew I had worked with Beth there, had seen her at a party doing strange stretching movements. He told me, "We all thought it was pretty weird."

I suggested to Beth that she increase her medication, girding myself for the obligatory abuse I knew such a recommendation would bring. I had already waited several weeks, hoping that psychotherapy alone could pull her back from her incipient descent into psychotic perdition, but in doing so I began to recognize the control Beth was exerting on me and, consequently, on the therapy. Like a diver peering anxiously over the edge of a platform, I had been afraid to take another step. Now I plunged in. As I had feared, Beth became enraged at the indirect message that I did not trust her judgment. I held my breath, hoping that my quiet reassurances would calm her frenetic fury. It is never easy to be yelled at, especially when you cannot yell back, but even remaining silent is infinitely easier than having to focus solely on another person's best interests while she is unleashing her wrath.

Beth did somehow manage, in the end, to agree to increase the medication. Unfortunately her side effects got worse, and soon she simply stopped taking it altogether, believing that causing her physical discomfort was my way to punish her for her decidedly unfeminist behavior. I tried to interpret to her that she was really trying to punish *me,* that stopping the medicine was an extremely self-destructive means of expressing anger at me, her parents, the senior partner, and anyone else she felt had ever betrayed her. But the combination of the abandonment by the senior partner and the absence of psychotropic thought-glue— the medication—made her downward spiral ever deeper. She began to think other people "knew" about her "relationship" with him. She wondered if he would be angry and retaliate if she dated other men.

I urged her to resume her medication, but she angrily spat back she would not. Surprisingly she seemed to pull herself back a bit from the brink when she acknowledged during our next session that thinking her boss would retaliate was not rational. I hoped this would presage a lull in her psychotic symptoms, never entertaining the thought that much of what Beth had told me about her senior partner, starting with his developing a personal interest in her, was probably as factual as Fran's delusional beliefs about me.

Beth had somehow managed to complete her limited duties for the semester, but the structure inherent in academic life, so crucial to containing her tattered psyche, was coming to an end. Without some additional support, getting through her upcoming summer break would be like wading through quicksand in a fog. To try to contain the potential devastation to her sanity, I recommended that she attend an outpatient therapy group and set about trying to find a gentle, supportive one in her town. The choices were limited and I am afraid in the end, it would have been better to have had no group at all.

A psychologist I barely knew ran a therapy clinic near where Beth lived. Her daughter, also a therapist, and I were close friends, and knowing that the daughter did good work, I foolishly assumed the mother did, as well. She had even won a local "Morningstar" award for the charity work she did through her center. I soon discovered she was more of a supernova: overbearing, overpowering, and completely overwhelming my patient. When Beth mentioned in group that she was having some trouble with her car, Helen responded that her husband, a mechanic, would take care of it. When she discussed feeling anxious at the prospect of developing a class schedule for the spring, Helen set up an appointment so she and Beth could work on it together. Unfortunately this only mirrored Beth's family dynamics, underscoring her feelings of helplessness, incompetence, and dependence. In her already-depleted state, she could not cope with this new onslaught by Robotherapist. Beth felt under fire, as if the last, albeit disorganized parts of herself were being ripped completely away. Like a Buddhist meditating on a single syllable to clear the mind, Beth created her own enlightened center by renewing her focus on the senior partner.

She told me that she had driven by his house, gotten out, and removed a pebble from his front yard that she now kept in her bedroom. Psychiatrists call this a "transitional object." Young children normally use such transitional objects as blankets or stuffed animals to represent a comforting figure, to substitute or transition for parents when they are not there. Beth had regressed to this point. I finally persuaded her, yet again, to take medication, and wrote out a prescription that she promptly "lost" by the next session. Then she dropped another bombshell.

"I've decided to ask him, in writing, if he plans to leave his wife. I don't understand what he wants from me, and this is the only way to find out for sure." It took me a full ten minutes to convince her that this was very poor judgment indeed and might prove the fatal blow to her already tenuous career. Just when I felt my eyes roll back into their sockets, Beth let loose with yet another jolt.

"You know, if I were a therapist, I would plant spies around my patients to see if what they report is true or not," she said, eyeing me coyly. "Is that what you do?" Normally when a patient presents a fantasy like that, the standard psychoanalytic response would be to explore with them what that would be like. Beth, however, was not a standard psycho-analytic patient.

"No, Beth," I said, "I never do that and never would. It is completely unethical. No therapist would ever do that."

"I've always thought you had people reporting to you about me," she said, almost as surprised by my answer as I was by her question.

It was ironic indeed that I had had someone, albeit unsolicited, report to me about her. But in Beth's delusional state, I could not ask about that specific person. That would have been like Dr. Trottle's telling Fran she and I could not have a relationship even if I wanted to.

"You mean you've thought this since we started seeing each other and never brought it up before?" I asked instead, incredulously. At her nod, I repeated again, "No, Beth. No. It just doesn't happen. Therapists do not plant spies." But the strangeness of that session was only just beginning. She went on to say that she had had a urinary tract infection over the weekend and had gone to the emergency room for treatment. There, a woman physician examined her.

"It was amazing. I instantly felt better when she touched my vagina, put something, a catheter, I think, inside me. I think I just needed to be touched." Then her face abruptly clouded as she turned angrily to me.

"And you . . . you did nothing for me. All she had to do was touch me, but how long have I been coming to you? For what? To feel like this?"

"Beth," I began.

"So you can't help me, so you send me to that *group*." She said the word as if it were an epithet. "What, did you do that to punish me? To show me how sick I was because I wouldn't take your medicine?"

"Beth, I wouldn't punish you. It's your choice whether or not you take the medicine, but I felt then and I feel now that it would help you."

"What's going to help me is to see someone else. I've made an appointment with Dr. Douglas. I want a second opinion."

That stopped me in my tracks. I had been preparing to provide more measured arguments against whatever she said; instead, I found myself agreeing with her. I thought a second opinion was a marvelous idea. I was afraid to sound too enthusiastic, however, for fear she might think I was colluding with him as well. I knew Dr. Douglas, her previous psychiatrist. He was very good with medications but did not do any sort of therapy. I was certain he would agree with my assessment; maybe he could convince her to take medicine.

During that arduous hour, I tried to remain calm, modeling the appropriate way to resolve differences, gently feeding reality back as she regurgitated fantasy. I began to realize that while Beth had been losing control over her thinking, she had been exerting progressively more control over me, in terms of my reticence to alienate her further by pushing her harder to take medication. As the situation became more critical, I recognized that I needed to discuss my helplessness so that I could better help her. I went to see an old supervisor from my residency whom I trusted and respected. After I related Beth's history and the history of our work together, he asked a few questions and after a long pause, commented, "This is a very difficult case." Although I certainly knew that already, I was relieved that it also seemed difficult to someone with a lot more experience and knowledge than I had.

"When the ER doctor touched her, she felt some kind of intimacy that immediately seemed to make her feel better. What do you make of that?" he asked. I had been thinking about that quite a bit.

"Well, it seems as if that woman doctor was a stand-in for me, yet when she feels close to me, she gets scared and acts out. She certainly doesn't feel better."

"No," he agreed, "but she can allow herself to feel better when the intimacy is less threatening, when it is one step removed from you." I nodded that I understood. "Closeness, caring, and intimacy always had strings attached in her family. Nothing good ever came from those feelings. There were no boundaries. Closeness was really a license to invade, but the only way to experience closeness was by being invaded. I think that's why she felt better immediately when that doctor invaded her, so to speak. Now as an adult and because of her thought disorder, she still has difficulty drawing boundaries with other people."

"Like with her senior partner," I interjected.

"Like with you." At my look of surprise, he continued. "She's terrified that if she has no boundaries, perhaps you don't either." He paused a moment so I could ponder this, then added, "She defends against her closeness to you with mistrust and rage."

"Yeah. She thinks *I* yelled at *her*." I said.

"Exactly. She turns it around because she doesn't know where she ends and you begin. That's why she gets suspicious when she thinks you care about her and when she feels close to you in return. What she does is project her suspiciousness and mistrust on you; that *you* don't trust her and send spies after her, that *you're* angry at her and yell at her. So she keeps her distance by acting like a little girl and doesn't do what her 'parent' wants, in this case take medication or come to sessions. Realize, too, that taking medication is a metaphor for taking something of you inside of her. Just like the ER doc; a kind of intimacy."

"But she needs the medications." I protested. "She's pretty psychotic right now."

"You're right. She does. But right now she may not be able to take them from you."

"So what do I do?"

"I think it's a good thing that she's going back to Douglas for a second opinion. What she really wants is to see if her other parent approves of you. I'm sure he'll agree that she needs the medicine, and she may be able to take it from him since they have a less intense relationship than the two of you do."

I left his office feeling more optimistic about Beth than I had in a long time. As helpless and out of control as she and I had both been feeling, I now had a much better handle on what was happening and how to help her. During our next session, Beth told me that her last class had not gone well and she blamed it on her senior partner.

"He did that. He wants me to fail so he can get rid of me."

"Beth, the senior partner has a professional stake in his associates doing well. He had nothing to do with the class. I think you want to believe that he is intimately involved in your life. You wish that he had more contact with you, so you make yourself believe that he does, even if it's in a way that hurts you."

Beth was silent a long time, thinking about what I had said. I had purposely been more direct and less empathetic because from my conversation with my supervisor, I believed Beth would be better able to listen to me if I presented things in a less sympathetic way.

"Okay, I can accept that, but I know he really loves me," she finally said, and added that she had an appointment with Dr. Douglas the next week.

"Good," I said as dispassionately as I could and added in my most disinterested voice, "I'll be interested to hear what he has to say."

When I next saw Beth, she informed me that she had canceled the appointment with Dr. Douglas.

"After last time, I realized that I *am* losing my marbles. You're right; I need to take medication." I hastily wrote out a script and handed it to her. Perhaps my pulling back during our last visit had enabled her to tolerate taking in more of all I offered: support, reality checks, interpretations, and medications. Unfortunately, Beth's psychosis had merely subsided momentarily. She had just found out that her parents were coming for a visit, and as she began to consider the familial onslaught, she again wove me into the frayed fabric of her psyche, accusing me, like her family, of betraying her.

"Just like you've been more loyal to him all along," she finally screamed.

"Beth, tell me calmly what you mean."

"You've been reporting to him all along. Telling him how I've been doing." I know my mouth fell open at that accusation.

"He's even been paying for my sessions." If it were possible for a mouth to open any wider in amazement, mine would have.

"Beth," I said, struggling to regain my composure, "you pay for each of your sessions by check when you leave. How could the senior partner possibly be paying for them?"

"I don't know how. But he is," she finished emphatically, angrily. I had momentarily forgotten the first rule of psychiatry: Never argue delusions with the delusional. I recovered quickly, closing my mouth so I could open it again, this time for speech, but she beat me to it.

"Now you're just going to lie to me again," she said.

"Beth," I began, but it was too late. She got up from her chair and purposefully strode out of my office. I never saw her again.

I left several messages on her answering machine, but she did not call me back. Finally I sent the following letter:

Dear Beth:
It has been a few weeks since our last meeting, and I have tried calling you several times because I was concerned about the way you left the session. It is obvious that you wish to discontinue ther-apy, but after all this time, I ask that you come in so that we can discuss this in person.

A week later, I received my answer, a letter in which she said that I was correct: She no longer wished to see me, and although she under-stood that I wanted to meet with her again, she was unable to do so. Later that week, however, she called and set up an appointment with my receptionist. She never showed up. I found out that she had admitted herself the night before to the psychiatric hospital where I worked but that she had requested another doctor. Given that there were several other such hospitals in her town, I could only assume that this was one last attempt to express her rage at me. This time she was placed on the locked unit, and since I had no patients there, I did not see her the entire time she was in the hospital, although I heard that she replayed all her rage at me with her new psychiatrist.

Several months later, I received two strange letters in her handwrit-ing with her law school's return address. The first one thanked me for sharing my memories of my early career with her, saying she would "cherish every detail." It was signed "Isadora Crotch." The second said simply that she was thinking of me, and she signed it "With love, hope, warm hugs, much heart" from "Spike Person." I had no idea what any of this meant, but at least she was teaching. Perhaps behavior that would not be tolerated at, say, IBM might be considered appropriately eccen-tric in a law school professor. With the protective distance of time, it seemed she could have warm, if sexualized thoughts of our work together. On further reflection I realized that intimacy was often sexualized in her family: Her father used to walk around the house with his fly undone while her mother loudly complained that all he ever wanted was sex. Beth was never allowed to lock doors in her house, so her parents frequently walked in on her while she was dressing or going to the bathroom. Perhaps in her psychotic state, her parents' inopportune visit as she struggled with feeling close to me had heightened her fears that I would cross the same boundaries they had.

I had hoped to hear in more concrete terms how she was doing. But I had to admit that with all that had happened with Fran, a significant part of me was just as happy not to receive any more overly familiar, bizarre mail from yet another psychotic woman. I guessed I would never know how much of Beth's story about her senior partner was true. Had they ever really had intimate lunches? Had they ever, in fact, even spoken? What was clear was that at some indistinct point, Beth's interest had turned into erotomania. It is not often that a psychiatrist gets to witness the development of a mental disorder before her eyes. More often, illness is firmly entrenched by the time treatment is sought. Why had I not seen it coming? Had my wish to deny that this was happening to me with Fran hindered my awareness of the same thing developing in Beth?

For some time after my last session with Beth, I took stock of how Fran had changed my life. How else was she affecting me in ways I had not even imagined? I felt that the fulfilling life I had looked forward to after suffering eight years through medical school and residency was being continually violated, made worse by the apparent randomness of Fran's contacts. But I had not realized that she had been so deeply affecting my work, an area of my life I had always considered an honor to partake in and one that I prided myself on doing to the best of my ability.

Too late I realized that my feeling helpless and out of control with Fran had seeped into my work with Beth, who had reinforced those very feelings, leading me to respond in kind. Just as Beth had transferred her feelings about her parents onto me, I had transferred my actions, or rather inactions, with regard to Fran onto Beth. I had to ensure that that would never happen again.

I redoubled my efforts to help myself.

Chapter Three

WHAT'S LOVE GOT TO DO WITH IT?

*A*YEAR AFTER WE HAD FIRST MET, FRAN continued to call me several times a week at my office and at the hospital, leaving messages with her home, work, and pager numbers so that I could always reach her. She even had her pharmacy call me to order a refill on a medication Dr. Trottle was prescribing. Although I had asked my receptionist and my answering service to let her know I would not accept any of her calls, Fran persevered with her telephonic onslaught.

The cards and letters also continued, sent by mail to my office, placed directly in my box at the hospital, or left on the windshield of my car, a method I found particularly intrusive. I had bought an old Corvette at an auction for a song as a graduation present to myself, and it had always been very special to me. It was the first nice car I had ever owned. Before that I had driven a beat-up, ten-year-old Toyota Corolla with faded paint and a dented bumper. But now every time I walked to the parking lot, I approached my silver baby with dread, stepping hesitantly toward it until I could see that the windshield was clear of one of Fran's deranged missives.

She was averaging one note a week, sometimes as many as three. Once she just left a blown-up photo, a close-up of a woman whose face had been severely beaten. It was so swollen, so grotesque and bloody, that I could not tell who it was, and it did not come with any explanation or note. Was she showing me what she had been through in the past? Or was she threatening what she might do to me in the future if I did not respond to her?

I started looking for someone to walk me to the parking lot every night. I would have asked Tim and he would have done it, but I knew he continued to feel that my fear of Fran was out of proportion to reality. Instead I tried to join groups of people or individuals who happened to be leaving when I was.

As Fran continued her pursuit, my own constant second-guessing was making my erotomanic ordeal especially difficult. I would often wonder what I had done wrong, because surely this whole mess could have been avoided somehow. Every time Fran wrote me or phoned, I would spend several sleepless nights ruminating about my own unwilling role in this psychotic melodrama. Had I been too nice? Should I have insisted she pay my fee in full? Why didn't I recognize her meager attempt at flirtation? The truth was, none of that probably would have mattered.

Gradually I realized that the only thing that might have saved me was transferring her care immediately and without further contact to a male psychiatrist. I certainly blamed Dr. Trottle for not warning me, but I also think Fran's parents shared some culpability. Barring sewing a scarlet letter *E* on her clothes, they knew enough about their daughter's mental illness and past history to keep her far away from, or at least warn, any female authority figures who might unwittingly cross her path.

But even that might not have saved me, because with Fran, as with many erotomanics, that first contact is what catalyzes the almost instantaneous cascade from delusional, mutual magnetism to boundless bond. As if drawn from the National Organ Donor Registry, I became the perfect match, with the potential to save her life; her own personal avatar of *amore*. It is not uncommon for victims in many difficult situations to blame themselves. No one wants to feel helpless. If we believe we have in some way caused what is happening, perhaps we can also make it stop.

At first my embarrassment about what I might have done to encourage Fran's targeting me made me want to keep my ordeal a secret. I had confided in only a few close friends about my "relationship" with Fran, and none of them were psychiatrists. I suppose I took the blame I was putting on myself and projected it onto others, assuming they would also blame me. But by the second year of her pursuit, when she started coming to the hospital more often to give her letters directly to

the receptionist, I began to fear that she might try to get herself admitted there in an effort to have me treat her again. I decided to ask the
head of the admissions department, a social worker I had befriended, to
have a woman named Fran Nightingale admitted elsewhere if she tried
to get in. Of course, he wanted to know why.

"I treated her here over a year ago, and she's been stalking me ever
since. I'm afraid even if she's assigned to another psychiatrist, I'll run
into her," I said, trying to sound professional and matter-of-fact.

"What's wrong with her? What's her diagnosis?" he asked.

I didn't really want to get into any details. I remembered how easily
Fran had found out that Tim and I were "an item," and I knew that a staff
psychiatrist's being stalked would be a tempting tidbit for hospital gossip.

"I don't really remember much about her, but I would appreciate it
if you would not admit her here."

"Okay," he said, "if Fran Nightingale shows up, I'll have her taken
somewhere else."

I knew he would agree. It was a reasonable request, and besides, Tim
had recently been promoted to associate medical director of the hospital.

That very question of what was wrong with Fran was the one that
continued to nag at me for months after my conversation with the social
worker. How could Fran have erotomania? She had been diagnosed with
schizophrenia, and her behavior on the unit had been such that she
clearly had more than just erotic delusions. I knew the difference
between delusional disorders, such as erotomania, and other psychiatric
disorders, such as schizophrenia, in which delusions are only one part of
a complex of serious symptoms.

Schizophrenics have bizarre, completely implausible delusions that
often change over time. They may also suffer from hallucinations—
hearing voices or seeing things that are not there. Whereas someone
with a persecutory delusional disorder might believe that the government is spying on him and offer elaborate proofs (like the black car
cruising down his street or the new neighbors just moving in), a schizophrenic might believe that the CIA has implanted a microchip in his
brain and may even hear voices telling him so. Unlike patients with
delusional disorders, schizophrenics often cannot function well on their
own in society even if their delusions are under control. When such
patients are not experiencing their delusions, they often come across as

"flat" or unanimated to others. If their disease is in full throttle, schizo-phrenics may be incapable of caring for themselves: not eating, not bathing, not paying the rent or taking out the garbage. Fran certainly seemed to fit the more global illness, yet she clearly had erotomanic delusions. Perhaps if she did not have erotomania after all, my situation would not be so hopeless. I needed to learn more.

I returned to the library, and to my pleasant surprise I found that several more articles had been published since my disillusioning quest almost two years before. Some of the articles mentioned celebrity stalk-ers with erotomania, so on a hunch, I also checked popular magazines. To my astonishment, I discovered almost as much information in *Vanity Fair* and *People* as I had in *The Journal of the American Psychiatric Association*. Perhaps it had even been the increased public awareness of the disorder that had sparked renewed psychiatric interest—and fund-ing. When my ordeal started in 1989, most people, even professional therapists like myself, had never heard of erotomania. Yet the disorder was already at that time glimmering on the national scene. The ero-tomanically deluded Robert Bardo, who murdered the young actress, Rebecca Schaeffer, just two months before Fran began stalking me, had since been convicted of first-degree murder and was serving a life sen-tence without parole.

I recalled that erotomania recently had become part of our national dialogue when Americans sat transfixed by the Senate Judiciary Hearings in which Professor Anita Hill was accused of suffering under the delusion that Judge Clarence Thomas loved her. Since then, eroto-mania has continued to glow in the national, and even the international, spotlight. Although far from being a disease affecting only the rich and famous, erotomania has increasingly impacted celebrities, whose lives are dissected daily in the media. It is precisely for this reason that public awareness of erotomania has exploded in the nineties. Madonna, Whitney Houston, Vanna White, Kathie Lee Gifford, Janet Jackson, Michael J. Fox, Suzanne Sommers, Anne Murray, Barbara Mandrell, Sharon Gless, and David Letterman are just a few of the celebrities who have been stalked by erotomanics who were convinced these stars were in love with them. The deluded individuals wrote them lovesick or overtly threatening letters, trespassed onto film sets, invaded their homes, and otherwise disrupted their lives.

Sharon Gless, like me, had been stalked by a lesbian erotomanic woman, who finally, armed with a rifle, broke into a house Gless used as an office. Luckily Gless was not there. Her stalker's intention had been to sexually assault the "Cagney & Lacey" star, kill her, then kill herself. Instead this disturbed woman—against whom Gless had obtained a restraining order sixteen months before—surrendered to police after a seven-hour standoff.

"Late Show" host, David Letterman, unlike me, seemed able to find humor in an inherently humorless situation. The erotomanic who stalked Letterman believed herself married to him, repeatedly broke into his house, even "borrowed" his car, and was rewarded with jail time for her efforts. Nevertheless, he was often able to work his plight into his comedy routine. Before moving to CBS he had on his top-ten list of things to do: "Number eight: Give the woman who keeps breaking into my house Conan O'Brien's address."

In the cases of both celebrity and noncelebrity stalkers, I learned as I read, some were not mentally ill at all, but most appeared to be. Of those, some were erotomanics; but many more seemed to have other mental illnesses, such as schizophrenia with erotomanic delusions. And just how common were erotomanic delusions? No one knew for sure. Most statistics appeared to exclude the significant number of patients whose erotomanic delusions were "secondary" to some other mental illness that dominated their lives in a more global way. Even figures for "pure" erotomania were hard to come by, but according to the *DSM*, 0.03 percent of the population, or 3 in 10,000, were said to suffer from some type of delusional disorder.[1] A later study estimated that of those, approximately 10 percent, or 3 in 100,000, had erotomania.[2]

Seeking more statistics I grabbed the library's copy of the *DSM* and browsing through, counted more than twenty mental illnesses in which erotomanic delusions could manifest, illnesses as disparate as schizophrenia, depression, and manic-depression. This ability for one characteristic symptom to permeate so many varied illnesses, and even have an illness named after itself, seemed to make erotomanic delusions extremely difficult to quantify. I therefore wondered about the accuracy of these statistics.

When I had finished poring over the various studies I still had no clear idea exactly how many people suffered from erotomanic delusions, or even a clue about how to accurately compute the number. What was all too clear in the research, however, was the agreement that erotomania in its so-called "pure" form was the most tenacious, chronic, and difficult illness to treat because, as in all the delusional disorders, the delusions themselves are "fixed," or unchanging, and notoriously unresponsive to medications.

Patients with delusional disorders, in which erotomania was classified, rarely seek help on their own because they do not feel they have a problem. Since they appear normal, apart from their delusional preoccupations, and are usually loners, erotomanics, the literature suggested, seldom reached the point of inviting intervention by their families or by the courts unless they actively pursued their objects—as Fran had been pursuing me and other women before me. Many apparently harbored their deluded beliefs in silence, perhaps even for years, their erotomania surfacing only if stalking began and if the object of pursuit became aware of the stalker. Compounding the difficulties of quantifying erotomania, most of the studies seemed to agree that there are far more people with erotomanic delusions than there are "pure" erotomanics.

I was trying to put together a prognosis for Fran's and, therefore, my own condition, but that was no easy matter. How long would her attachment to me go on? How could I stop it? I was not finding any clear answers. I recalled the case of a patient I had seen in a nursing home during my residency. She was a terribly sweet seventy-two-year-old, who thought the thirty-something male physical therapist there was in love with her. She often told me about their plans to marry. The staff thought the patient's beliefs rather precious and teased the poor therapist mercilessly. In her case, erotomanic delusions arose out of her primary mental illness, dementia. At least she could not stalk her object beyond the confines of the facility—or her wheelchair. I wondered how many other cases of erotomanic delusions, let alone erotomania, were missed, as I had done with Beth, and with far graver consequences?

During that second foray into the literature, I learned that Fran could not be properly called "erotomanic," but rather, "schizophrenic" with erotomanic delusions, just as other schizophrenic patients might have religious, grandiose, or persecutory delusions. That Fran's primary diagnosis was not erotomania seemed to indicate that her delusions would be easier to manage. In theory, the studies agreed, erotomania manifesting as a symptom of a broader mental illness, rather than the illness itself, was easier to treat than the "pure" syndrome: Just treat the underlying pathology and the erotomanic delusions would disappear. That was the theory.

In practice, however, the various authors were quick to admit that in the most serious and persistent mental illnesses, such as schizophrenia, medications could only control the symptoms, not provide a cure. In such cases, the underlying disease seemed to present a chronic threshold of disturbance that could not be breached, with the erotomanic symptoms waxing and waning with the natural course of the primary illness. Some experts even believed that when erotomania occurred in its "symptomatic" form, or as part of another mental illness, it was more likely to involve different objects over time, as well as more overtly sexual desires and behaviors toward those objects.[3]

Fran certainly had had multiple objects, but I was relieved that so far, at least, she had not exhibited any more carnal interests or gone to the extent of physical violation of another. A man who had stalked Kathie Lee Gifford was arrested for raping his aunt and seemed to be suffering from a serious mental illness of which his erotomania toward Gifford was only one symptom. Subsequent to the attack, he told his aunt that he was going to leave her to be with his girlfriend, Kathie Lee. After his arrest, police found he had compiled scrapbooks with the star's pictures. He told them he was following Gifford as part of a surveillance mission for the government, although he also believed that same government had abducted and impregnated her. Although on the surface his bizarre delusions about Gifford seemed almost laughable, they took on a much more sinister tone when viewed in light of the rape of his aunt and his subsequent statement, "I need to make her [Gifford] my wife and bring into this world my child."[4]

I was also learning more about the objects of erotomanics, although it was a bit discomfiting to read about myself in a profile. I was more used to reading the profiles of others or profiling them myself, but there was no denying it—there I was. The majority of unfortunate persons who become victims of an erotomanic's unwanted attention tend to be in some position of authority. They also tend to be of superior looks and intelligence, but before I allowed my head to swell too much, I realized, of course, that this perception, along with the conception of love, could be nothing more than erotomanic invention. While some true initial superiority or desirability might, in fact, be present, it is then grossly elaborated on and distorted by many other supposed attributes.

Unlike Fran, who is seven years older than I, erotomanics are generally younger than their victims, who tend to be about forty years of age, contributing to the perception of authority. Most victims also seem very nice and very approachable. While it is the obnoxious celebrity who gets the lion's share of hate mail, it is the sweet, girl-next-door type who, in fact, is in the most danger of being erotomanically stalked. One researcher stated this well: "Their public personae foster an illusion of intimacy and receptivity and a willingness to come close in a nonthreatening manner to subjects who generally have difficulty with social relations."[5]

Theater actors were perhaps the most vulnerable celebrities of all because they truly were approachable; anyone can buy a ticket and be in the same room as their chosen star, night after night for hours.[6] Robert Bardo may have fixated on Rebecca Schaeffer precisely because she was not yet a major star; she still seemed attainable. This seemed applicable to my own situation with Fran. As I understood from Dr. Trottle, all the other women she had stalked were her advocates, attorneys representing her in various matters. Similarly my own initial relationship with Fran was entirely based on my role as a helping professional, trying to appear nonthreatening to a disturbed patient so I could better care for her. From there, Fran seemed to assign all sorts of false attributes to me: that I was a lesbian, that I wanted a relationship with her, that I was psychically connected with her, that I could help her career. Who I really was became unimportant, buried under a myriad of delusional beliefs. If I could have snapped her out of her psychosis for a second, I doubt she would have even recognized me—like the pregnant internist who told a seemingly too attached male patient that she was going to be taking some time off.

"Why?" he asked.

"I'm pregnant," was the obvious reply.

Although this internist had never heard of erotomania, her patient's stunned expression was all the doctor needed to confirm her worst fears. In erotomania, the object is like a *tabula rasa* onto which the erotomanic projects her every desire, because she needs to manufacture some highly sought-after person's coveting her to have self-worth and to feel worthy of love. Dean Martin compellingly crooned what could be considered the erotomanic's anthem: "You're Nobody 'Til Somebody Loves You." I was probably nothing like the Dr. Orion that Fran had manufactured in her mind.

Unfortunately at the time I met Fran, I felt that to establish a working alliance with a severely disturbed, suicidal, schizophrenic patient, I should appear very nice and very approachable. Since my experience with Fran, I have begun to question that tack.

As a physician and especially as a psychiatrist, part of the training I received was geared toward learning how to leave my work at the office. This phrase took on new meaning soon after I met Fran. I had always had a particularly difficult time with that aspect of my work, often getting too emotionally involved with my patients, thinking of them, their problems, even their children's problems, outside the office. During residency, my supervisors were well aware of this tendency and tried to help me channel some of that overabundant empathy into a greater capacity for insight so I could more effectively help my patients while not burning myself out.

I had often thought that to prevent burnout, therapists needed to have thick skins. Yet I never thought one could be a particularly good therapist without a fairly thin one. Inherent in the special sensitivity that good therapists must possess are often the insecurities that go along with being sensitive: self-doubt and the constant questioning of one's abilities. Although painful, it is this questioning that makes for a good therapist. It is a mediocre therapist who is always sure that his or her comments are best. As a private practitioner, I had come to understand that for basically competent therapists, there are generally no bad responses to patients; but there are almost always better ones. After almost two years of Fran's continued contacts, this self-doubt and questioning made me continually wonder, "Could I have done anything differently so that this would not be happening? Could I do anything differently now to make it stop?"

Yet I had discovered through my continued reading that erotomania could stop—sort of. Often erotomanics simply moved on to other objects, as Fran had done in the past. Even for those with "pure," or "primary," erotomania, the objects could change over time. David Letterman's erotomanic, as attached as she appeared to be to him, used to stalk Yul Brynner when he was appearing on Broadway in a revival of *The King and I*.[7]

Robert Bardo stalked the singers Debbie Gibson and Tiffany before killing Rebecca Schaeffer. Even as a severely disturbed thirteen-year-old, he ran away from his Tucson home to Maine seeking Samantha Smith, the young girl who gained prominence writing to Soviet president Mikhail Gorbachev about world peace. Fortunately for Smith, Bardo's parents alerted the police, and the boy was picked up and returned to Tucson.

Even while in jail after his murder of Schaeffer, Bardo began fixating on Dyan Cannon.[8] Could that have been another illustration of the way erotomanic delusions erode the love object's real identity, substituting fantasy? Schaeffer had played a younger version of Cannon's character in a television movie the older actress had directed. Perhaps Bardo believed that Cannon really *was* Schaeffer. One man with erotomania thought the male doctors attending him in the hospital were really his wife in disguise.[9] While erotomanic behavior toward a particular object might cease, the erotomanic delusions themselves rarely seemed to end. In fact, according to a study I would later read, about 17 percent of erotomanics have stalked more than one victim.[10]

What makes erotomanic delusions so tenacious? Perhaps it is because erotomanics feel utterly incomplete without their objects. They need to be made whole by some highly esteemed other. This is underscored by the fact that in classical cases of erotomania, the delusion begins with the belief that it is the *object* who started the relationship. It is as though the erotomanic thinks, "There I was, minding my own business when this incredible person made the first move. If such a God-like creature noticed *me*, well, maybe I'm not so bad after all."

That "first move" is usually something completely innocuous, something the object would not normally think twice about: a kind word at work, a good grade at school, or a door held open for a stranger. Fran, for example, told Dr. Trottle that she knew by my "nonverbal communication" that I was in love with her. How does one guard against that? Even more vexing, the first move is often something that never occurred at all. Ralph Nau, a severely disturbed schizophrenic with erotomanic delusions, stalked several female celebrities for years. He is believed to have murdered his autistic eight-year-old stepbrother because the boy interrupted gymnast Nadia Comaneci's plea through the television that Nau come live with her. He was also told by a supernatural being that Cher and Olivia Newton-John were in love with him.[11]

People with erotomania and erotomanic delusions seem to come from abusive, emotionally distant families. They suffer from an extreme self-consciousness and lack of self-esteem, factors that contribute to the drive to find romantic fulfillment through fantasy. Often there are signs of trouble from an early age. As a teen, Ralph Nau killed and mutilated animals, burying them on the family farm. His parents allegedly had orgies that the young boy and his siblings watched. When he was sixteen, his father reportedly made him engage in incest with his mother, his first and last sexual experience. The security firm hired by Cher and by Newton-John was so concerned about Nau that it even interviewed his father, who told them, "He's another John Hinckley. We're all afraid of him."[12]

Robert Bardo also showed early erotomanic tendencies. Although a straight-A student, he had no friends. In junior high, he wrote bizarre letters to a female teacher. At various times he threatened to kill himself and others. As a teenager, he was admitted to a psychiatric hospital, but his family pulled him out, consistently denying that he had mental problems and ignoring school authorities' repeated pleas to get him professional help. Even Bardo himself seemed to recognize that he needed someone to come to his aide, writing on a school form, "Help. This house is hell. I'm going to run away again. I can't handle it anymore. Please help. Fast."[13]

The psychiatrists who examined him before his trial concluded that his father was an alcoholic, his mother paranoid, and his older brother abusive, making him drink urine and forcing him to steal. Bardo never had a date, never, in fact, had been so much as kissed by a woman, except for his mother. Rebecca Schaeffer had responded warmly and personally to one of his letters, writing that it was "the nicest, most real" she had received, signing it with a heart and the words, "Love, Rebecca," unwittingly encouraging his erotomania toward her. Schaeffer thus became the only woman who had ever responded to him, and he could not let go. As he said in an interview after the murder, "I didn't have anything else in my life to look forward to."[14] He and Nau are typical of patients who have erotomanic delusions, where an emotionally barren and abusive upbringing sows the seeds for an intense longing to be loved and made whole by a superior someone.

There seemed to be no magic formula for determining who would develop erotomania. Just as some lucky people with all the risk factors never develop diabetes or heart disease, the vast majority of people who are loners and products of dysfunctional families will never develop this delusion. It seemed that although a certain foundation is necessary, with genetic, familial, intrapsychic, and social factors coming into play, once that foundation is laid, a certain precipitating event, usually some kind of loss, must often occur before the development of full-blown erotomanic delusions.

The case histories I read were replete with instances of such premorbid personalities developing erotomanic delusions after losing their one meaningful connection in life, such as a parent or job. Erotomania has even been theorized to be a form of mourning, with more than 25 percent of recorded cases occurring after the patients experienced a significant loss.[15] I did not know if this were true for Fran. She had told me about being raped years earlier, certainly a devastating loss for anyone. Yet I did not know if all her erotomanic attachments began after that. In cases where such a loss occurred, the delusional, erotomanic relationship compensated for some ultimate privation in patients faced with an even bleaker life.

Atypically, one devout woman with erotomanic delusions was married, but due to illness, her husband had been impotent for ten years. Rather than face the permanent loss of sexual gratification, she developed erotomania toward her priest, and her psychiatrists reported that: "At night she felt her hand 'being moved' to the 'sensitive areas' of [her] body. She believed that this action was completely beyond her own control and would take place whilst she was in a 'trance.'" She felt strangers were manipulating her thoughts and "that the only way to stop such outside interference was to achieve sexual orgasm, and to 'free' her mind and body she would spend many hours masturbating."[16] Thus, this strict Roman Catholic could erotomanically gratify her sexual needs without guilt, by attributing her own actions to the priest's control of her.

As did Robert Bardo and Ralph Nau, many erotomanics developed signs of something amiss in adolescence and, indeed, ever after seemed stunted at this level of maturity. Fran would sign her letters with such sentiments as "Thank you for being" or "Happy spring," and embellish her sign-offs with hearts and smiling faces. Once she had even drawn an outline of her hand on the letter she sent. I recalled the juvenile compositions she had sung for me in the hospital and her inept attempt at flirting toward the end of her stay there. Perhaps this was the driving force behind erotomania: an adolescent fantasy of a magical love that would somehow right all wrongs. Similarly, the focus of an erotomanic like Fran seemed to be on what I or any of her would-be lovers could do for *her,* how being loved by some supposedly special person made *her* feel. Her "love" for me felt even more regressive, even desperate; like an infant's love for a mother she was still dependent on for survival.

Erotomanics, being both socially and emotionally immature, seem to maintain the adolescent fantasy of an ideal love through physical adulthood, ominously carrying with it the means of realizing the fantasy. As Arthur Jackson, a paranoid schizophrenic who developed erotomanic delusions toward actress Theresa Saldana (years before her starring role on "The Commish") wrote in his diary: "Theresa Saldana is the countess of Heaven in my heart and the angel of America in my dreams. Theresa Saldana is a soulmate to me. I have psychedelic fantasies of romance about her in springtime—enchanting visions of our walking together through the gardens of magnificent palaces in Heaven."[17] In an adolescent boy such fantasies would seem harmless, even sweet. They become menacing in an adult man with the physical and intellectual means to attempt to carry them through. For Arthur Jackson, they led to his 1982 multiple stabbing of Saldana, after he had methodically stalked the then rising star by honing in on those closest to her, traveling around the country upon arriving from his native Scotland with the express purpose of murdering her, to be united with her in the hereafter. Impersonating a reporter when talking to her agent and then an agent when talking to her parents, he slowly zeroed in on his target. The majority of adolescents could not manage such skillful subterfuge.

Fran, like many others with erotomanic delusions, seemed to avoid any direct contact with me, another holdover from adolescence. In the manner of a gaggle of pubescent girls, erotomanics giggle and point to their crushes, never dreaming of actually approaching them; instead, collecting momentos of their objects, much as adolescents surreptitiously hoard telephone numbers and discarded scraps of paper, even "stalking" their chosen ones by finding out when he has math class or where her locker is. In fact, one study reported that the only type of contact erotomanics were much less likely to engage in than other stalkers was face-to-face. They avoided direct contact with their objects.[18] The author of the study explained that these relationships become "mythical" for the erotomanic: "The erotomanic does not want to burst the bubble. They don't even necessarily want to have a sexual relationship with their victim. They're more interested in a perfect union. . . . To go up and approach is too threatening to them."[19]

In adolescence, when my friends and I pinned up glossy posters of our latest celebrity crushes in our rooms and obsessively read and collected everything ever written about our favorite stars, our behavior was considered normal and expected. While cute in adolescence, such an all-consuming passion matures to the sinister in an adult.

One particular erotomanic victim, a biochemist, has been stalked by a technician in his lab for years. He has been afraid to press charges against her for fear that he might lose his job. Instead he has chosen to move from state to state, but she always manages to follow him. Early on, trying to determine if indeed it was she who was stalking him, he broke into her house when he knew she was at work and in the process, discovered horrifying confirmation. She had built an addition to her home that was an exact replica of his bedroom, down to the size, shape, layout, furnishings, and decor.[20] It is as if merely possessing this private information conveys the illusion (or for erotomanics, delusion) of intimacy, whereas more direct contact would be all too threatening.

In my experience with Fran, I often wondered, with her many calls to my office, why she hadn't simply given my receptionist or answering service a made-up name so that she could talk to me, or why she never just waited in my waiting room? It seemed more important for her to let me know that she continued to think about me, that she, at least, was keeping our love alive, despite my not responding to her many overtures. It was as if she did not want to risk yet another rejection, and by staying involved, even at a distance, she was able to remain a constant, consistent part of my life. Since she had never been in an intimate relationship (except in her mind), she may not have been able to cope with more direct, close, and implied sexual contact. Perhaps, too, she did not want to risk the harsh reality of finding out that I was not the ideal lover she had set me up to be, thus protecting our delusional bond.[21] Reality can even disappoint the deluded.

Erotomanics cross the line between interest and obsession when the delusion ripens into running and ruining their lives, not to mention the lives of their objects. Erotomanics, like adolescents, misinterpret their objects' responses, albeit through a prism of psychosis. An adolescent girl may feel all a-flutter when the captain of the football team happens to wink in her general direction, as she mistakes some lint in his eye for a flirtatious signal. In a grotesque distortion of this hopeful adolescent embellishment, erotomanics exhibit a seemingly endless capacity for creative misconception, reinterpreting even the clearest rejections as declarations of love.

One erotomanic man approached his "lover" in the street. She told him in no uncertain terms to "fuck off." When discussing this with his therapist, the erotomanic happily anticipated their developing intimacy, for after all, he maintained, fucking was a part of love.[22] Some erotomanics apparently interpret the autographed pictures sent out by stars' agencies as meaningful personal missives. That is exactly how Robert Bardo perceived such a photo of Rebecca Schaeffer and why so many security experts now advise their celebrity clients never to send out signed photographs.

While erotomanics operate under the patently false belief that their objects love them, loving their objects back is not a given, because erotomanics may rarely profess indifference to the objects delusionally pursuing them. When this occurs, however, at least one expert noted that the erotomanics seem to eventually succumb to their objects' charms.[23]

Much more common is the erotomanic conviction that a relationship already exists. The woman pursuing David Letterman has called herself Mrs. Letterman since 1988. Madonna obtained a restraining order against the man who claimed to be her husband and scaled her eight-foot security fence. After her Olympic victories, two-time gold medalist Katarina Witt was stalked and threatened by a man who thought the figure skater was his wife. A man believing himself to be Paula Abdul's lover showed up at the home of her mother.

Justine Bateman was stalked for five years by an erotomanic who believed he had had an affair with her years before, during which she repeatedly raped him. To prove his love to her, he arrived armed with a .22-caliber pistol at a theater where she was rehearsing, threatening to kill himself. After a three-hour standoff, he surrendered to authorities. A male erotomanic who stalked a well-known female celebrity with phone calls and letters, finally showed up at her home one day in a tuxedo, telling her security guards, "I'm here for the wedding." This would-be bridegroom thought it was the happiest day of his life until he realized the car coming to whisk him away was no limo.

Although many erotomanics stalk, not all stalkers are erotomanics. In fact, studies have found that only about 10 percent of stalkers carry erotomania as their primary diagnosis.[24] Most erotomanics appear to be women, while men tended to stalk nonerotomanically. John Hinckley, Jr., for example, who stalked both Jodie Foster and President Ronald Reagan, was not erotomanic. Although Hinckley sent Foster many bizarre letters and was clearly obsessed with her, the prosecution maintained he had a personality disorder and sought a prison sentence; the defense christened him schizophrenic and pled insanity.[25] Eventually found not guilty by reason of insanity, he remains in a psychiatric facility to this day where he has continued to fixate on Foster.

Hinckley's 1981 attack on President Reagan seems to have been an attempt to impress Foster, to get her to notice him. Just two hours before the assassination attempt, Hinckley wrote Foster a telling note: "I've left you dozens of poems, letters and love messages in the faint hope that you could develop an interest in me. . . . At least give me the chance, with this historical deed, to gain your respect and love."[26] He had also written her, "Even a phone conversation seems to be asking too much, but really I can't blame you for ignoring a little twerp like me."[27] If Hinckley had been erotomanic, he would have already thought Foster was interested in him and would have explained away her ignoring him, rather than having understood it. Erotomanics *know* they are in a relationship with their unsuspecting objects.

The resolve of the erotomanic to pursue his amorous goal at all costs and the profound disruption this causes in his life and that of his victim also seem applicable to many cases, like that of John Hinckley, Jr., that cannot be correctly classified as erotomania simply because the delusional aspect of being loved is lacking. Instead these individuals are driven by their not quite deluded devotions to believe that if only they persevere, they will win the heart of their heretofore indifferent loves. Such a single-minded, all-consuming belief occupying the psychological no-man's-land between fact and fiction, sanity and psychosis, is called an "overvalued idea."[28]

Overvalued ideas differ from delusions only in intensity: Delusions are unshakable beliefs. With an overvalued idea, the individual may be able to acknowledge that he is exaggerating or being oversensitive. I saw that Dr. Reid Meloy, a forensic psychologist, had written several papers and a book on pathological attachments. In one article, he coined the term *borderline erotomania* to describe an individual who holds a particular overvalued idea toward a love object that if only he pursues her hard enough and long enough, the object will reciprocate his affections.[29]

Because overvalued ideas are more grounded in reality than are true delusions, Dr. Meloy believes that borderline erotomanics, unlike their delusional counterparts, have usually had some contact with their objects, no matter how tenuous, before the development of their pathological attachments. However, as with their frankly delusional cousins, borderline erotomanics may engage in the same stalking behaviors and prove just as difficult to dissuade from their amorous advances. While some stalking studies mentioned Dr. Meloy's term, *borderline erotomania,* most seemed to be making up their own categories of stalkers, and I found that comparing and piecing together all the research I was reading was extremely difficult.

All the studies did agree that as with other delusions, confronting an erotomanic on the implausibility of his or her fantastic beliefs simply does not work. I found no case in which this had been successfully tried. This was true whether the person doing the confronting was a policeman, judge, psychiatrist, the victim, or the victim's 250-pound linebacker husband. One district attorney, in trying to talk a particularly persistent erotomanic out of his pursuit, let him know in no uncertain terms that his victim did not want to receive his visits, letters, or telephone calls. The deluded defendant angrily responded, "Well, fuck her, then. Let her call me."[30]

While never doubting the love of an object, the erotomanic will rationalize, often quite irrationally, the reason the object does not act on the attraction. Maybe it would be damaging to his or her career, maybe there is too great a gap in social standing, maybe he or she is married. Robert Bardo thought Rebecca Schaeffer was becoming arrogant. Ralph Nau believed that the same supernatural being who told him of Cher's and Olivia Newton-John's love, cast a spell on the stars, rendering them incapable of answering his letters. Finally when Newton-John still did not respond despite his increased efforts to contact her, Nau thought she had been replaced by an evil double he had to kill in order to save the singer. Kathie Lee Gifford's stalker believed that government-inserted implants were the reason Gifford remained unaware that she was his girlfriend.

The stories were alarming, and many, many more than I ever cared to know about. I soon felt I had gotten what I could from the literature. There were several papers on the history of erotomania that I had not yet read, but I put them aside for the time being in favor of pursuing a different tack. Now that I had learned so much more about erotomania in general, I realized I needed to learn as much as I could about Fran in particular. I needed to know how far she was capable of going, and the best predictor seemed to be how far she had gone in her past delusional "relationships."

Dr. Trottle put me in touch with the social worker who was seeing Fran for psychotherapy. This was the first I had heard that Trottle was only managing Fran's psychiatric medications, and I was astonished to discover that the person she saw for therapy was a woman. I telephoned her, unsure of how much she would be willing to share with me. She was very helpful, technically even too helpful. I knew that therapist-patient confidentiality issues did not allow her to give me any information about Fran without Fran's permission. I, on the other hand, was bound by no such ethics because all of Fran's inappropriate contacts with me had taken place outside the doctor-patient relationship. Since the therapist was willing to talk to me, I was certainly not going to stop her.

She basically confirmed the information I had already received from Dr. Trottle, adding that she thought several women in Tucson had, over the years, taken out restraining orders against Fran. Subsequently I did contact the county court but was told that such records were destroyed biannually, and there was no record of any motions against a Fran Nightingale for the last six months. At the end of my conversation with the therapist, I asked a question born of both curiosity and hope: Why had Fran not developed erotomania toward her? She explained that she was quite a bit older than Fran, in her sixties, in fact, and felt Fran had developed more of a "mother transference" where she was concerned. My curiosity was satisfied but my hopes were again crushed. I suppose I had wished for some magic answer, an amulet I, too, could use to ward off Fran's abhorrent attention. But even if I had wished for it, I could not instantly age more than thirty years, although since meeting Fran, I often felt I already had.

Several of Fran's letters included invitations to join her at meetings or cultural events; some even had a ticket enclosed. I was especially dismayed to receive a particular invitation to a play, curiously titled, *Confessions of a Female Disorder*, being performed at a small repertory theater located in the downtown arts center. My ticket came complete with instructions on when and where to meet her in the complex before the play, but what bothered me most was the date. Tim and I already had tickets to a different play in the same arts center complex for the same date and time. We could not exchange the tickets, and I did not want to miss an evening I had looked forward to because of Fran.

The night of the play was typical for spring in Tucson: clear sky, endless stars, and mild enough for only a sweater. I do not even remember what it was we saw performed that night, only that during intermission, we took our customary walk around the compact complex, which was set up like the courtyard of a hacienda. Tim, although not concerned himself, offered to forgo our usual promenade and stay inside the auditorium for my sake. But I stubbornly refused to let Fran run or ruin my life more than she was already doing.

As we strolled around the darkened perimeter holding hands, we passed an outside stairwell and I saw, out of the corner of my eye, a woman who looked vaguely familiar standing on the bottom step, starring down at me. Unsure of how I knew her, but thinking she must be a former patient, I started to smile reflexively when I suddenly realized that she was, indeed, a former patient. *The* former patient. It was, of course, Fran, and my interrupted smile quickly flattened as I looked away, muttering to Tim, "It's her" under my breath. We continued walking back to the auditorium, and I could not enjoy, let alone concentrate on, the rest of the play.

In the note I received the following week, Fran described her version of events in a rambling, often unintelligible poem, scrawled over three pages that seemed to have no beginning or end. Although the return address said, "From the woman who thrives on being put down," the tone alternated between anger and contrition. She accused me of playing games by not accepting her ticket yet showing up anyway, then assured me that she wanted to be my friend before she became my lover. She commented on what I wore that night, as well as on my "cracked" smile.

Again, I felt responsible. Had my trace of a smile encouraged her? I simply had not recognized her immediately because it had been almost two years since I had last seen her. As I neared the end of her letter, I felt my hopes rise as she promised to say good-bye "for now" because she was so heartbroken at my latest rejection. That lasted three days. I really shouldn't have expected anything less. Ralph Nau made two trips to Australia, both times expecting Olivia Newton-John to meet him at the airport. He stalked her just as persistently after she didn't show.

Fran had also been sending me copies of letters she had written to someone I gathered was her former boss, seeming to dispute the circumstances of her termination and asking for some sort of compensation. She sent me these copies without any explanation, and like the poems and cards, they did not make much sense. Finally one letter explained why I had been made privy to all the rest. She asked to speak to me about her termination since I had never "confessed" my involvement. I had not fully realized until then how completely she had woven me into the delusional fabric of her life. What else might she think I had been responsible for? But that was only the beginning.

Freud would have had a field day with the flotilla of phallic symbols that came my way from Fran. There was the time she hung a balloon with a picture of a unicorn on my car with a note explaining that she had heard I was pregnant and knew a couple in California who wanted to adopt a baby. She said that I should let her know if I was interested in having her pursue this option. I already knew from her letters about her former employment that she had created quite a delusional system about me in an attempt to believe that I was as involved in her life as she wanted me to be. At least those delusions seemed to contain a certain thread of reality; she probably really had been fired during a time when her schizophrenia was not well-controlled. But I was not pregnant. What purpose could possibly be served by believing that I was?

Tim and I discussed it that night and agreed that for Fran, my pregnancy might serve as a plausible explanation about why I had not yet left Tim for her. We guessed that to make ready for our reunion, Fran had offered to get rid of the one thing, a baby, that she could never give me and that might be standing in the way of our relationship. Her letter typically assumed I would want the same thing she did. Why shouldn't I? In her mind, I loved her as much as she loved me. Up until then, in spite of my wariness and fright, I had tried to ignore her. Now I wondered, what if I did have a baby? Tim and I might want to someday. Would she take or harm my child as a way to remove a tie to him?

Chapter Four

FUROR AMORIS

IN DESPERATION, AFTER THE NOTE ABOUT my "baby," I dug up the research on eroto- mania's history that I had not yet read. Perhaps some clue to thwarting Fran lay buried under a millennium of medical dust.

The word *erotomania* has been used as a catchall phrase for cen- turies, and it was only early in this century that it was precisely defined as the mental illness recognized today. Despite this indefinitive free- for-all, I had discovered that history was full of fascinating stories of erotomanics, dating as far back as ancient Greece, although it was not until 1640 that the word *erotomania* was first used, and then only to describe an illness that we would not recognize as erotomania today.

With his "Erotomania or a Treatise, Discoursing of the Essence, Causes, Symptoms, Prognosticks and Cure of Love or Erotique Melan- choly," the French physician, Jacques Ferrand, became the first to coin the term *erotomania,* or "love madness," from the Greek, *eros* or "love," and *mania* or "madness." In deeming it a "depravity of the imagination," Ferrand thus began the trend that would last for nearly the next two cen- turies, in which erotomania almost exclusively described aberrations of sexual desire, or "erotic manias," most often nymphomania, but also satyriasis, its male equivalent.

Erotomania, Ferrand believed, was "a state of the most unbridled excitement, filling the mind with a crowd of voluptuous images, and ever hurrying its victim to acts of the grossest licentiousness in the absence of any lesion of the intellectual powers."[1] In attributing such socially reprehensible behavior mainly to nymphomaniacs, Ferrand was only furthering the belief, spawned over a century before during the Dark Ages, that women were the source of sexual excess, even evil.

During the Dark Ages, with the publication of the infamous hand-book of the Inquisition, *Malleus Maleficarum*, (*Witches' Hammer*), the sinister seed had been sown for future, more "enlightened" generations, like that of Ferrand, to attribute ills, especially mental ones, to women. As the *Malleus* dogmatically declared, "All witchcraft comes from carnal lust, which is in women insatiable . . . the mouth of the womb . . . says not, It is enough. . . . Wherefore for the sake of fulfilling their lusts they consort even with devils."[2] With the *Malleus* in tow, men continued to misogynistically persecute women as witches.

Equally remarkable were the medical consequences to be attributed to women's unbridled uteruses. The sixteenth-century Parisian physi-cian, Bartholomy Pardoux, distinguished between *furor uterinus* in women and *amor insanus* in men. The female ailment, *furor uterinus*, originated in the uterus and referred to an inordinate desire for sexual intercourse so unrestrained and wanton as to cause brain injury, ulti-mately driving the lustful ladies mad. The male counterpart, *amor insanus*—love sickness—could also ultimately cause brain injury, even death, but was thought to originate in the liver, and thus no aspersions were cast on a male organ situated farther south.[3]

The trend of viewing women as slaves to the salaciousness of their sex organs continued into the eighteenth century. By 1771, more than a hun-dred years after Ferrand's first use of the term *erotomania*, patients, mostly women, suffering from the disorder were defined as those "who engage in the furious pursuit of vagrant and illicit lust."[4] In Bienville's *La Nymphomanie ou Traité de la Fureur Utérine*, not only were women more frequently stricken with the dire ailment, but conveniently, men could provide the cure for the ladies thus stricken. The eminent eighteenth-cen-tury physician, Jerome Gaub of Leiden, concurred. He wrote in his famous essay, *De Regimene Mentis*, love "can even replace medicine if the desired object is attained."[5] His interest in thus "treating" the lovelorn was perhaps revealed when he reflected that "physicians sometimes uncover to their own advantage," instances of women "languished with desire."[6]

Although Gaub is also credited with changing the notion that femi-nine love, or rather lust, might be a symptom of mental illness rather than the cause,[7] he was not the first to note the curative powers of love, and he certainly will not be the last. Indeed, modern erotomanics themselves would undoubtedly agree that the love of another possesses almost magical powers and would be heartened to learn that their conviction would be seconded by the most distinguished of opinions. Hippocrates diagnosed that the nervous condition of a prince was due to "restrained. . . ardor within. . . and after having thus uncovered the cause of the disease. . . rendered him at last partaker of the desire."[8] In a seemingly lone dissenting view, the great Roman physician, Soranus, although known for his humanitarian treatment of the mentally ill, disagreed with the then prevailing view that "the insane be permitted to indulge in the pleasures of love." In furthering his point, he also noted, for perhaps the first time, the delusional aspects of love when he described erotomania without actually naming it:

> *Some have imagined themselves descending into Hades for the love of Proserpine; some have believed they were favored by a promise of marriage to a goddess, although she was the wife of another. One man enamored of the nymph Amphitrite cast himself into the sea. . . . It is absurd to believe that love, which itself is so often a fury, can suppress furious agitation.*[9]

The first real description in psychiatric literature of what we now consider erotomania has been credited to another prominent French psychiatrist, Jean Etienne Esquirol. Ironically, given how intractable erotomania appears to be, he was also the first in modern medicine to believe that not all mental illnesses were incurable. Writing in his classic 1837 textbook, *Maladies Mentales*, Esquirol differentiated between erotomania, or "love in the mind," *l'amour de la tête*, and the voracious sexual appetites of nymphomaniacs.[10] Yet the debate over the cause of erotomania, although it continued to be known by various terms, remained heated for the rest of the nineteenth century until physicians concurred that in contrast with the "physical" disorders of nymphomania and satyriasis, the "erotomanic was the toy of his own imagination."[11] Thus, the ailment was finally recognized as a bonafide mental illness.

Once the concept of erotomania took hold as a mental disorder rather than a moral depravity or aberration of sexual organs, many more cases came to the fore in the psychiatric literature, even though different terms were still used to describe them.

A German textbook from the turn of the century described symptoms of "erotic paranoia" that match precisely what we call erotomania today and particularly took note of the poor prognosis and lack of a cure, an outlook that has not unfortunately changed with time: "The malady is subject. . . to exacerbations and remissions. . . . I have never seen a case recover." The author, in recognizing the frustrations and ineffectiveness of treatment, detailed the case of a fifty-four-year-old single coachman. "Of limited mental endowment, peculiar, and given to solitude," he worked for a baron and developed erotomania toward his employer's sister-in-law. By her "friendly manner and inviting glances she had given him to understand that she wished to marry him." He believed that other servants in the household and even the baron himself approved of the union.

Finally he approached the baron and asked for the lady's hand. He was fired from his post and hospitalized, where he apparently only learned not to give voice to his delusions. On his release and away from the confines of the hospital, he was able to act on them. When he again went to his former master, "The baron received him very ungraciously and hastened his descent down the steps." The coachman was finally placed in an institution for incurables.[12]

At about the same time, the potential violence of erotomanics was finally recognized, a potential of which modern society is all too aware. It was eerie reading about an erotomanic, long since dead, who resolved to murder to achieve her amorous ends. If an erotomanic from a more genteel society could resort to violence, I wondered how Fran, who had already been the victim of violence herself, would respond when her desires were continually frustrated?

Describing "insane jealousy," an 1892 dictionary of psychological medicine mentioned a "famous case of a lady" who "believed a doctor wished to marry her, and she found that his wife was fond of chocolate creams, and most ingeniously managed to introduce poisoned creams into the stock from which the doctor's wife bought her sweets, and poisoned several children, though the intended victim escaped." It seemed the "lady" thought the doctor could not extricate himself from his marriage without her industrious help. As the author noted, in cases of women suffering from the ailment, "If the man happens to be married or engaged, the jealousy may lead to serious social troubles, and may give rise to attempts at murder."[13]

The same author, in describing how to treat "insane jealousy" illustrated that there has been little improvement in therapy since then, because patients with erotomania continue to require forcible separation from their objects. He, in fact, recommended a regimen almost identical to the best modern medicine has to offer:

> *Removal from home is necessary. . . as long as she harbours. . . false ideas. She needs generally some bodily treatment, and hypnotics for a time may be required. She should have a sensible middle-aged companion of her own social station to occupy and amuse her. . . . She may be tried at home after six months' absence, but if any signs of the old symptoms recur she must be sent off again, this time for a shorter period, and thus she may be tested. This treatment is tedious and costly, but if properly carried out and begun early enough, the result is often good.*[14]

One wonders if this remedy actually cured the delusions or as with many erotomanics today (and the German coachman), compelled by the courts to undergo prolonged inpatient treatment, they quickly understand what the acceptable behavior is that would allow them to remain at home, keeping their delusions to themselves.

The continuing evolution in the understanding of erotomania took a giant leap backward under Victorian influences when the word *erotomania* was yet again relegated to the domain of sexual perversions, bearing no resemblance to the disorder we recognize today. Typical of that era was an 1899 definition of erotomania as a form of "moral insanity" that included "an abnormal desire for coitus, or habits of masturbation up to indecent exposure of the penis, rape of children, connection with dead bodies, pederasty, sodomy and bestiality."[15]

By the early twentieth century, any traces of sexual depravity were expunged from theories on erotomania for good, but the moral pendulum seemed to have suddenly swung in the opposite direction, replacing perversion with inhibition, as in an influential text that described *paranoia erotica* as occurring:

often in individuals of defective sexual life, not much inclined to copulation. Sometimes the subjects are old maids who have never had an opportunity of marrying. . . . They are eccentrics, dreamers, idealists, indifferent to passion. . . . In other cases, although more rarely, the sexual desire exists and torments the subject; but domestic circumstances, education, timidity, or ugliness conspire against the poor woman, on whom no one ever casts a glance of love.[16]

It was not until 1921 that yet another Frenchman, Gaetan Gatian de Clérambault, first reported erotomania as a specific psychiatric syndrome with clear, identifiable symptoms. He considered erotomania, or "de Clérambault's syndrome," as it is still sometimes termed, to be one of the *psychoses passionnelles* that resembled the delusional disorders of today. The unifying theme among the *psychoses passionnelles* was a relentless drive toward a specific delusional goal along with the fact that despite all obstacles, these patients felt completely entitled to their objectives, undeterred by the disruption caused to their lives or to those of others.

De Clérambault believed that the *psychoses passionnelles* were precipitated by some crisis, plunging the patient into a prolonged, powerful pathology of passion, the same belief many researchers of today hold about erotomania. He also differentiated "pure" erotomania, in which the onset was abrupt and explosive, from "secondary" erotomania, which arose more gradually as one symptom of another psychiatric illness. De Clérambault's fundamental postulate, however, that "It is the object who began the process and is most in love, or even the only one in love," has since lost its importance and is no longer considered key to the diagnosis.

Today to be considered erotomanic, a patient has only to delusionally believe that another loves her, not that the other initiated it. Fran, in her very first letter, expressing her "surprise" at my "interest," undoubtedly would have been diagnosed as erotomanic by de Clérambault because she met the criteria of his fundamental postulate. Additionally, she had reached many of the other delusionally drawn conclusions de Clérambault noted in his erotomanic patients: Despite any outward ties, the object was available—Fran almost never mentioned Tim, as if acknowledging his existence put a damper on her delusions; the object watched and protected her—Fran felt I was intimately involved in her life through controlling the actions of those around her; the object had many indirect conversations with her and could not be complete without her—Fran described how I sent her messages through other people; the object used enormous resources to surreptitiously signal devotion—Fran believed I paid for her hospital stay; and the "relationship" incited nearly universal sympathy.

Although de Clérambault noted that not all these delusional conclusions were present in every case, the fact that the object behaved in a paradoxical and contradictory manner—in other words, that the object might seem to ignore or even rebuff the erotomanic while really loving her—was unequivocal.[17] Fran "knew" I really loved her, and made frequent references to my ignoring her, even while believing I had gotten her fired. Yet she had written that while she did not understand my thoughts and actions, she felt that when people told her to "take care," this was "an extension" of my "good will" toward her.

One of de Clérambault's cases, which illustrates well many of his conclusions, was that of Léa Anne B., a fifty-three-year-old milliner. Léa Anne, like Fran, would travel a great distance to be nearer to the object of her delusion. For eighteen years, from the age of twenty-two, the Frenchwoman really had been loved, or at least "kept" by a socially prominent man until his death. Perhaps it was this loss that triggered her erotomania a few years after. Erotomanics do not necessarily live by one love object alone, as her case so aptly illustrates. By World War I, she not only thought an American general was in love with her, but also thought other officers of many ranks had made overtures. Her real lover had made her a woman of means, so she could afford to travel widely, and did, accruing numerous, prominent, albeit delusional "lovers" along the way.

Léa Anne set her delusional sights higher and higher: It was not long before one would-be lover sat firmly on the throne of the loftiest of social stations. She became convinced that the King of England himself, first Edward VII, and then George V, was in love with her. Her fixation on the latter seemed to have been the strongest; she knew he sent secret emissaries under the guise of sailors and tourists to proclaim his love for her. She believed all of London was aware of their affair and wished them well. The tenacious Frenchwoman persistently pursued him, spending large sums of money on extravagant trips to England where she stalked the royal residences, including Buckingham Palace, awaiting the monarch with amorous anticipation.

I suppose the inhabitant of a less grand residence might have noticed this would-be intruder, but she continued to watch for the king undisturbed. Once she interpreted the movement of a curtain as a signal from her monarch. Yet she also noted his paradoxical behavior, believing that he placed obstacles in the path of their love, including preventing her from finding lodgings in London, making her miss hotel bookings, and causing the loss of her luggage. When she was finally incarcerated due to her increasingly flamboyant actions, agitation, and assaults on strangers in the street, she gave her convoluted explanation for the royal's seemingly baffling behavior: "The king might hate me, but he can never forget. I could never be indifferent to him, nor he to me."[18] To the end, true to the spirit of the erotomanic, she believed that he returned her affection—even while awaiting him along with her freedom.

Similarly Fran's belief that I had gotten her fired did not seem to obstruct her obsession, despite "a lot of tears," "great grief," and my "most assuredly" causing her "more harm than good." I only wished Fran would change delusional objects with the alacrity Léa Anne seemed to possess, because after almost two years, Fran's ardor toward me showed no sign of abating.

Although after de Clérambault's landmark work, the word *erotomania* would never be used as a catchall again, he did perpetuate the centuries-old tradition of overwhelmingly diagnosing women with a disorder of love. Although he did report one case of a male patient in his initial pool, he considered that case atypical, feeling that the syndrome almost always occurred in females. He even declared erotomania *le délire professionel de la femme*—the professional delusion of women—who needed security and legitimacy from men.[19] Although by the time of de Clérambault, erotomania was no longer considered an aberration of sexual desire, aspersions on sexual organs were slower to be shed. As recently as 1959, a prominent psychiatrist seemed to harken back to the Middle Ages, when he placed the blame for erotomanic delusions squarely on the uterus, noting that "Many erotomanics show a state of oestrogenic exhaustion. . . . [t]he low level of sexual hormones and the decline of feeling were the cause of all sorts of compensatory fantasies which might take the form of erotomania."[20]

It was only a matter of time before Freudian psychoanalysis, with its emphasis on unconscious motivations for conscious, especially sexual, behavior, analyzed erotomania. Freud theorized that erotomania developed as a defense against (what else) latent homosexual urges and "remains totally unintelligible on any other view."[21] In his conception of the disorder, a male erotomanic, in essence, would say, "I don't love *him*, I love *her*, because she loves *me*." In other words, a man's homosexual feelings would be so intolerable that the love of a woman is manufactured to ward them off.

I'm not quite sure how Freud would explain someone like Fran, an avowed lesbian. Was she experiencing heterosexual panic, and as a result did she desperately need to believe that I, a woman, loved her? Yet, Freud's view of the "family romance" was quite instructive in illuminating the delusional "purpose" of erotomania: In the family romance, Freud believed that prepubescent children imagined that they were really the product of more prominent parentage and that their "real" parents would someday spirit them away from their "adoptive" ones, restoring their proper importance.[22] How similar to erotomanic delusions, in which the object is perceived as possessing the ability to completely transform the sufferer's undistinguished life, providing more potent persuasion that erotomanics function at a stage of development arrested in adolescence.

The psychoanalytic theories of Freud and those who followed him are not incompatible with more recent findings of the biological basis for many psychiatric illnesses. Based on the work of the British psychoanalyst, John Bowlby, erotomania has been conceptualized as a pathology of attachment.[23] Bowlby observed that in World War II England, children who were separated from their parents and sent to the countryside for safety were more prone to depression later in life. As a result he proposed that one of the major evolutionary purposes for parental attachment to offspring was to provide the infant with security.[24] I had even seen, in a college psychology class, the grainy black-and-white film of his work, showing a young boy left for weeks in the care of nurses while his mother had a new baby. The camera recorded the wrenching stages of separation experienced by the unfortunate toddler: protest, despair, grief, and denial. Given his trauma, we were left to wonder how trusting, engaging, and social an adult the temporarily abandoned child could possibly grow up to be.

Recalling this painful incident, it became apparent how a child might maladapt to more prolonged detachment from his caregivers. If erotomania is a disorder of attachment, resulting from distant, unnurturing parenting, the fixation of the erotomanic on a higher authority could be a psychotic reattempt at bonding with a previously unavailable parent. There have even been several cases of erotomanics fixated on objects who they felt resembled their mothers. At times, for example, the man who has, for over a decade, erotomanically pursued singer Roberta Flack has thought the pop diva *was* his mother.[25] John Hinckley's mother, Jo Ann, was known as Jodie to her family and friends until her son's assassination attempt on President Reagan. Presumably the nickname was then dropped because it was identical to the name of the object this "borderline erotomanic" had tried to win in the attempt— Jodie Foster.[26]

Since attachment to another is biologically based—as infants, it protects us from predators, and as adults, it compels us to reproduce and perpetuate our genetic material—then perhaps a pathology of attachment, like many pathologies, physical and mental, is also rooted in the genetic code. Scientists learn more about the genetic basis for many diseases every day and about the key role of environment: not in whether a disease *will* manifest, but in *how* it manifests. Even given that a predisposition to psychosis is rooted in the genes, the *content* of the delusions may be determined by a particular aberration of nurture rather than nature.

If one was genetically predisposed to heart disease or diabetes, one could modify one's diet or increase one's exercise, and the disease might not express itself, or if it did, would do so to a lesser extent. Likewise, an individual with a genetic predisposition to psychosis raised in a nurturing, loving home might develop a psychotic illness, if one developed at all, other than erotomania, while the same individual growing up in a home devoid of affection and encouragement, might be more prone to this particular disorder of attachment. Perhaps added experiences later in life, such as multiple rejections by prospective partners, coupled with a strong sense of entitlement (erotomanics do, after all, feel they deserve to be united with their "lovers" no matter what), would render such an individual additionally vulnerable. Certainly many complex factors that are not yet understood come into play, but at least psychiatry has moved away from the stereotypical blaming of a mother's behavior for her child's mental illness to blaming the mother's (and father's) genes.

The intricate interplay of environmental and genetic factors is hinted at in the case of one British erotomanic who has stalked a famous female celebrity for over two decades. He is an identical twin, whose brother, despite sharing all his genetic endowments, has never become erotomanically evolved to the same extent: the brother "still lived at home and also had problems of an emotional nature with a woman. She had to resort to calling the police, but according to [his] mother, 'at least he knew when to quit.'"[27] If we are to believe the mother, the one son could control himself, whereas the other became a full-blown stalker. Each might have been predisposed to the same mental illness, with only one able to modify his behavior. Perhaps different life experiences accounted for the fact that in the case of these identical twins with identical genes, only one could not cease stalking.

For as long as the term *erotomania* has been used to describe the illness we now know, women were almost universally believed to be its primary sufferers. The dependency inherent in the delusion that someone of a higher social status could, by virtue of his love, dramatically transform an otherwise doomed life, seems to be more easily attributable to women and their traditionally more passive role in society. A woman's station has, after all, until relatively recently, been determined by whom she married. I chuckled when I came across one early 1970s author's assertion about erotomania:

> *With the revolutionary sociocultural changes that have taken place in the Western world over the last half century coupled with the far greater freedom of expression in sexual matters now enjoyed by young people it seems likely that this particular syndrome will become an even greater rarity that it is at the moment.*[28]

I wish. Contrary to this author's view, recent history has not born out his prediction. In fact, greater opportunities for women in our culture may be contributing to an increased incidence of erotomania in men. Since someone of higher authority is almost always chosen as the object and since more women than ever before have become higher authorities in their own rights (with the exception of Greek goddesses), perhaps the risk of women becoming erotomanic objects will approach that of their male counterparts. Yet some feminists have asserted that erotomania does not exist at all, that it is "just another form of misogyny. . . like nymphomania." Something men dream up to make themselves feel desirable.[29]

There have probably been many cases of erotomania throughout history, including today, that go unnoticed. And it may well be true that it is the inherent nature of erotomanic delusions that prevents study. Proclaiming that someone loves you is not nearly as remarkable as asserting that Romans, Napoleon, or Martians are invading the city. That I could not initially find many articles on erotomania seemed to reflect that psychiatrists had long been divided about whether it existed all. An influential text-book of only the last decade stated, "It would be advisable not to perpetuate the existence of this questionable syndrome in the literature."[30] A few authorities even asserted that if most cases of so-called primary or pure erotomania were followed long enough, symptoms suggestive of some other, more common psychotic illness, such as schizophrenia, would manifest.

Research also indicates that female erotomanics are more prone to the mania, or mood symptoms, in erotomania, suffering more often than their male counterparts from depression. If true, this would further complicate the diagnostic picture and render the study of erotomania more difficult. It would also mean that women, rather than men, with the disorder, would be more likely to seek treatment, thus contributing to the perception of women being more prone to the illness in the first place.

Regardless of who stalks whom, male after female or female after male, the media explosion around the globe in the last decade seems to have enhanced the problem for both sexes. The immediacy with which current technology allows people from all over the world to connect with one another imparts an implied intimacy. This is especially true for celebrities. While the "celebrities" of prior ages were (and continue to be) the objects of delusions, whether Greek gods, Jesus Christ, Napoleon, or royalty, we seem to have so many more potential targets now, thousands of celebrities who because of television, movies, and tabloids are known just as well in other countries as they are close to home. How many of us who consider ourselves "normal" feel almost as if we know our most beloved stars? A person predisposed to psychosis could believe that he really *does* know that person, even that a particular star, newscaster, or radio personality is talking directly to him. As a lonely teen described his fascination for his favorite actress:

> *It happens because they're in the limelight. . . [she] was on TV. She appeared on a commercial advertising her show and her personality came out. I'd read those magazine articles. You feel like you know these people. It's not like they're strangers. . . it's like they've been with you all your life, 'cause you're always hearing about them. . . . To me, [she] wasn't a stranger. . . I felt like [she] was accessible.*[31]

> —Robert Bardo explaining his delusional fixation on Rebecca Schaeffer after he murdered her.

Another possible factor contributing to the exploding number of celebrity stalkers, including erotomanics, is that celebrities are no longer as guarded about their private lives as they once were. An entire industry has flourished surrounding the not-so-personal lives of celebrities, from unsanctioned paparazzi photographers with telephoto lenses to television quasi-news shows like "Entertainment Tonight," endorsed by the celebrities themselves, to the tabloids with their completely fabricated stories. Even respected network news programs now "report" about celebrities as if this were real news, precisely because of the success of the tabloids and shows like "Hard Copy" and because of the public's craving, the world over, for tantalizing tidbits about the rich and famous.

In the last twenty-five years, cases of erotomania have been reported around the globe in such faraway lands as Brazil, Tanzania, Kenya, Malaysia, Hong Kong, Singapore, Saudi Arabia, Great Britain, Canada, and Australia; in such diverse cultures as Hindu, Afro-American, Islamic, Jewish, Chinese, and Greek; between the ages of thirteen and seventy-six and among straights and gays. What could explain the worldwide prevalence of a disorder that has really only been formally identified since de Clérambault published his studies in the 1920s? Surely the fact that erotomania has been seen in such diverse settings is testimony to some common, underlying psychopathology at work, as is true for depression, schizophrenia, and other psychiatric illnesses that occur across cultural and geographic lines. But as with other mental illnesses, it seems that the manner in which erotomanic delusions are expressed and even *whether* they are expressed are influenced by the society in which they occur.

Not long ago, an elderly Chinese woman in a Hong Kong nursing home developed erotomania toward an even older retired doctor who was also living there. Although certain of his love, she had never approached him, and her delusion was discovered only after she complained to the nursing home supervisor that her "lover" had told all the other residents about their "affair," causing her great embarrassment. In this case, it was supposed that she had never pursued the doctor because "Chinese elderly are still very traditional in their attitudes to love and marriage and it is very shameful for a Chinese female to speak directly to a man about her feelings."[32]

Culture may also influence how family, friends, and community treat the erotomanic and victim. At least in 1980, it was reported that for erotomanics in Tanzania, "The natives realise that there is something odd about their behavior and no marriage is formalized until after some ritual ceremonies have been performed."[33] Perhaps as our society has become more mobile, individuals predisposed to erotomania have also grown more removed from the natural social structure of family and community, forces that have traditionally provided a safety net with which to deal with destructive and obsessive impulses, inhibiting their expression.

A Hindu male who recently emigrated from Sri Lanka to England developed erotomania toward his sponsor's daughter after living with the family for just a few days. He believed they had fallen in love at first sight because of the way she had handed him a towel and became convinced that the young college student was his wife, harassing her incessantly with telephone calls, letters, and expensive gifts. He even tried to abduct her in the temple, right in front of the entire congregation, and persisted in his pursuit despite police injunctions and a beating at the hands of temple members. Her family believed that dishonor had been brought on them and, in fact, in their native Sri Lanka their daughter could have been forced to marry her erotomanic stalker.[34]

Today an extraordinarily high percentage of erotomanics, 43 percent in one 1993 study, appear to be foreign born.[35] Some authors believe this is due to acculturation gone awry, when men from sexually repressive cultures with a certain premorbid personality, immigrate to more open, Western societies. Once there, they misinterpret the normal social behavior of Western women by attaching romantic meaning where there is none.[36] Indeed, the misreading of sexual signals in the *same* culture, exemplified by the popularity of such books as *Men Are from Mars, Women Are from Venus* and by such nineties disagreements about whether no really means no, underscore how much more confusing it may be for immigrants from foreign cultures to adapt socially.

Culture shock has been defined, in psychiatric terms, as "a reactive process stemming from the impact of a new culture upon those who attempt to merge with it as a newcomer. [It] profoundly tests the overall adequacy of personality functioning, is accompanied by mourning for the abandoned culture, and severely threatens the newcomer's identity."[37] When culture shock, coupled with a vastly disparate code of sexual conduct, overlies a specific constellation of preexisting psychological problems, the result may be the societal bane of erotomania. Loss is often a precipitant for the development of erotomania, and in the case of those experiencing culture shock, the loss of an entire way of life may trigger its onset.[38]

If a man believes a woman from his new, strange society loves him, he may feel more accepted and understood by his adopted land because he is sanctioned by one of its most desirable members. Once the disorder develops, the rationalizations that accompany it are all too familiar: misinterpreting, embellishing, and even completely fabricating the love object's actions so that the fantasy love can exist. A man from Libya erotomanically pursued an American woman who happened to have the misfortune to sit in front of him in a college course, sending her gifts, flowers, letters, and a blood-soaked feather. He telephoned not only her, but also her mother and employer, stalking her for over five years, violating several restraining orders, all the while believing she was encouraging him by "the way she looked at me, the way she did her hair." He explained that "She gave a smile from a distance like she wanted to engage in a puzzle. . . ."[39]

By that summer of 1991, I had learned quite a bit about erotomania, more than I had ever expected to know. It was almost seventy years since de Clérambault first systematically categorized erotomania and it had taken almost all this time, until 1987, for American psychiatry to formally recognize the disorder, even though the illness itself had been known, if not named, since ancient times. With all the many misnomers used to describe it as well as the other disparate illnesses that had usurped the term, it was no wonder that erotomania had had a rather psychotic history, describing everything from sexual depravity to lovelorn longing. Given all its varied manifestations, erotomania had nevertheless been understudied and seemed to be one of the few areas in psychiatry one could research and honestly say one had read everything ever written about it.

So far Fran had proven relatively harmless, but since there was such a paucity of information on successful treatment, I felt I had little more than my instincts to guide me on what to do next. To be sure, discovering that various nobility from baronesses to kings, not to mention Greek goddesses, had been saddled with erotomanics throughout the ages provided me some comfort, for I perceived myself to be in illustrious company, indeed. But it was now almost two years since I had met Fran, and her telephone calls to my office showed no sign of abating. My small solace at being part of a distinguished cadre quickly evaporated as I found myself wishing I could simply rely on my antecedents' powers of *noblesse oblige* to banish Fran from me forever. Alas, it was not to be.

For now I decided to tolerate her distant advances. Since the incident at the theater, I had not seen her again. I was still afraid of angering her with a restraining order, perhaps inciting her to further, even violent action, as she had done in the past. Although I knew she would rationalize it away, I still hoped that my constant and consistent unresponsiveness to her letters and telephone calls might eventually lead her to lose interest and focus on someone more engaging.

Chapter Five

RESTRAINT

B
Y NOW FRAN HAD BEEN IN HOT pursuit of me for almost two years. Sometime after the note about my "baby" I had called the police to see what my options were and was informed that Arizona did not have a law against stalking. Unless I obtained a restraining order, nothing could be done. If Fran violated a restraining order, the police assured me, she would be arrested. Although I had previously resisted this course, fearful it would incite her to violence as it had apparently done in the past, I seriously considered obtaining such an order after finding a particularly disturbing series of notes on my car within the span of two weeks. They seemed to illustrate how detached from reality she was, at least reality as I knew it to be, and to confirm all the delusional assumptions I had assumed she was making about me and our "relationship."

In one note, she wondered if I would ever give her my home address or telephone number because she knew she should not call me at work. She even admitted feeling awkward about sending letters, cards, and songs to my office and ended by expressing, yet again, that she would like to see me. In the next letter she confessed that she thought about me "all the time," yet was "confused" by my actions. She suggested we meet at her church, but at the same time chastised me for waiting for an invitation from her to express my feelings. She said she had seen evidence of my humor but had been hurt by my "tenacious ability" to contact various individuals in her life, influencing them to change their minds about matters that affected her. She felt there were not many people left that she could trust who would not be subject to some "interjection" from me. As an example, she said her ex-boss had told her that I had helped him write the agreement under which she had resigned from her company, an agreement that she felt was unfair. She wrote that my "stealthy activism" never ceased to amaze her, and concluded with, "I love you."

But the *pièce de résistance* came in a quick one-two punch that left me reeling: She invited me to a party in a card that had printed on the outside, "If you don't come back soon. . . " and on the inside finished, "I'll just have to come and get you." Then the rambling and largely intelligible letter I received soon after had a P.S. repeating over and over that it was "Okey–dokey [sic]" for her to "steal" me.

Feeling more and more vulnerable from these tacit threats and having long ago given up all hope that Dr. Trottle could stop her, I made the decision to obtain a restraining order. I was sorry that a mentally ill person I had treated and that I still felt somewhat responsible for would be spending time in jail, but after her last series of letters, I was becoming more and more frightened. I had stopped keeping Dr. Trottle informed of Fran's attempts to contact me a few months after the incident in the hospital parking lot, when he had written to ask that I send him copies of her letters. I was livid when he wrote that this was to help Fran understand my response to her. He was a doctor who had been venerated for his therapeutic skills, yet he was apparently breaking one of the basic rules of psychiatry: Never argue delusions with the delusional. He just did not get it. Fran would win every time. It did not matter what the content of her letters or our one meeting had been. It was inappropriate of her to contact me—period.

I sent the copies he requested but ceased communicating with him because I believed it might be doing more harm than good. I could see that Fran might interpret any contact I had with him as an interest in her. So when I received Fran's latest correspondence, I knew that I was on my own. What I did not expect was that this feeling would only be heightened by Tim's response to my announcement that I had decided to get a restraining order. He downplayed my discomfort.

"I really think she's harmless," he said.

"How do you know?" I asked, incredulously.

He could only shrug, but I knew he was referring to his own stalker, Joanne. She was a middle-aged patient Tim continued to treat despite her once following him home to find out where he lived. Neither of us was ever aware of her watching the house, but she had told Tim of her visits during one of their recent sessions. This woman had multiple personality disorder, and, she explained to Tim, one of her child "alters" felt more secure just being near him during times of stress. When this alter felt better, the "host" personality took over and the woman was able to go home. Joanne had been a sore spot in our relationship ever since Tim had told me about her surreptitious visits. I had asked him to dismiss her as a patient if she would not stop them.

"You have a patient watching you, too," he shot back.

"Former patient," I corrected. "There's a big difference. If you continue to see her, you're just giving her the message that what she is doing is fine."

Tim disagreed. He thought Joanne's visits were harmless and he continued treating her. To me it seemed clear that both Tim and I had stalkers. It was just that I was the only one who realized it. I tried to see things from Tim's point of view. Was he assuming that just because Joanne's visits were innocuous, that Fran, who hadn't even reached the point of coming to our home, was innocuous as well? Still, I found his lack of support for me disheartening.

Tim and I had always been so in sync about so many things. We knew on our first date that we would always be close, although at the time we had no idea that we would ever get married. It was so unlike the two of us not to understand and share each other's feelings. I was worried about my stalkers, our stalkers, so he should be, too, I reasoned. Yet whenever I announced Fran's latest contact I felt him withdraw. It was as if her letters and telephone calls were tangible evidence that he could not protect me from harm and as if my further suggestion of a restraining order only reinforced his feeling of helplessness. Perhaps he felt my desire for outside aide pointed to his weakness, as if I were implying, "If you can't protect me, maybe the police can." But I *was* afraid, and by now not just of what Fran might do, but also of the effect her emotional assaults were having on my relationship with Tim.

I was only too aware, from my work, that couples seemed to deal with crisis in only one of two ways: Either it made them stronger or it pulled them completely apart. I wondered if Tim and I would come through this harassment from Fran with our relationship intact. Neither of us had broached the subject of marriage in some time, although we still considered ourselves engaged. With the growing distance between us, talk of a wedding would have seem forced and unnatural. Without much success, Tim and I had tried to discuss the emotional distance we were experiencing, and I had assumed that some of it was due to the natural ups and downs in any relationship, but now I wondered how much of it was caused by Fran and by the continuous drain on our lives from her many contacts.

Ever since the day Tim and I had met, I as a fourth-year medical student and he as the second-year resident assigned to supervise me, Tim had maintained some of that initial mentoring, protective role throughout our relationship. It had been a source of pride for him and comfort for me. One of the things I loved most about Tim was that I knew I could count on him for anything, from knowing what was wrong with my car, to how to console me when I needed it. Fran was eroding what had once been a foundation of our relationship; her erotomanic delusions about me were something he couldn't fix, and his response was to downplay their impact, only serving to draw us further apart. Ironically, I found myself wondering if Fran might just get what she believed she already had: a free me.

When I called the county court, I learned I had to appear in person to obtain a restraining order. This meant a trip to the downtown courthouse, a thirty-minute drive from my office. My practice had gotten quite busy, and I just could not seem to find the time for such a long break during the day. I also resented having to cancel current patients to take care of unfinished business with a former one. I kept putting it off, telling myself that perhaps Tim was right, it wasn't so bad. I could handle a few (hundred) letters.

Finally my not-so-subconscious fear of Fran collided with a real-life Fran "invasion," propelling me to take action. It had been several months since I had treated Beth for the last time. But one night I had a dream, a nightmare really, in which Beth was calling out to me, screaming with terror. In the dream I stumbled out of bed and made my way to the front door in the dark. Beth was banging on it from the outside, yelling for me to help her. She didn't have to say what the crisis was; I knew. Fran was there, somewhere in the night, terrorizing her and through her, me.

I tried opening the door, but it was locked on both sides. I went to the windows and threw myself against them, but they did not budge. On either side of the door, Beth and I were becoming frantic. Suddenly she let out a shrill scream that drowned out the sound of my own panicked breathing—until her scream turned into the piercing ring of the telephone. I heard Tim sleepily answer the call, roll over and say, "It's for you." I finally opened my eyes, groping for the receiver. I could barely hear the voice of the operator at my answering service over the sound of my still labored breathing and pounding heart.

"Dr. Orion, you have an emergency call from Fran Nightingale. Shall I put her through?"

"What?" I asked in a daze, wondering if I was still dreaming.

"You have an emergency call from Fran Nightingale. Can I connect you?" she said indifferently, repeating her standard protocol.

"No. Don't put her through," I said, and I heard a faint gasp from the startled woman. "Don't you have a note there not to contact me when she calls?"

"Well, let's see. . . no I don't see any. . . oh, wait. Here it is. I'm sorry, Dr. Orion. I'm new and I just didn't see it."

"That's fine," I lied. Then fueled by leftover adrenaline from my dream that had been instantly recharged by the mere mention of Fran's name, I managed to say, "Tell her if she calls me again, I'll get a restraining order."

I lay there the rest of the night, wide awake, seething because Fran could get to me even in my sleep. Next to me in bed, I did not hear the sound of Tim's usual snoring. I knew that he, too, for once, was awake, his feeling of helplessness reflecting Fran's own perception of him as inconsequential. The nightmare also confirmed the conclusion I had already reached about my experience with Beth, that Fran's intrusiveness was affecting others whose care I was responsible for. Now I saw it was also affecting the one I cared about most.

The morning after that noxious night, I arrived at my office and picked up my messages. Two from Fran. She certainly had not wasted any time. I could no longer do so either, and rearranged my schedule so I could get downtown a few days later. Of course, I realized that obtaining such an order was giving Fran exactly what she wanted—contact with me, albeit indirectly through the courts. But almost two years of offering her no response had not seemed to change her pursuit of me in the least: If anything, she was becoming more threatening. Since she seemed to think I was contacting her all the time, anyway, I reasoned, perhaps an actual contact would do no more harm. Most important, it seemed safe to assume that she had stopped stalking the other women sometime after they had obtained their restraining orders. Dr. Trottle had, after all, told me of two other women who had filed restraining orders against Fran, but since my periodic checks with the county clerk's office uncovered no other orders of protection against her, it seemed reasonable to conclude that she had long since ceased her pursuit of them.

I purposely did not go to the courthouse at lunchtime, thinking that time of day would be particularly busy, and was rewarded with only one person ahead of me in line when I entered the small room in the county court building. The woman talking to the clerk about getting a restraining order was casually dressed in a skirt and blouse, holding her application in one hand and the hand of a small child in the other. From what little I heard, it sounded as if she needed protection from some sort of male significant other who had been abusing her for some time. How sad, I thought, that while I needed protection from the threat of someone who I had never loved, she needed to be protected from someone she had and who would always be connected to her through their child.

I waited only a few minutes, and when the woman took her little girl over to a bench to begin filling out the paperwork, I told the clerk what she had probably heard hundreds of times before, "I need to get a restraining order." I felt silly saying those words in my Ann Taylor suit, as if being a professional should automatically mean that I was insulated from getting into such a predicament. I wanted to tell the clerk that I was not like that other woman, that I had not been beaten down, had not stayed too long in an abusive relationship out of some futile combination of hope and fear. But in a sense, I had. I had allowed Fran to abuse me for almost two years and was only now taking legal action to protect myself. I, too, had stayed in the "relationship" out of fear; fear that a restraining order would only incite her further. When the clerk handed me an application, I simply said, "thank you," instead of explaining myself to her as I had wanted to do. I sat down at another bench and started to fill in the blanks, feeling perhaps a trace of the shame the other woman felt and a deeper understanding of how those in domestic violence situations can stay with their abusers.

I was stumped at the first question, or rather the first series of questions, which asked for a physical description of "the defendant." I did not remember how tall she was, how much she weighed, what color her eyes were, even the color of her hair. So much for a psychiatrist's powers of observation. I had seen a pay phone in the hall, so I called the medical records department at the hospital and asked the clerk to look up Fran's chart. I knew the initial nursing evaluation from when she had been admitted would have all the pertinent information. Glancing down the rest of the triplicate form, I realized I also needed Fran's social security number, address, and telephone number, so I asked the clerk for these as well, although I could easily have obtained the latter from almost any one of her numerous notes and messages I had brought with me. It was less painful to have the information provided to me than to subject myself to handling any of her papers.

The rest of the questions were easier to answer. I noticed with some bemusement that, for once, pressing hard enough with my pen was not an issue. I could feel my anger swell as I dutifully detailed and relived my many communications from Fran. Yet with each stroke of the pen, I felt a growing confidence that I was assuring my own safety and that of Tim's, as well as our uninterrupted sleep. I had only six lines to answer the statement, "I have been harassed by the Defendant as follows: (Important: Harassment involves a *series* of acts. Be specific about each event, the date and place it occurred)." I felt I could write volumes, but I had to be succinct: No room to detail the incalculable emotional damage she had wreaked in my life for more than twenty long months.

I provided the dates and times for her most recent letters and phone calls, which I had dutifully documented in anticipation of this moment, and I indicated that there had been numerous other contacts. I added that early on she "followed me out to my car and was told then not to contact me, but she continues." I characterized some of her letters as "angry/threatening and psychotic." The next question, "If this petition is not granted immediately, the following may occur:" was more difficult to answer. I wanted to write, "more of the same." Wasn't that enough? Remembering the conversations I had had so many months ago with Dr. Trottle and Fran's therapist, I finally wrote: "Her past therapists told me she did this to other women, followed them home, and damaged their cars." I also added, "She knows who my fiancé is, and I am concerned for his safety."

And I was concerned. I knew from my research that some experts felt those most at risk of violence from erotomanics are not the objects themselves but their loved ones, especially if perceived as obstacles to the erotomanic's love. Just as Fran had offered to get rid of my delusional baby, she also might want to dispose of my very real fiancé. Even other family members can be in danger, if they are perceived as threats. Tragically, the Lennon Sisters became the first well-known family so affected.

Bill Lennon, the patriarch of the family and father of eleven, quit his job as a milkman to manage and travel with his four singing daughters after they became regulars on *The Lawrence Welk Show* in 1955. Despite their subsequent marriages and having children of their own, he continued to keep a fatherly eye on his grown-up girls in this close-knit Catholic family. Perhaps that was his downfall.

Chet Young, a disturbed man with a history of mental problems, began to believe that Peggy Lennon, married with a family of her own, was his wife, and repeatedly tried to contact her. He sent Peggy numerous letters, constantly showing up at the studio, seemingly only to stare at her. After he appeared at her home and church, he was finally arrested and sent to a mental institution. He escaped months later. In several letters to Peggy, he had clipped photos of her father, circled them, and written, "This man is keeping me from my true wife."[1]

Finally a year after the stalking began, believing that Peggy's father was still against their union, Young waited for him in the parking lot of the Marina Del Rey golf range where Bill Lennon worked as a pro. As Lennon approached, Young jumped out from behind a car with a gunny sack and pulled out a rifle. According to a witness, the two men struggled:

> Bill broke away and started toward the entrance to the parking lot. . . . [t]he man fired, hit him once, Bill staggered and ran toward a corner fence. The man fired again and hit him in the back. Bill crawled around the fence, the man ran right up to him, put the gun to the side of his head by the ear and fired again.[2]

Almost immediately on hearing of their father's murder, the sisters knew who was responsible. Later that day they discovered a letter from Young in their unopened pile of fan mail. It contained another cutout of their father from a magazine with a picture of a gun aimed at his head and the words, "High Noon" scribbled nearby. Bill Lennon had died that day at noon. Young escaped but was found two months later in his car, dead of a gunshot wound, an apparent suicide. The gun he had used to kill himself was the same one he had used to kill Bill Lennon.

I felt chilled in the oppressive heat of the Tucson summer as I remembered what had happened to the fifty-four-year-old Lennon and thought about what that could mean for Tim. When I handed the clerk my completed application for the restraining order, she glanced over it and read Fran's name out loud as a look of shock came over her face.

"She's stalking you?" she asked, but it was more of a statement.

"Yes, she is," I replied, producing for her the foot-thick stack of letters, cards, and phone messages from Fran that I had collected and brought in as evidence. I started to explain to her what erotomania was and that a woman could very well stalk another woman under its influence, but she cut me off.

"That's nothing," the clerk laughed. "You should have seen the pile some woman brought in on her a few years ago!"

In that instant I realized that what had been a painfully long, drawn-out ordeal for me was really just a miniscule moment in Fran's never-ending, erotomanic story.

I took an oath that what I had written was true, and the judge quickly granted my petition. Then I paid thirty dollars to a process server whose card said, "Serving Tucson since 1958." I wondered how many other men and women had applied for restraining orders against erotomanic stalkers since then.

Returning to work, I waited for Fran's response, which I knew would come. It did not take long. Within just a few hours of being served, she called my office. I immediately called the police. They said they would arrest her, and for the first time in almost two years, I was elated. For once I felt in control again. Why hadn't I done this before, I quizzed myself.

But my newfound confidence did not last long. I quickly discovered that "arrest" has a different meaning to the police than to ordinary citizens. In lieu of being sent to jail, an arrest for those crimes considered minor, misdemeanors such as spitting, loitering, littering, and violating restraining orders, can be dealt with strictly on paper. This type of arrest was the one made on Fran. She was issued a citation.

After being served with the temporary restraining order, or TRO, she had two weeks in which to appeal, but even if she lost and the restraining order was made "permanent," it would still expire after six months. The court promptly notified me that Fran had, indeed, appealed, and I was given a date to appear before the judge. If I did not appear, the TRO would be dropped. In the meantime, however, Fran was supposedly bound by its restrictions. After that first telephone call, I did not hear from her again during the weeks before the court date.

I arrived at the courthouse at the appointed date and time, once again resentful that I had to cancel several patient hours in the process, but hopeful that this would finally signal the end to my ordeal. There were eight rows of benches in the spectator section of the courtroom. I thought I recognized the back of Fran's head in the first. A young woman whom I did not recognize was sitting next to her in the nearly empty room, and she and Fran were whispering back and forth.

The judge was also a woman, and as she ruled on some previous motion, I quietly found a seat toward the back. When my case was called, Fran stood, and I saw that it was indeed her. The woman with her did not rise, and I felt relieved that Fran had not hired an attorney. Fran was sworn to tell the truth and sat down at the defendant's table.

I approached the bench and was told to sit at the table usually reserved for the prosecution. Fran was asked if she wanted to question me, and she, of course, answered yes. I had not expected this. I thought we would both present our cases to the judge. It had never occurred to me that justice would be served by forcing me to interact with the woman who was stalking me. I was disgusted, outraged, and a little frightened. I tried not to shake as I walked toward the witness stand where I, too, was sworn to tell the truth.

Although it was my life that had been disrupted and violated, we were now on equal ground before the court. We were complements of the legal system, face-to-face for the first time since that night I had briefly glimpsed her at the theater. I do not know if I would have even recognized her on the street. It had been too long. She seemed to have put on weight, and my professional eye could detect the dulling of features and expression caused by the antipsychotic medication she must still have been taking.

Other than that, however, I would not have been able to tell there was anything wrong with her. She was not disheveled as I remembered her from our last interaction in the hospital parking lot. She had obviously been able to pull herself together for her court appearance. I was suddenly not so sure that the judge would grant my request for a permanent restraining order. I would have to prove my case.

As I sat waiting for the stalker to question me, I felt my anger build, not just at Fran, but at the legal system that had led us both to this. The courts had finally allowed her access to the one thing she had professed to have wanted for so long: me. Well, she now had her wish. And unexpectedly I felt victimized more than I ever had been in the last two years by being forced not only to face her, but also to speak with her.

I decided right then that even though I had to answer her questions, I did not have to submit to her, to encourage her any more than my mere presence was already doing. By responding tersely and looking at her only when I had to, I could give her as little satisfaction as possible. If she violated the restraining order, I reasoned, she would have more opportunities to see me in court. I needed to make this one as ungratifying as possible.

"Why have you gotten this order against me?" she asked, quietly.

"I want you to stop harassing me," I said as evenly as I could while trying to look straight through her.

"Harassing you how?" she asked, emotion straining her voice.

"You come to where I work and leave me notes, you call me at all hours, and you send me letters through the mail." I answered in a monotone.

"But, you wanted me to. . . and my job. Why did you tell my boss. . . I—"

Under the pressure of finally getting her wish and perhaps seeing that I wasn't as attractive and kind and caring and nice as she had made me out to be, reality was beginning to tear at her delicate delusional bubble. She could not keep herself together much longer under this pressure, and I felt petty in my anger toward her. Her uncanny ability to insinuate herself in my life and my relationship had, up to this point, led me to think of her as an equal in this contest, but truly we were not even playing on the same field.

I had not fully comprehended until that moment how much her delusions about me were driving her behavior. It was one thing to read about them in her letters; it was quite another to be confronted directly with them and all the passion in her they incited. Given the only truth she knew, perhaps she could not help herself. But I could not show her any of my misguided sympathy. We were no longer in a professional relationship. I had to show her we were in no relationship at all. Sympathy might be interpreted as compassion; even love.

"I just want you to stop." I said firmly, still trying not to look at her.

"But, then, why do you keep doing things—"

"I just want you to stop," I repeated.

"Then why did you talk to my boss and have me fired and my insurance taken away?"

I looked over at the judge, and it was obvious that I did not need to say another word. Her expression indicated that she had heard enough.

"Ms. Nightingale, you are ordered not to come within five hundred feet of Dr. Orion, her house, her car, or her place of work."

The judge turned to give some paperwork to her clerk. I was relieved and grateful until I heard Fran start to cry.

"But, Your Honor, if I can't go to the hospital where Dr. Orion works, I won't be able to attend my support group there."

I instantly shook off my sympathy, finally banishing it forever as I considered this new ploy. Perhaps she was not as helpless and uncalculating as I thought. A free support group for the mentally ill did meet there Tuesday evenings, but I knew that she rarely if ever attended. I often stayed late at the hospital and was there when the meeting started. The small group met in the cafeteria with the door open, and I had never seen Fran in the room. I also had other patients who attended the group, and they had never mentioned her.

"Your Honor, she rarely if ever goes to this group and if you grant this request, she will just use it as a sanctioned means to continue to harass me at my workplace. Besides, there are other such support groups at other locations in the city. You should also know that the defendant has already violated the temporary restraining order."

Fran started crying even louder and then pointed to the woman who had sat beside her.

"My therapist—she's with the mental health center—can tell you how important that group is to me!"

The judge, however, said she did not need to hear anymore. She informed me that punishment for the restraining order violation was another matter altogether and would be considered at another time. She then amended her order, in effect rewarding Fran's violation by giving her legal blessing to her proximity to me one day a week. Sure enough, from that day forward, I could regularly count on finding letters from Fran in my hospital box on Wednesday mornings. The receptionist told me that Fran would come by to deliver her letter on Tuesday nights and leave, never even staying for the group.

Through various connections, I easily discovered who her new therapist was. I assumed that after Fran lost her job, the loss of her insurance followed and that neither Dr. Trottle nor the woman therapist I had spoken to were still treating her. When I finally located the new therapist, I did not waste any time. After the introductions, I got to the point and we quickly fell into the natural rhythms of therapist doublespeak, usually reserved for therapists who do not agree on how to handle a case. While I did not appreciate her accompanying Fran to the courtroom, I did not know how much I might have to depend on her good graces in the future.

"My concern and the reason for my call is that going to court with her may have given her the wrong message." Meaning: Fran thinks you agree with her.

"At the time, I wasn't clear about what was going on. I understand now that going was probably a mistake." Meaning: I'm new in the field and I've heard all the horror stories about psychiatrists having relationships with their patients. I didn't know if you were one of them. Sorry.

"Well, I can understand that hearing the situation only from Fran's side, it would be easy to be confused. Please keep me posted on any threats or intentions I should know about." Meaning: You owe me.

"I will." Meaning: Sorry (again).

"By the way, you may want to transfer her care to a male therapist."

Once again, Dr. Trottle had probably not warned the mental health center about Fran's special needs with regard to gender.

"I was wondering about that." Meaning: Now I'm scared.

In all probability she was not at risk. She was considerably younger than Fran and, without a "Dr." before or an "Esq." after her name, was probably not perceived by erotomanic, piranha-like Fran as high enough on the food chain to lure her.

I had naively assumed a restraining order would keep Fran away from me once and for all. I could not have been more wrong. The restraining order did not help; she ignored it. Even more to my chagrin, the police seemed to ignore it as well. I soon found myself wondering if

I had filled out the wrong paperwork. Who was being restrained here, Fran or the authorities?

Within hours of leaving the courtroom, Fran called my office. I immediately called the sheriff's department. They cited her. With the next phone call, they cited her again. Another phone call, another citation. The letter I soon received angrily accused me of obtaining the restraining order under false pretenses, since I had written in my initial application to the court that she waited for me that day in the hospital parking lot, when, she maintained, she had only "happened by." She wrote, sarcastically, "Who cares about the truth." Yet despite her obvious ire, she still asked me to call her, enclosing her telephone number.

Her fury, however, never seemed to last long. Even after that latest letter, the next might have sounded tender coming from anyone else, in other circumstances. She thanked me over and over for all I had done for her. The trouble was, the only thing that had even the slightest basis in reality was her belief that I had paid for her hospital stay. She also seemed to think I was the one who brought her to the hospital in the first place and further, that I had given her church one hundred thousand dollars earmarked for her, which she now was trying to retrieve from them.

Yet she seemed to have *some* awareness of my wish not to see her: She said she cried often because of all the "mixed messages." Still, she continued to feel a strong attraction to me even while she felt embarrassed that she might be perceived as a "gold digger," since "in some ways, our lives do not integrate."

After every contact, by phone or letter, I would call the police. Armed with my restraining order, I would expect them to arrest her. But nothing happened. She was simply given a citation, assigned a case number, and added to the backlog in the county court system.

The only effect the restraining order seemed to have was on my relationship with Tim. Whenever the police came to our home or office to get my statement, he was reminded even more about how powerless he seemed to be. Although he didn't say it, I got the distinct impression he thought my getting the restraining order was overkill, especially now that I was practically on a first-name basis with the entire Tucson Police Department. He still did not view Fran as a threat. Unfortunately the police seemed to agree.

One Saturday afternoon, a few months after I had obtained the restraining order, I was puttering around the house when Tim got back from the hospital. I had not gone in that day and was still in my nightgown, a luxury I allowed myself on weekends when I didn't have to work. Since our mailbox was at the foot of our driveway, about five hundred yards from our home, I had not retrieved the mail that day. Tim had, and left it on our kitchen table while he fixed himself something to eat and began to tell me about an interesting case he had seen that morning. So much of our conversations those days had seemed to revolve around work. I half listened as I sorted through the letters.

There was one envelope addressed to me in a child's handwriting. It had a return address, but no name. Curious, I opened it first. I did not know any children who would write to me. Inside was only a poem entitled, "Let's give up these stupid fights." My heart raced as I skimmed to the end. It was signed, "Love, Fran." I let out a small cry, and Tim looked up from the meal he was preparing. Seeing my expression, he immediately asked, "What is it?" as he strode to my side. I handed him the letter. We both knew what it meant. Fran had somehow found out where we lived. He studied the envelope.

"It doesn't have a stamp, or a postmark," he said, gently, knowing how the news would affect me. Fran not only knew where we lived, she had been there. That day. While I was home and in my nightgown. I felt sickened, but at the same time, I felt Tim's presence in a way I had not for months.

"What's different?" I asked, and he immediately understood what I meant. We knew each other too well.

"I guess I didn't realize how intrusive she was and how violated you felt until now," he said tensely. "I don't like the idea of her coming around, especially when I'm not here."

Now that he could understand why I had been so fearful, since he feared for me himself, his anger was finally mobilized. I had also felt helpless with Fran for so long but obsessively reading everything I could about her illness had allowed me to feel as if I were dealing with her in some small way. Tim had not had that advantage. Even though Fran had just been at the house, I was relieved to feel that Tim and I were in sync again.

"So are you going to get rid of Joanne?" I asked, playfully.

"No," he said, without hesitation, grateful that I could now joke about what had been a sore spot for us. That Joanne came to our house didn't seem to matter as much to me after that. As long as Tim understood the fear Fran instilled in me, I could live with one more inappropriate visitor. I also began to realize that one of the ways Tim had dealt with his powerlessness to stop my stalker was by being too lenient with his. Letting Joanne continue to come to the house had proven to him that stalkers were not dangerous and had led him to downplay my discomfort. Since I knew he would not discount my feelings again, I could handle Joanne's visits. Fran's were another matter.

After six months the restraining order expired and I had to wait, despite her numerous violations, for her next intrusion before I could reappear in court to request a renewal. She also had the right to appear to challenge my request that she be forced to stay away from me, for all the good it did. I dreaded seeing her again but was confident this time the judge would grant the injunction. Fran's continued pursuit, despite a court order, proved that she needed to be restrained.

I had gotten to the courtroom a few minutes early and looked around. No Fran. Maybe she had decided not to come? Weren't patients with erotomanic delusions supposed to avoid face-to-face contact? She certainly had up until now. I found a seat in the nearly empty room and listened as the judge finished hearing another case. Soon I felt someone sit directly behind me as I waited for mine to be called. Whoever came in had to climb over several people to get to that particular seat. I literally felt the hairs on the back of my neck stand up and turned around. It was Fran. I slid to the other end of the bench. I know that meant, in effect, that I blinked, and she got me. But I couldn't stand the thought of her literally breathing down my neck when she had done it figuratively for so long.

Of course, the judge granted my request. Of course, she again told me that punishment for Fran's violations would take place at a different hearing. I had actually gone to the trouble of getting a notarized affidavit from the hospital receptionist stating that on Tuesday nights, Fran typically came to the hospital, left a note for me, and did not stay for the group. The judge took out the provision that Fran be allowed to attend the sessions. But I didn't feel relieved. By now I had learned that it wouldn't make any difference; I would still continue to hear from her.

The officer who served that second restraining order had my answering service call me at home.

"Are you aware that she is no longer at the address you gave us?" No, I was not. I had simply given them the address from the restraining order served on Fran the first time, six months before. "Well, I thought I'd better let you know that she's moved," he said, and gave me her new address.

"Oh my God, she lives less than two miles away!"

In a city of half a million people, this could be no coincidence. I never knew how she had obtained my address. I assumed she simply followed me home from work one day. Dr. Trottle had said that was what she did with the other women. Now she and I shopped at the same supermarket, filled up our cars at the same gas station, had an evening snack at the same Baskin-Robbins. I felt as if my life was no longer my own; that I was forced to share it with a totally unwelcome, unwanted, potentially dangerous intruder. Far from restraining her activities, the order of protection had simply emboldened her, giving her license to intrude even more into my life because she saw that her continued inappropriate behavior was, nonetheless, acceptable to those sworn to protect me. Her violations cost her nothing.

Unfortunately the issuance of a restraining order's provoking an erotomanic to more brazen acts is not unique. Mona V. found out that hell hath no fury like an erotomanic scorned. She first met Stephen G. when she worked in a mall in Scottsdale, Arizona. She was concerned enough with his unwanted attention that when she moved to Denver for graduate school soon after, she instead told him that she was moving to Seattle. When he gave her a one hundred dollar bill for moving expenses, she returned it with the note, "When a lady says no she means no, a gentleman respects that."3

Stephen proved he was no gentleman. He looked for her in Seattle, and when he could not find her there, managed to learn she had moved to Denver. He not only moved to the same city, but also to the same apartment building, right down the hall. He even planned to enroll in the same graduate studies program. Soon he was leaving her such books as Stephen King's *Nightmares and Dreamscapes*, Anne Rice's *Lasher*, and Dean Koontz's *Mr. Murder*.

Feeling threatened, she tried to return them, telling him repeatedly to leave her alone. In desperation, she even threw the books over a fence but found them on her doorstep the very next day. He started talking to their apartment manager about the object of his obsession.

"She's so magnetic. Don't you feel it? Don't you feel her magnetism?" he would ask.[4] Mona obtained a restraining order. Stephen was stunned.

"I couldn't believe this was happening to me," he said later. "I didn't follow her here."[5] Far from stopping him, the restraining order drove him underground. Literally. Three-and-a-half months after she first saw him in Denver, Mona spotted a freshly drilled hole in her bathroom floor. The maintenance man came over the next day to investigate.

"When I went underneath the building I found the whole bottom side of her vanity had been dug out and made so. . . somebody could get inside. I all of a sudden heard noises from a grate outside. . . and the grate came open and [the stalker] crawled in."[6]

Stephen denied he had ever been down there before and maintained he had only done so that one time out of his concern for Mona's safety.

"I heard this sound, this banging," Stephen insisted. "My curiosity got the best of me. I knew something was wrong."[7]

The police found that the floor under Mona's bathroom had been altered so that all Stephen had to do was push up the bottom of the vanity to gain entrance. A search of his apartment revealed a hammer, work gloves, binoculars, and a book. They also found Mona's name written in large letters across a calendar, momentos from the photo lab she had worked at in Scottsdale, and a heart Stephen had drawn with their names in it and the words, "For Eternity."

Stephen was sentenced to five-and-a-half years in prison, but the "tunnel stalker," as he came to be known, only served about a year. For the rest of his sentence, he was transferred to Phoenix, where he remains under house arrest. Mona has since left the state, as well. The prosecutor on the case thinks Stephen will never give up and has said, "He's going to find her."[8] As Stephen wrote to Mona after his arrest, "You've misjudged me. That alone entitles me to one more chance to earn your respect."[9]

By Christmas 1991, Fran was a frequent visitor to the home Tim and I shared, although thankfully, she confined all her visits to above-ground activities. I still never actually saw her. But I knew she had been there whenever she left notes stuck in our front door or kitchen window. Then, while Tim and I were away for a two-week vacation, our housesitter twice saw Fran beating her chest in our yard. She left before the police arrived. I already knew she watched our house, which was not visible from the road, but set in a ravine at the end of a five hundred-yard driveway. Nothing illustrated that fact to me as vividly as the day she left her guitar and flute in our garage.

It was a Saturday afternoon and Tim had been working in the front yard for hours. During his one brief break, Fran had managed to walk unobserved all the way down our driveway and put her flute and guitar in our garage with a note. Largely illegible, it seemed to say something like, "win Dr.Orion, win" and was written on the unopened envelope of a letter sent to her by the county hospital. She further wrote that she did not want the instruments until I arranged for her to get her job back with the insurance company that fired her and that I could bring them to the "trail [sic]" when I did. I assumed she was referring to her upcoming hearing on her numerous restraining order violations.

I did not know what do to with the stuff, but knew I did not want anything of hers in the house. It made me feel as if she herself had finally gained entry. So while waiting for the police, we left the instruments in the garage. Amazingly Fran somehow slipped in and took them before the officer came. When he arrived, Tim suggested that she might even then be watching our home. He and the officer searched the desert while I remained behind locked doors. I had wanted to search, too, but Tim pointed out that if Fran saw me, that would only encourage further visits.

We lived in a residential neighborhood, yet because of the way our house was situated, surrounded by desert washes, building nearby was impossible. So there was nothing but several acres of sagebrush and cactuses surrounding our ranch-style home. I had never particularly liked the desert and never ventured beyond the confines of our yard to explore the terrain beyond. It had seemed unwelcoming, even threatening with all its prickly plants and camouflaged, stinging creatures. Now knowing that Fran could be out there watching at any time, the desert felt even more treacherous. It was as if she were waiting, curled behind some large rock, spines at attention, ready to strike.

When Tim had convinced me not to accompany them, I hadn't wanted him to go search with the officer either, but he was fuming that Fran had been watching our home—watching him all day. He was now completely involved, the threat she represented to us having been brought home by her—literally. They searched the surrounding area for about a half hour but did not find her. Chalk up two more citations.

There was still more evidence of Fran's surveillance of our home, and we learned of it from the unlikeliest of sources. During one of their sessions, Joanne, his patient with multiple personality disorder told Tim, "You know, it was the strangest thing. I woke up outside your house the other night and saw some woman looking in your window. Boy, did she run when she saw me!" That night, when Tim related this conversation to me, he obviously thought it was hilarious and suggested, "They should just take a number." I had to laugh at the image of each of our stalkers, Joanne and Fran, politely waiting their turn to be called. He was relieved I could see the humor in the situation, even as I wondered in revulsion about what Fran might be seeing. Yet, there was some satisfaction in pondering how she felt, for once being the object of observation herself.

I still couldn't sleep after each contact with Fran and continued to look behind me wherever I walked. Now I found myself doing this in my very own home, the one place I had formerly felt safe. I gave up my habit of remaining in my nightgown on weekends. Now whenever I picked up my mail, whether at work or at home, I dreaded finding another note from her. And I got dressed in the closet—it didn't have windows.

A pretrial hearing for Fran's multiple violations of the court order was finally set for February 1992, almost two and a half years since the stalking had begun. A few weeks before the court date, I received a letter from the private attorney her parents had hired. She wrote that she hoped my goal was not to punish Fran but to end her harassment of me and that in talking to her client, it was her belief that that goal had already been achieved. She explained that Fran had been taken to the county hospital after a security guard at a local mall had seen her in the parking lot beating herself with her fists.

Fran had remained hospitalized for two weeks, undergoing intensive group and individual therapy in which her harassment of me was thoroughly addressed. Fran told her attorney that she now clearly understood the purpose of the restraining order and that it was inappropriate of her to contact me in any way and, furthermore, that she agreed never to contact me again. She was taking a new antipsychotic medication, and I was welcome to contact the psychiatrist, Dr. Gertler, who had treated her in the hospital, to get his assessment. The attorney concluded by asking me to drop the charges.

I never really considered doing so. Even if Fran really were sincere, which I sincerely doubted, she would stay away from me whether or not I did what her attorney wanted. I had nothing to gain by signing the paper and everything to lose. If I dropped the charges and she continued to stalk me, I would have to start any legal proceedings against her from scratch. Besides, dropping the charges might well be interpreted by Fran as proof of my love for her. She had been in treatment the entire time since I had first met her, on various antipsychotic medications, with many people confronting her about her erotomanic delusions toward me. It had not done any good until then, and I seriously doubted anything had changed substantively.

Nevertheless, to try to get an objective opinion and in the faint hope of gaining some piece of mind, I telephoned Dr. Gertler. He told me that the psychological testing done during that admission was consistent with schizophrenia and that in contrast with what the attorney had said, he felt Fran was still quite delusional about me and that my chances were only "fifty-fifty" that she would cease her harassment. Unfortunately his prediction turned out to be wildly optimistic.

Her attorney was also wrong about me. I did think Fran deserved to be punished. Although I agreed that she was delusional and, therefore, had no control over her thoughts, I felt that she could and should control her actions. Her letters to me clearly indicated she knew what restraining orders were, but she was choosing to ignore them. Still, if I had thought dropping the charges would provide any chance of stopping her harassment of me, I would have done so in a heartbeat. My fear was quite the contrary, that doing so would "prove" to Fran what she had apparently been thinking all along: That I loved her and was testing her to see if she was worthy of that love. I had to proceed with the charges. Tim agreed.

Of course, the stalking did not stop. On the contrary, as the hearing approached, Fran stepped up her own efforts to contact me, asking me to drop the charges. The tone of one letter left on my car during that time was typical. It expressed her bewilderment and anger at my seeing the matter through, saying she didn't have money for an attorney. Wouldn't I please show some Christmas spirit by dropping the charges?

The letter's P.S. said it all: "I love you and I have a Christmas present for you." Two weeks of intensive, inpatient therapy and continued anti-psychotic medication were obviously no match for Fran's erotomanic delusions.

The prosecutor explained that even though Fran had racked up quite an impressive series of restraining order violations, these were only misdemeanors and Fran would get no jail time. She plea bargained the case, and in March 1992, almost a year after Fran's initial violation of the first restraining order, I received the following letter from the county attorney's office:

> *The final outcome of the case in which you were a victim is as follows: The Defendant, Fran Nightingale, has pled guilty to the charge of interference with justice. It is ordered that the defendant be placed on unsupervised probation for a period of six months and participate in domestic violence counseling and will not have any contact with the victim. The County Attorney's Office, the Law Enforcement Agencies involved, and the Victim Witness Program wish to thank you for your cooperation and assistance in this matter.*

Fran would remain free. She would not be incarcerated. Fran, of course, had already joyously contacted me to tell me the outcome even before the court had. In fact, for the two consecutive days before I received this notice in the mail, I had also received letters from Fran taped directly to my kitchen window. The first had a feather stuck to it, was addressed to "sassy woman," and offered me that feather for my cap.

In the second she asked if "redbeard" and I were getting serious. Of course, she had seen Tim at the hospital when I had first treated her, so she knew that he had red hair. But he had only recently grown a beard. Was she watching him as well? She also expressed her chagrin that despite working "on getting my act together" for two years, she still did not get to see me. But not to worry, she promised. She would return "stronger and more creative." I would not have long to wait.

Chapter Six

No Order in the Court

FRAN WAS FINALLY ARRESTED—REALLY arrested—in June 1992, after many more restraining order and probation violations. By then I had given up hope that she would ever see the inside of a cell. But one Saturday afternoon, nearly three months into her probation, I was at home alone, making lunch, when I noticed an envelope taped to the outside of my kitchen window. I knew immediately what it was because that had become a fairly typical way for Fran to leave her cards and letters. Even though I was used to this encroachment onto my property and into my life, her notes never failed to bring with them the dread that I could now feel rising. Had she watched me get dressed that morning? Seen me get out of the shower? Heard me sing to the radio? The integrity of my home once again had been breached by Fran's furtive scrutiny. She was out there—somewhere. At the same moments I had believed myself alone and unobserved, she could have been watching my every move. Once again she had stolen my sense of security.

My hunger vanished as all my senses focused on that envelope. Slowly, I walked to the window next to the front door where I could observe not only this latest tangible evidence of Fran's invasion in my life, but also the entire yard. No Fran. How long had she been watching the house today? And was she still out there? Now my pace quickened as I called the police. As usual, the dispatcher needed a telephone number where I could be reached so an officer could call before coming. I was afraid if I gave the number of my answering service, the police would either ignore the call or give it even less of a priority than I knew it was going to get anyway. Plus it would take longer for me to get to speak with the police if the answering service was involved. Alone, with Fran possibly still watching the house, I did not want to wait, so I gave the dispatcher my home phone number, pleading, "Please don't put this number on any piece of paper she could possibly get a hold of. She doesn't know my number and I don't want her to get it."

"I won't," she assured me.

An officer quickly called back and was on my front porch within minutes. Only then did I feel safe enough to retrieve Fran's note, a short poem that seemed to be about world peace. I handed it to the officer with resignation. Because this note, like the others, was not threatening, I expected him to merely make a paper arrest, as all the other officers had done for all her previous violations. After scanning my copy of the restraining order and hearing my story, which I could by now pop off in just under thirty seconds, he shocked me by saying, "I'll just go take her in. I have nothing else to do right now and besides, she lives right up the street."

"Take her in?" I asked, hesitantly. "You mean arrest her?"

"Yeah, I'll go arrest her," he casually replied.

"Let me get this straight. You're going to go to her apartment, arrest her, and put her in jail? Not just give her a citation?" I knew that suspicion had crept into my voice, but I could not help it. I had gotten my hopes up so many times before.

"Yeah," he answered, quizzically and with a bit of irritation. "Isn't that what you want?"

"You bet I do!" I exclaimed, allowing myself the relief and gratitude that was long overdue. I thanked him profusely but could not help wondering out loud what made this time so special. The difference turned out to have less to do with me or Fran than with the experience of this particular police officer.

"I've been stalked myself," he confided.

"Really?" I blurted out, as my psychiatric training deserted me. Stupidly, I was surprised that this could even happen to a police officer. But that was point with erotomania: Anyone could become its victim.

"Some elderly lady I helped on a burglary case years ago began following me around and sending me letters at the station. She thought I loved her," he said, shaking his head as if to ward off the memory. "It went on for years."

"How did it end?" I asked, hoping for some clue to my own situation.

"It didn't stop 'til she died." Sensing my disappointment, he quickly assured me, "I can understand your situation. I'll let you know what happens."

The next day at work I got his brief message: "Officer Cortez said he made the arrest and that you'd understand." Understand? For the first time in two-and-a-half years, I felt safe. Maybe if Fran finally reaped some legal reward for her behavior, she would stop at last.

Despite all I knew about erotomania, both from my personal experience and the research I had done, I was utterly flabbergasted the next morning when Fran called me collect from jail. Because she had never called me at home before, I could only surmise that the promises I had received about the care that would be taken with my home phone number were as empty as all the previous promises that Fran would be stopped. As soon as she was let out, I would have to change the number. For now, after she made five more attempts to call me collect at home, the jail suspended her telephone privileges.

Since Fran was actually in jail, the prosecutor could and did argue to the judge that she should remain there until her trial without bail. That she had violated her probation was only the latest evidence that she would continue to ignore the court orders. To my amazement—because up to now, I had not exactly felt that the legal system had been on my side—the judge agreed. Fran was to remain in the county jail.

Her parents had again hired an attorney for her. Even though they were not making it any easier for me in the courts, I felt sorry for them. Although we never spoke, I would see them on the few occasions I was in the courtroom. Motions were always being filed, and the prosecutor felt the judge would be more likely to keep Fran in jail if I were in court, both to show my concern and to answer any questions. Fran's parents looked to be in their seventies and seemed as weary dealing with the latest result of their daughter's mental illness as I was.

I felt truly sorry they had to suffer because of her behavior, but I did not believe that they were acting in her best interest, or mine, by hiring attorneys for her. I recalled that her father seemed to blame Fran for her psychotic breakdowns. Why was he not insisting, then, that she take responsibility for herself when she broke the law? Along with my personal feelings, my psychiatric training could not help surfacing, and I wondered how such mixed messages and misplaced concern on the part of Fran's parents might have contributed to the development of her erotomania in the first place.

In any event, it was now clear that her parents' inappropriate attempts to mitigate the consequences of their daughter's actions would not encourage her to stop. Although she would probably always believe that I loved her, the only hope of getting her to leave me alone was if the punishment for acting on her delusions was severe enough. If her parents stopped bailing her out and if the courts stopped merely slapping her on the wrist, perhaps she would feel that our great "love" was just not worth the price.

Fran remained in jail for four months while the legal system figured out what to do with her. To help in this task, she also received court-ordered psychiatric evaluations from two psychiatrists, who also happened to have been my supervisors during my residency just a few years before. Their job was to determine whether Fran understood she was acting illegally when she violated the restraining orders and whether she was competent to stand trial. If so, they were to make recommendations for sentencing. Both psychiatrists readily agreed she was currently competent, but whether or not she understood the consequences of her actions at the time was a little tougher for them to tease out.

Despite their conducting separate interviews, each psychiatrist obtained remarkably similar information from Fran, which they duly noted in their reports. She continued to believe that I had paid for her hospital stay and that even after getting the first restraining order, I had tried to contact her by attempting to give her several cars and jewelry. I was apparently still sending her masked messages in jail through some of the staff, who under my guidance were also altering her medications. Moreover, she thought I had given diamond earrings to a guard to give to her.

She also knew I was in a position to have her songs published (several of which she continued to write for me while in jail) since my family was in the entertainment business (Orion Pictures, again). Through this connection, she said, I had even tried to get her married to Paul Simon. Last, but not least, I was providing her with opportunities to escape, and if she did, I would drop the charges against her. As if the psychiatrists needed further confirmation, Fran admitted to them that she was still obsessed with me and that even if released, she would have a difficult time staying away.

Although throughout the interviews the psychiatrists had considerable trouble making sense of what she said in relation to me, both agreed that in all other areas, and on every other topic, she seemed completely lucid and logical. For this reason, one of the psychiatrists diagnosed erotomania, whereas the other believed, based on Fran's history, that she had schizophrenia with erotomanic delusions.

Finally both concluded that at the time of the offenses, she did not understand that her actions were wrong and, therefore, was neither mentally competent nor responsible. This was the conclusion despite her telling one psychiatrist that "She believed she was sane, but intended to claim that she was insane at the time of the offense."

He, in turn, felt that although Fran was delusional, she had the ability to "pull herself back" from her delusions, and observed that there was "a reluctance to act on her knowledge of reality." He believed Fran exhibited "some choice in giving in to the delusional system." Noting that Dr. Gertler had said Fran did not always take her medications, the psychiatrist felt "appropriate sanctions that would weigh that choice in favor of reality" and better compliance with her treatment would be helpful. Still, he opined, "Imprisonment would seem a harsh method of delivering those sanctions, given her severe mental illness" and instead recommended long-term hospitalization to deal with her "compulsions."

The other psychiatrist added that every possible effort should be made to keep Fran away from me because, he noted, eventually some individuals with erotomania become violent toward their victims. One sentence above all others in his report stood out, the one in which he briefly described a significant bit of Fran's history I had never heard before: In 1985, four years before we met, she had developed erotomanic delusions toward a female attorney. Fran had tried to strangle her. Had Dr. Trottle known about that?

I was incredulous that given her history, the psychiatrists would recommend against incarceration, but that is exactly what they did. I felt bitter disappointment as the last of my hopes were driven away, replaced by an irrational feeling of betrayal. These doctors had been my supervisors, and they were now my colleagues. Although I knew they had an obligation to be objective in their reports for the court, I had expected more from my own.

While the psychiatrists argued that Fran should not be imprisoned because of her compulsions, even they would have had to admit that many criminals have "compulsions" to act on their criminal behavior, but society expects them to control themselves. If they do not control themselves, regardless of whether they cannot, they are incarcerated—namely, arsonists, rapists, child molesters, and drunk drivers, despite the potential presence of bonafide mental illnesses such as pyromania, sexual sadism, pedophilia, or alcohol dependence.

Fran had even admitted to one of the psychiatrists that she knew what she was doing was "inappropriate." Didn't that mean that despite "compulsions" to give in to her behavior, she understood right from wrong? That she was choosing to illegally act on her delusions? I was not demanding that Fran stop fantasizing about me or stop thinking that I loved her or even stop believing that we had a relationship. Clearly, that was too much to ask. I did not care what she did in her own psyche as long as it did not impinge on mine.

Even if Fran truly could not control her behavior toward me, she *was* choosing not to be compliant with her medications, potentially the only effective treatment for her condition. I knew from Dr. Gertler that Fran had already been tried on Pimozide. Some of the psychiatric literature had reported that this rarely used antipsychotic medication was supposed to be specifically efficacious for erotomanic delusions. In these cases, although the delusions sometimes remained, they were apparently muted to the extent that the patients were no longer preoccupied by them and stopped trying to contact their victims.

Fran had also been treated with numerous other medications, appropriate not only for erotomania, but also for schizophrenia, depression, and manic-depression, none of which seemed to have touched her erotomanic delusions. Regardless, the attempts at medicating her symptoms were not having the desired effect. Research indicates that if medications are not working, which they rarely seem to anyway, the only treatment that offers hope for the victims of patients with erotomanic delusions is enforced separation. I was truly sorry that jail was a harsh method of punishment, but wasn't that the point? By deciding not to take her medicine and by ignoring the court orders, it seemed to me that Fran had already made her choice.

During one court appearance for a motion to grant bail, Fran looked particularly disheveled. When the judge called a brief recess, she was escorted, manacled and handcuffed, in her bright orange jail jumpsuit, to a holding area just outside the courtroom. The county attorney and I sat together in the hall, discussing the case, waiting for court to resume.

Suddenly, we heard a loud noise as Fran came crashing through the swinging double doors several yards away. She was headed straight for us. Her guards quickly pulled her back, but as the doors continued to swing to and fro we caught glimpses of Fran, as if caught in a strobe light, wrestling with them as more ran to their aide. Did she still think I wanted her to escape? Or was she trying to hurt me?

I saw the county attorney roll her eyes in bemused disbelief at Fran's feeble attempt to flee her captors, but when she looked at me, her expression immediately changed. I had been mesmerized by Fran's violent dance with her guards and had felt renewed terror at the thought that the judge might grant her request for bail. The attorney must have read my mind because she said, "Why don't you just go home. There's no way the judge will grant the motion after this. I'll call you if anything happens."

I thanked her and left, but I couldn't go home. I had patients to see, and somehow I had to manage to see them. Reading about Fran's agression toward another victim had been bad enough. Seeing her agression toward a bevy of burly guards she could not hope to thwart had nearly destroyed my resolve.

Why had I ever gotten that restraining order? I was no burly guard. Fran easily had fifty pounds on me. Once she got out, would she hesitate to try her luck with a more manageable target, the target who was responsible for her current predicament in the first place?

I made my way to my car for the thirty-minute drive from the downtown courthouse to the hospital. I tried to concentrate on the afternoon ahead, but thoughts of Fran's surreal struggle clamored for attention. I could not rid my mind of the image of her violence. Once again, I feared my patients would be shortchanged.

When I got to work, I tried to find Tim. He was not in his office, and thinking that he might be at lunch in the hospital's cafeteria, I looked for him there. Still no Tim. Some of my colleagues were sitting at a table and invited me to join them, and I did because I did not feel like being alone. Noticing that I was particularly dressed up, they asked what the occasion was.

"I had to go to court," I said, without thinking of the consequences of being honest. I was still preoccupied with the sight of Fran's thrashing against her keepers. My announcement was met with raised eyebrows. Now I had done it. They would think I was being sued.

"Oh, what the hell," I thought, "I really need to talk about this," and I began to briefly relate my story, ending with what had happened earlier that morning. Some of the psychiatrists already knew I was being stalked. It is almost impossible to curtail hospital gossip, and someone from the admissions office must have said something.

One of the psychiatrists had recently treated a woman who was being stalked by her ex-husband, and he promised to provide me with references for papers and other resources that had newly surfaced for stalking victims. My prior forays to the library had revealed next to nothing on this particular topic because stalking victims were not an area of interest for researchers.

My colleagues, in general, were very solicitous, very sympathetic, but I sensed they were holding something back. I was left with the distinct impression that they thought what was happening to me could never happen to them. The logical conclusion was that there was something about me, something I had done that had encouraged Fran's fixation.

I had sensed that presumption many times before, when I had talked with the various police officers who had handled my many telephone calls. The first question invariably was "Were you in a relationship with her?" When I answered firmly, "No," the next question, "Are you still treating her?" inevitably followed. I was never sure what difference any of that made. I had a restraining order and she had violated it. Were not criminal acts just as criminal whether perpetrated against intimates or strangers?

Could the fact that Fran was a female be another reason that my case was not receiving serious attention? If she had been a man, would the potential threat have seemed greater? Were the police uncomfortable with the lesbian overtones inherent in a woman stalking a woman?

I found myself quickly explaining the situation, invariably inserting the line, "Even though she knows I live with my *fiancé*, she does not stop," because in conservative Tucson I believed that if the responding officers thought I, too, were a lesbian, they would do even less than they were going to do anyway. Overall, their questions only left me with the impression that those responsible for my safety thought I was to blame for putting myself at risk.

My colleague with the stalked patient made good on his promise and provided me with a few recent psychiatric journal article citations on stalking and stalking victims as well as some telephone numbers of various victims' groups around the country. I immediately called for brochures from several of the organizations, and about a week later after work, I made my way to the library yet again to retrieve the new articles. There were only a few, so without looking at them too closely, I made copies and drove home, where I was pleasantly surprised that some of the information from the victims' organizations was already waiting in my mailbox.

I retrieved the articles from my briefcase, got out of my work clothes and made myself some tea. I did not know exactly what to expect, but I was not terribly hopeful that I would learn much more than I already knew. After all, I reasoned, as a psychiatrist I had treated many victims of many trying situations, far more serious than the one I found myself in. Surely I knew all about victim responses, especially to stalking, from my own experience.

I brought the tea and papers into the living room and made myself comfortable on the couch. My cat, Shula, as was her custom, waited for me to get settled before settling herself on my lap. I had laid down like this to read, with my soothing tea and my beloved cat so many times before that I was completely caught off guard by the familiar, calming routine. These seemingly innocuous pieces of paper were about to effect a profound change on my outlook and attitude, for above all, the research made it clear to me that I was not alone in feeling that others were somehow holding me responsible for Fran's attentions.

I had been unaware of how deeply a sense of guilt had invaded my psyche, sapping my spiritual strength, until I sensed the release that came in reading what was before me. The words of two Australian psychiatrists who run a clinic that exclusively treats stalkers and their victims could have been written about me and the impact of an erotomanic obsession on my life:

> *The notion of someone standing silently outside a house at night nursing their unrequited love may be redolent of the romantic, but when protracted it becomes intimidating. It is difficult to overstate the fear produced in most victims. . . simply by the repeated and intrusive contacts. . . .*
>
> *The victim's discomfort may be augmented by acquaintances, relatives and even partners assuming that some encouragement must have been given to the erotomanic. Instead of receiving sympathy and assistance, victims. . . are often confronted with suspicion and raillery.*[1]

As I read the last sentence, I let out a small gasp of recognition, waking Shula, who eyed me with evident disdain. Chastened, I quickly put the paper down to pet her back into her catatonic stupor. The Australian researchers had captured exactly how I had been feeling. Up to that moment I had even doubted my own perceptions about how others were reacting to me.

From the beginning, with Dr. Trottle, then with Tim, the police, and now my colleagues, whenever I had felt blamed for Fran's stalking me, I could almost understand it, because I had inwardly blamed myself. After all, I was a psychiatrist. If I did not know any better than to get into a predicament like this, I reasoned, I should at least be able to find a way out of it. I would wonder if others were indeed silently suspicious that I had somehow caused the problem or if I was just projecting my own self-doubt onto them?

When I reasoned this way, I recalled how I had second-guessed myself hundreds of times, speculating on what I might have done to encourage Fran's obsession. It seemed logical, then, that I might falsely assume that others blamed me, too. Once Shula's purring was replaced by her soft, high-pitched snore, I picked up the paper and reread the line, "Instead of receiving sympathy and assistance, victims. . . are often confronted with suspicion and raillery." It was so comforting to have this validation at last, even if only as typed words on a page.

As I pored over this new information on stalking victims, the papers sprawled about me on the couch, Shula was disturbed one too many times. Thoroughly disgusted with my priorities, she retired to a nearby chair, where she could still keep me, or more accurately my lap, in her sights. At first I devoured the papers in a frenzy, as if I had been starving for this information for years, even without knowing it. But then, as if to savor the sweetness of my new awakening, I reread them more slowly, reveling in the banquet of my new knowledge. I felt strangely satisfied, even while coming to a greater understanding of how profoundly Fran had affected my life. I had finally, fully pieced together all that had transpired in my own psyche: how Fran's erotomania had affected me and my relationships with Tim, colleagues, friends, and patients.

Before, understanding erotomania itself, from the erotomanic's perspective, had given me only part of the picture, something I did not realize until I saw myself in these papers and brochures printed thousands, even tens of thousands of miles away.

The information for and about victims had forced me to recall my own emotional evolution and assign some order to the muddle of responses I had felt since Fran had been stalking me. As I reflected back on almost three years of torturous and confusing reactions to being stalked, I was suddenly aware that my reactions seemed to follow the five stages of grief outlined by Elisabeth Kübler-Ross: denial, anger, bargaining, grieving, and acceptance.

At first, in the denial stage, I could not believe what was happening to me. I now realized that this stopped me from taking the proper precautions and blinded me to the inherent danger. As a result I had waited too long to get a restraining order, and had not been as vigilant as I should have been about Fran's ability to follow me home. I read how other victims' denial could even lead to counterproductive acts, like reasoning with their stalkers or returning their letters or gifts, thus encouraging continued pursuit.

Then, in the anger stage, I had fought against allowing myself this natural response to being stalked because Fran was a mentally ill, former patient. I was fearful, too, that if Fran was aware of my anger, she might have felt threatened and might escalate her harassment into more menacing and violent behavior. But it was my very resistance to becoming angry that, in fact, had made my ordeal more difficult. When I finally grasped how Fran had affected my work with patients, through reevaluating the therapy with Beth, I had indeed become angry at what Fran had done and what I had let her do, and I was able to move into the third stage.

In the bargaining stage, I got a restraining order, believing that if I set such a firm boundary, backed by the threat of legal sanction, Fran would not breach it. Obviously, I had been mistaken and could no longer assume that Fran's behavior, or any stalker's for that matter, could be controlled. I read that other victims similarly believed that if they took certain steps, such as getting a boyfriend, an attorney, or a dog, the stalker would stop. The legal system often reinforced a victim's false hopes in the efficacy of "bargaining" by recommending a restraining order. Those hopes were undercut, of course, when that same legal system became caught in this stage itself, reinforcing the victim's false hopes by encouraging the stalker's continued pursuit with light sentences and (plea) bargaining.

In the penultimate stage, grieving, which I could feel myself entering, my new awareness allowed me to appreciate all that had been lost, perhaps forever, due to the pernicious pursuit by another. I thought it ironic that loss was the most often cited trigger for the development of erotomania as well as what the erotomanic's victim will unerringly feel. Being stalked by a relentless tormentor had resulted in a tremendous loss of my privacy, security, and sense of well-being, instilling in its place a constant level of fear that ate away at both my professional and personal lives even while I was not overtly aware of its insidious presence.

In the last stage, acceptance, I expected that I would learn how to live with being stalked, and that all the essential precautions I needed to take would become automatic, incorporated into the other, more normal activities of my life. Although I realized that attaining that stage was an inevitable part of the healing process, I did not want to accept Fran's stalking me. I did not want to live my life anticipating or preventing or in any way reacting to her presence. As Kübler-Ross pointed out about death and dying, these five stages were fluid, not absolute, and I could feel myself, even as I grieved, still bargaining, hoping that the legal system would be able to keep Fran away from me.

In applying these five stages of grief to my plight, my self-awareness deepened, and I was gently nudged closer to eventually accepting all that being stalked had meant in my life. But at that moment, newly grieving,

I continued instead to sort through the materials strewn before me to glean more about my current feelings.

One researcher believed that the most difficult issue for the objects of erotomanics was the very persistence of the disorder. He had himself seen symptoms of post-traumatic stress disorder (PTSD) develop in victims of erotomanic and other stalkers. PTSD may develop after one has been exposed to an overwhelming trauma such as rape or war. But similar symptoms such as chronic anxiety, a foreshortened sense of the future, an exaggerated startle response (for example, jumping when the phone rings in anticipation that it might be the stalker), intrusive thoughts of being stalked, avoidance of situations with any potential to come in contact with the stalker, and a reliving of the stalking in nightmares may also develop in stalking victims.[2]

Given that erotomanic delusions last on the average slightly more than a decade,[3] this becomes a tremendous number of events to relive and an even greater number of situations to avoid. Research by the psychiatrists who run the stalking clinic in Australia reached similar conclusions, adding that anticipation and not knowing when the stalker might strike next heighten the sense of impending doom and consequent omnipresent anxiety. Over half the stalking victims studied there had PTSD, and research with them revealed that:

> *It was the stalker's constant intrusions and menace that created the most fear and distress. Indeed, several victims indicated that they might have coped better with the more tangible damage of physical assault; certainly, this might have produced a more sympathetic response from their helpers.*[4]

The description of how the experience of being stalked eroded the victims' confidence and ability to function normally seemed painfully familiar to me. I cringed as I recalled how often I had looked apprehensively in my rearview mirror, how afraid I had been to walk to my car, how many sleepless nights and nightmares I had endured.

Ninety-four percent of the Australian victims reported having made major lifestyle changes in response to being the objects of pursuit. Three-quarters expressed overwhelming feelings of powerlessness, and nearly a quarter acknowledged serious suicidal thoughts.[5]

As one stalking victim quoted in the British press put it:

I feel angry and frustrated about what this one person has done to my life. For a long time I experienced guilt, partly due to the helplessness and powerlessness that I felt. . . . I felt hunted, like an animal for the entire period that I was being stalked. I did not feel flattered; I did not enjoy the attention; the ordeal was not a pleasant experience. . . .

The worst thing about being hunted in this way is that one has no sense of where or when the hunter will turn up, or what he is likely to do. . . If you tell others about your ordeal, you still find them not believing you. People frequently hold the opinion that you must have known the stalker, or encouraged him or that you must have led the stalker on. It is very important to remember that a stalker needs no encouragement.[6]

As I read further, I found confirmation of other subtle changes I had sensed taking place, dampening my spirit and wounding my soul. Generally trusting by nature, I had quickly developed a sense of mistrust in other people, and so, too, now understood that stalking victims:

have a more difficult time developing [relationships]. It basically destroys a person's life. It's the same kind of thing a child molestation will do to a child in terms of their sense of attachment to people and their perception of their own self.[7]

I had experienced this mistrust in my reluctance to take on certain types of new patients. I became suspicious, even a bit paranoid of other people, especially of strangers and new acquaintances. Unfortunately, in many cases, the paranoia and mistrust the victim feels only serves to further isolate her during a time in which she, above all, needs the support of friends and family.

I had also mistrusted how colleagues and friends would react to me, thus effectively closing myself off from any potential help I might have received. This seemingly protective paranoia can backfire when the victim attempts to form new relationships: The mistrust perceived by others may drive away the kinds of people a stalking victim most needs to have in her life. Those who value mutual respect in relationships, who enjoy sharing their lives and their interests with others, can be understandably unwilling to get involved with someone who appears suspicious, paranoid, and withholding.

I could now appreciate how I had been weakened by my erotomanic experience in a myriad of ways. But I had more to discover about the profile of stalking victims in general and myself in particular, to learn how to better adapt.

Bonita Hammell, PhD, administrative director of the Stalking Treatment Options Program (STOP) in San Diego, California, a program that treats both stalkers and victims, identified additional issues that she believes stalking victims must recognize and face.[8] Many victims, she said, struggled with uncertainty about which events were related to stalking and which were not.

She recalled one victim who had the brakes go out on both of her cars at the same time. She suspected her stalker, even though her mechanic had other plausible explanations. Similarly, even before Fran was given our home telephone number, I had always wondered if she was behind any hang-up calls to our house.

Victims, Hammell noted, were also often disappointed in the limitations of law enforcement and in the bad advice given by mental health professionals who were not well versed in stalking—again, an issue with which I was all too familiar. In addition, victims experienced what she called, "anticipatory terror": waiting, not knowing when the stalker's next contact would be.

How familiar this particular kind of agony was to me. One victim she treated spent all her free time sitting by the phone, waiting for her stalker's next call. "Well, at least I didn't do that," I silently congratulated myself. But then I remembered the paranoid ritual I performed dozens of times a day, every day—glancing out the front window as I walked by, to ensure Fran was not lying in wait.

Dr. Hammell also identified several issues for therapists who treat stalking victims, such as the need to be aware that a victim might purposely not schedule appointments at the same time every week, for fear the stalker would learn her schedule. The therapist also needed to be flexible in the case of cancellations of appointments, for reasons such as "I can't come in today because my tires are slashed." While Dr. Hammell spoke of the impact on the therapist, I was now focusing on the dynamics of the stalked, the victim—in this case Doreen Orion, not Doreen Orion, MD.

Dr. Hammell also elaborated further many of the visceral responses of stalking victims, ones that I had experienced as well: isolation, loss of security, helplessness, rage, and difficulty with trust. For me, the most troubling feelings to sort out had been my complex reactions about a former patient, the woman who had stalked me now for three years, Fran. As I read on and learned more, I came to understand that any feelings I had were in response to Fran's actions rather than to Fran herself.

Responding on an emotional level would only give Fran in reality what she already believed she had attained in fantasy: a relationship. Even if she had no way of knowing how I felt, *I* would know, and my hating her would also mean to me that a relationship, of sorts, existed between us. On the other hand, if Fran were aware of my angry feelings, they would only encourage her. Just as neglected children do anything to be noticed, for erotomanics, even negative attention is better than none at all. I began to focus my feelings on what Fran did, rather than who she was.

Along with the information I now possessed from professionals, there would also be new information for stalking victims from stalking victims themselves. Soon I was learning to take precautions my local police department had never even mentioned.

In 1991, Jane McAllister, a former victim of a mentally ill stalker, founded Citizens Against Stalking in Virginia, one of the first such victim support groups in the country. She came through her own terrible ordeal, stalked by a mentally ill stranger, forever transformed into a fountain of knowledge with practical how-to advice any stalking victim could follow.

For example, she advised victims to document their harassment by taking pictures, using video cameras, and collecting statements from witnesses. Even though one incident may be insignificant by itself, she counseled, it is important to establish a pattern of harassment. Another active measure was for victims to tell neighbors, friends, family, and co-workers about the stalking to enlist their help, giving them a picture of the stalker, vehicle description, and license plate number if available. Notifying everyone is not only important for protection, but also for countersurveillance.

Stalkers can be extremely devious in acquiring personal information about their victims from unsuspecting persons surrounding their prey. McAllister emphasized that the first time the stalker appeared was not the moment to begin explaining the situation, because the stalker would deny the problem and try to discredit the victim. She also advised victims to call the police every time the stalker made contact even if the stalker's actions were legal, because it might become crucial to have a record of each incident later. Victims should also ask the police for periodic drive-bys and a free home-security check. Finally she suggested victims join a support group, such as the one she herself had founded.[9]

Having a record of a stalker's acts seemed all-important in prosecuting stalkers. One detective specializing in such cases noted, "Stalking is a paper crime. It's all about documentation."[10] I had always kept all of Fran's notes and cards and a record of all her telephone calls and visits to my home, but that was more a rote result of my psychiatric training, to document every contact with a patient, even a former one.

Unfortunately, most victims do not know enough to do this, just as I probably would not have done so if I had not once treated my stalker. Rhonda Saunders, the Los Angeles deputy district attorney widely credited with pioneering stalking prosecutions, noted:

> *I think the feeling is, when people get these letters or these phone calls, they feel so violated, they'll throw the letters out or they'll erase the phone calls and that's the worst thing they can do, because we need it as evidence.*[11]

In learning how to better protect my physical safety and emotional well-being, I found I was also becoming more aware of how others treated stalkers and their victims. I soon discovered that even mental health professionals may not fully appreciate the significance of someone's inappropriate interest toward another. Shortly after Fran's wrestle with her guards, a woman was admitted to the hospital I practiced at, and even though she was not my patient, her case was so titillating to the staff and to the other patients that I soon heard about it.

Although married with three young children, the woman had been having an affair with her clergyman for the past few years. She claimed her youngest child was, in fact, his. She had been able to hide all this from her husband until the clergyman announced he was leaving town with his wife for a congregation in a distant city. At this, the woman became depressed and suicidal and was admitted to the hospital.

We all, of course, were horrified that a clergyman would betray his trust in such a manner, and even more so when the minister started visiting his congregant/conjugant in the hospital. When the patient's husband visited, however, it was apparent he did not believe his wife's story.

It finally emerged that she was erotomanic, and the misguided minister in his efforts to counsel one of the woollier members of his flock, unwittingly perpetuated her delusions. Like me, he had been caught off guard by her erotomanica. Fortunately any harm done to the patient was short-lived, and none had yet been done to this particular object. Once the staff understood what was happening and explained it to the pastor, he readily agreed to stop visiting the woman.

Other mistakes may not be as easily rectified as the minister's. All too often, therapist ignorance and insensitivity can cause true harm to victims and patients alike by recommending actions that only reinforce destructive erotomanic behavior, thereby empowering the stalker to commit further abusive acts. As I became more comfortable in heeding McAllister's advice and shared my story with others, they, in turn, shared their stories with me. A social worker I knew told me of his sister, a young psychiatric worker, whose erotomanic ordeal aptly illustrated the dangers of professional naivete.

Amber W., fresh out of college, was employed as a psychiatric technician at a local community health center in a small Southern town. She was assigned to take care of the chronically mentally ill clients who lived in apartments subsidized by the center. She met with them either at her office or in their homes, took them grocery shopping, helped them fill out forms for government assistance, and ensured they took their medications and kept their doctors' appointments.

Bob, a twenty-six-year-old schizophrenic, was one of her first clients. Although he had developed an erotomanic obsession with the woman who worked with him before Amber, Amber's supervisor saw nothing wrong with assigning her to the case and, of course, did not warn her—just as Dr. Trottle had not warned me.

Within three months of meeting her, Bob wrote Amber a note, telling her he loved her. The next week, he came to her office to ask her out. When she informed him that they could only have a professional relationship, he said he understood. But he, like Fran, persisted. He played love songs for her when she went to her apartment and even called her at her home.

She notified her supervisor, and the center's board sent Bob numerous letters that his behavior was inappropriate. Unfortunately these letters were worded in such a way that he was given the impression that Amber would have returned his affections if it were not for her job.

When I heard that part of the story, I immediately recalled Dr. Trottle's inept comment to Fran that I could lose my medical license if I became involved with her. Like Fran, Bob had invented an entire relationship with his object. He told her employers that it had been Amber who had called him and that they had dated. He sent her many poems and letters, writing, "What will your dog do without his momma there? What will he do?" Adding, "I didn't want to kill someone who loved me. . . ." Even more disturbing, although the center knew of Bob's history of violence—he had once threatened to kill his roommate and had shoved his father's head through a windshield—still Amber was expected to work with him. His erotomanic delusions flourished under her reluctant care.

Typically, he stalked Amber in waves, sometimes not calling or writing for weeks, then bombarding her with fifty telephone calls in one night. She even put a call block on her telephone, but he thwarted her by repeatedly switching lines. He began sneaking into her office building, bypassing the receptionist so that he could leave letters and tapes for Amber directly in her mailbox.

Amber implored her supervisor to take her off the case, but was told it would be too difficult to change the personnel working with Bob. "You flex staff according to the client's needs, even if they're violent," not according to the staffs' needs, she was told. Finally she was allowed to cease activities with him outside her office, but by then, she had been made to feel that she was the one at fault.

Just as I had experienced the blame of professionals who should have known better, so did Amber. Someone had written in Bob's chart, "This guy should not be working with such a cute young girl." Amber told me, with anger in her voice, "They were making it my fault because I was young and cute. It shot any credibility I had, any skills or intelligence."

A meeting was finally held with Amber, Amber's supervisor, and Bob's psychiatrist, who told them, "He is a time bomb." Even then the supervisor downplayed Bob's behavior, saying, "We don't need to make him out to be a monster." Finally after six months of enduring Bob's center-sanctioned harassment, and only after its executive director got wind of what was happening, Amber was taken off the case.

Bob continued to harass her even after she was no longer working with him. She finally listened to her own instincts, and obtained a restraining order. After being served, Bob came to her office building and yelled at her across the parking lot, calling her "shit for brains." When she notified the police, who had advised her to get the order of protection in the first place, they said they couldn't do anything, but told her, "If he comes on your property, shoot him." For a time, the order did seem to restrain Bob from further acting on his ardor. Amber was eventually given another job at the center, but Bob has recently resurfaced, leaving a cassette on her car, with the song, "I Want You," circled.

Throughout her ordeal, Amber's supervisor had told her not to press charges, a decision Amber later regretted. "I really expected them to protect me, and I really expected them to know the right things. I was young and impressionable." Like me, Amber found out too late that she should not rely on "professionals" or anyone else to save her.[12]

Each story I heard about other stalking cases seemed to be a portrait of myself at one time or another as I struggled to deal with my victimization. One story illustrated how even victims themselves, in addition to therapists and law enforcement officials, may, in their denial, treat stalkers with indifference, sometimes with tragic results.

A forty-nine-year-old male erotomanic stalked an Australian singer, twenty years his junior. He went to all her public performances and even followed her to social events. When her friends expressed their concerns to the young woman, she told them he was simply sad and harmless. There was no warning before he finally did approach her in the street, fatally stabbing her. Weeks before he had confided to his mother that he was going to marry the singer. What changed his plans from marriage to murder? A newspaper article reporting her engagement to a prominent local businessman.[13]

Cases such as these, beginning with the death of Rebecca Schaeffer, have led Hollywood celebrities, at least, to no longer brush off or deny potential threats. Jeannie Wolf, a television commentator, explained:

We get fan mail at Entertainment Tonight, *Mary Hart, Lisa Givens, and I, and it used to be kind of a funny thing. We'd post the most romantic or the sexiest ones above the coffee machine and everyone would walk by and laugh. We don't do that anymore. You get that fan mail now, you turn it into the security office.*[14]

Many producers of the television shows taped in Los Angeles have installed metal detectors at the entrances and routinely position armed plainclothesmen in the audience.[15]

In my anger, there had been many times I was tempted to confront Fran directly and tell her to leave me alone, but I had intuitively resisted such a tack. I learned later, through additional materials I received, that following my instinct was wise. Confronting or threatening one's stalker is *never* a good idea because *any* contact reinforces the stalking behavior.

Renee Goodale, a stalking victim and founder of the nonprofit Florida group Survivors of Stalking (SOS), noted:

The unwanted pursuer calls you ten times a day for three consecutive days. Each time you did not answer the phone, and let your answering machine pick up. On the fourth day when the phone rang you picked up the receiver and screamed, "Stop calling me!" You just taught the harasser that it takes four days, and/or thirty-one telephone calls, to get your attention. This dance can go on for years.

Behavioral therapists call this "intermittent reinforcement." It is the most powerful reinforcement of behavior known, even stronger than consistently doling out positive rewards. Still more distressing for victims are counter charges. According to Goodale, "Counter charges are more common than we would like to admit." She observed:

I know of several cases in which the victim called the stalker to inform him/her to stop their harassing behavior. The victim was then charged with harassing telephone calls. Criminal charges can also be filed against you if you retaliate and take the law into your own hands. This is never a good idea, and it is also never a good idea to investigate or tail the stalker yourself. Think about it. In a court of law it would come down to who's stalking whom.[16]

Yet when faced with the blame of loved ones and the reluctance of the courts to punish stalkers, some victims have been driven to take matters into their own hands, with tragic results. One married man had been pursued for more than two years by an erotomanic woman who claimed that he was planning to leave his wife for her. She telephoned him incessantly, even contacting his wife and children. On two occasions, she went so far as to physically assault his wife, once severely enough that she required hospitalization.

Although the erotomanic had been arrested several times for the assaults and for restraining order violations, she remained at large. The wife eventually moved out, taking the children and telling her horrified husband she would come back only after he dealt with "the problem." She had always suspected that her spouse had, at the least, encouraged his stalker if not actually had an affair with her.

One night, after drinking, the man went to his tormentor's home, first pleading then threatening that she'd better leave him and his family alone. The situation quickly escalated out of control when he put a final end to the pursuit, strangling the woman who had ruined the last two years of his life, thus ensuring that the rest of it was ruined as well.[17]

While actual violence against stalkers by their victims is rare, fantasies of violence are not: 65 percent of stalking victims are reported to entertain aggressive thoughts toward their tormentors.[18]

I was now more open about being stalked, especially whenever I gave someone my home telephone number. One such person was a psychiatry resident in another city, who was thinking of moving to Tucson after graduation and had contacted the hospital Tim and I worked at. We both spoke to him at length about what it was like to start a practice in our town. At the end of the telephone call, I encouraged him to call us any time with questions, but asked him not to give out our number to anyone because I was being stalked. He then related a harrowing story. Once again, the inaction of victims who never move out of the denial stage and continue to pretend that their stalker will go away had devastating consequences.

Isabelle M. was twenty-nine, single, Catholic, and convinced that she was irresistible to priests. She determined that her local parish priest was in love with her and believed he was sending her special messages from the pulpit, staring at her, and directing his sermons her way. She began to take communion only from him. She went to mass daily and waited to greet him afterward. She would ask him if he liked her dress and when he answered that he did, she took this as a sign that he wanted to see her in more provocative attire.

She complied with his demands (his delusional ones, that is), and as she did so, the priest started to feel that there was something peculiar about this particular parishioner. When she began writing him sexually explicit letters, he confronted her on the inappropriate correspondence. She became enraged, seeing this as a betrayal of their "relationship."

While he was teaching a class in the church's basement, she put nail polish remover on his seat on the pulpit and set it afire, burning down a significant portion of the building. Although other parishioners and the priest himself were there at the time, no one was significantly injured. The priest did not press charges, but instead simply banished her from his parish. As a result, Isabelle suffered no real legal consequences and received no psychiatric treatment.

Subsequently, Isabelle began attending a new church, and two years later became fixated on a priest there, believing that he, too, was in love with her. When this priest asked if she wanted to ride a horse in the Christmas pageant, she interpreted that to mean that he wanted to watch her buttocks rub up and down on the animal. When one day he commented in passing that she looked nice, she believed that he wanted her not only to dress more provocatively, but also to have sex with him.

She became convinced that he was also directing his sermons to her, staring at her from the pulpit, and holding her hand longer than anyone else's on the receiving line. She began to wear revealing clothing to church and to flash him glimpses of her private parts. When he told her that her clothing and behavior were inappropriate, she turned his obvious displeasure with her around, thinking he wanted her to do even more.

She began to write him sexually explicit letters and even went to see him at the rectory. He again told her that her behavior must stop but while he was doing so, Isabelle happened to notice another woman and became convinced that the priest was cheating on her. This prompted Isabelle to step up her sexually explicit letters to him, but this time, she signed the other woman's name. She went even further creating a flyer naming the "other woman" a whore, and distributing it in the mailboxes of the church members.

Finally the police were asked to investigate, but no charges were filed. To Isabelle, this proved that the priest and the woman were indeed having an affair, and she became even more enraged, vowing that if she could not have her priest, no one could. She snuck into the rectory and put rocks into the exhaust system of his car, leaving a letter to the authorities explaining her ghastly deed as revenge against the priest for rejecting her, but signing the *other* woman's name.

Fortunately her plan backfired; the priest smelled the exhaust, discovered the rocks, and immediately suspected his most disturbed parishioner. When confronted, she confessed to her near deadly deed. She was told no charges would be filed if she agreed to a psychiatric evaluation. She went to a nearby facility and was, of course, quickly admitted.

One priest's denial nearly led to another's demise, but both priests' disregard for the potential danger Isabelle posed was, in fact, mirrored by her own detachment. Isabelle's admitting psychiatrist was struck by "an incredible. . . *la belle indifférence* in terms of. . . talking about everything that she did without any sense of remorse or guilt or even awareness that the priest's life was in jeopardy."[19] Isabelle clearly felt the priest deserved to die because of his betrayal and showed no insight at all into why her behavior was, to say the least, inappropriate, despite treatment with various medications.

Her psychiatrist discovered that, typically erotomanic, Isabelle had been in the same, low-paying job for fifteen years until her admission, and no one there, not even her family who lived nearby, ever had any indication that there was anything wrong. She had female friends, but no real relationships with men. Her parents, in fact, were totally dumb-founded by her admission to the hospital, and even though their daughter readily admitted to everything attributed to her, they refused to believe that any of it was true.

After six weeks of inpatient treatment, Isabelle began to develop some insight into her behavior, understanding that the priest could not have loved her, that it was morally wrong to distribute the flyer, and that it was crazy, not to mention unlawful, to try to kill him. She even expressed remorse for her actions. She was told she would be discharged without any charges filed against her if she attended daily intensive outpatient treatment at the hospital and never again returned to the church.

Once more, an erotomanic's dastardly deeds went unpunished, a practice that sets up a continually escalating circle resulting in ever more vicious acts, even murder, that finally can no longer go unpunished. With misguided mercy and wanting to turn the other cheek, the church and the priest agreed to this plan, promising that if Isabelle was ever again seen at the parish, they would immediately notify the hospital. In denial of the seriousness of the situation, the priest and his church had been reticent to cooperate with anyone treating her. This reticence would later come back to haunt them.

After a few months of treatment at the day hospital, Isabelle again started to show up at the church for daily mass. She, of course, did not tell her psychiatrist of this development, but neither did the church. After three more weeks, she broke the priest's windshield and was readmitted to the hospital. Seeing him again had reinforced to her both the strength of her love and her fury over his betrayal of it. She now felt that her previous attempt on his life had been justified because he had hurt her more than she had hurt him, again showing no insight into the gravity of her behaviors. Her inpatient psychiatrist, recognizing the intractability of her dangerous delusions, finally transferred her to a more permanent home in the state hospital.

La belle indifférence, a characteristic of erotomanics, explains how they can profess to love so much, yet are seemingly indifferent to the pain that love causes their objects. A French term meaning an emotional unconcern, in psychiatric parlance it usually refers to a patient's total disregard for symptoms that anyone else would find extremely disturbing. An erotomanic almost always displays *la belle indifférence* toward the suffering of the victim and the complete disruption in the victim's life she has caused. In this way, erotomanics are narcissistic in the true sense of the term; only the suffering *they* have experienced at the hands of their capricious "lovers" counts, because they believe, with all the unshakable conviction of delusional truth, that they are entitled to a relationship at any and all costs to their victims. Fran certainly did not seem to care how I felt. She even told one of the psychiatrists who examined her in jail that she knew I was angry with her and wanted her visits to stop. She continued them anyway.

I had learned so much about victims, about myself, seemingly at warp speed since Fran had been incarcerated. Perhaps it was because I knew that she could not contact me that I was finally able to let down my guard and examine my own responses to her during the four months she remained in jail. During that time, the attorneys and psychiatrists for both sides continued to have at her. As each psychiatrist had recommended against incarceration, there was really very little to be done.

The county attorney informed me of a plea bargain that had been offered by Fran's attorney: Fran would be required to remain an inpatient for six months in a psychiatric facility in Michigan, where her brother lived. If she did not contact me during those six months, all charges would be dropped. Given the psychiatrists' recommendations, the county attorney felt this was the best we could do.

Reluctantly, I agreed, thinking, "At least I'll have six months." Recalling all that Isabelle, Bob, and other erotomanics had been allowed to get away with, I was frustrated and angry at the legal system that could do no more to protect me. I had to face the reality that Fran would spend more time forcibly separated from me if I agreed to the plea bargain than if we proceeded with the criminal charges, which, incredibly, remained misdemeanors. Unlike Isabelle's priests, I wanted Fran prosecuted fully. The law just didn't seem to think there was much to prosecute her with.

I was bitterly disappointed at the outcome of my case. While six months in a psychiatric hospital would undoubtedly not be a pleasant experience, it was a far cry from a jail cell, and unlike the psychiatrists who had examined her for the court, I knew it would not be much of a deterrent. I also could not shake the fear that Fran's parents would finagle some type of reprieve for her. My anxiety only mounted as the day for her banishment to another state drew near. When I discussed my fears with Tim, giving voice to them made them seem even more paranoid, although he assured me they were understandable.

Little did I know the reprieve for Fran that I dreaded would nearly come from the police themselves. The morning of her transfer from the Tucson city jail to an airplane that would take her to her temporary exile, I was awakened by a call at 6:30 A.M. from the jail, informing me that the sheriff's department had "lost" Fran.

"What do you mean, you've 'lost' her?" I asked, alarmed.

The deputy explained that Fran was supposed to be released into her brother's custody so that he could take her to the airport and fly with her to the hospital, but that "somehow," Fran was released before he got there. No one knew where she was.

"We thought we should notify you," he said sheepishly.

"Thanks," I said, before realizing I had nothing to thank him for. "Please let me know if you find her."

He assured me he would. I crept silently out of bed. Tim, predictably, had gone back to sleep as soon as he realized the call was not for him. He must have thought it was a hospital admission for me. But I was now wide awake. I knew the jail was a half-hour drive from our house, and I had that long to ensure our safety. I checked all the doors and windows and sat in the living room where I had a view of the front of the house. I remained that way until I heard Tim stir for work an hour later. He was duly concerned and insisted that I go to the hospital with him, instead of leaving a bit later on my own, which was my usual custom. But before we left, the sheriff called to say that Fran had been found wandering near the jail. It seemed that she was as surprised as her former captors at the ease with which she had been released.

In this fiasco, Fran and I finally had an emotional experience in sync with one another. She, too, had expected her brother to be waiting for her and apparently had not intended to "escape." When her brother did arrive, he quickly processed her through the discharge from jail and whisked her off to her awaiting ward more than a thousand miles away.

That night Tim suggested we go out for a celebratory dinner, and despite my misgivings—because I still did not quite believe in my own reprieve—I agreed. I knew I had six months to feel safe. Six months of not looking in my rearview mirror everywhere I drove. Six months of not glancing around whenever I was in a public place, straining to see if I recognized Fran's face in the crowd. Six months of not having to worry if she was peering in my windows. It was going to be heaven.

Life without Fran was freer, easier. I felt as if my tank had been refueled, that without Fran's constant drain on my psyche, I had so much more energy to devote to the things in my life I truly cared about. I would relish those six months.

About a month after Fran finally flew away, Tim came home and announced, "I was offered a job in Colorado. I told them no, but that I'd better ask you first." He has since learned not to ask my opinion on anything. Tim was at the time the associate medical director at the hospital where I had first treated Fran. The hospital's former administrator had been promoted a few years before to regional vice-president for the entire chain. When one of his hospitals in Colorado needed a new management team, he thought of Tim. Tim had never been to Colorado and liked the job he had in Tucson, thus his immediate, negative response.

My reaction, however, was completely the opposite. I had visited Colorado briefly years before and found it not only stunningly beautiful, but also unexpectedly temperate. Having seen a scorpion in our Tucson living room just that morning, I said "Are you kidding? It's beautiful there! We can have four seasons again." I was, of course, referring disparagingly to Tucson's two seasons: hot and hotter. What a pleasure it would be to see the leaves changing colors in the fall instead of the cactus needles falling to the ground.

We flew out to see the community, and even Tim had to admit it seemed like paradise. Although we made our decision and moved four months later based on the considerable merits of our adopted town, I had to admit that in the back of my mind, I thought moving would make it that much harder for Fran to find me. But I also knew that such thoughts were typical of victims in the bargaining stage who often drastically altered their lives in response to unrelenting erotomanic pursuits, changing social activities, gyms, jobs, addresses, cities, schools, occasionally even countries—to avoid their stalkers.

Andrea Evans, a popular daytime soap opera star, quit her role as Tina Clayton on *One Life to Live* in 1990 to get away from her stalker. For three years, the schizophrenic man with erotomanic delusions had threatened to kill her. Each time he did so or was caught with a butcher's knife or meat cleaver and her picture, he would be institutionalized for two to three months and then released to a halfway house just ten blocks from where she lived. Believing the only way to survive was to end her career and go into hiding, Evans did just that. Painfully she admitted, "For a long time, work meant possible death to me."[20]

She could not even go to the grocery store by herself. Three years after she quit the soap opera, she decided to slowly start working again, but said, "I don't know if I'll ever feel safe."[21]

If Tim and I were going to move, in part bargaining that this would finally thwart Fran, I was determined that moving to our new town would bring with it a new resolve. Some victims are eventually able to progress into the acceptance stage and thus channel their helplessness and rage into action. I knew I needed to emulate them.

Like a beleaguered general granted a temporary reprieve, I immediately began shoring up my defenses. I had to make it as difficult as possible for Fran to find us in our new city. I felt I had finally arrived at acceptance, and to my surprise, rather than an odious burden, this last stage became a welcome challenge as I mobilized my response and sought ways to integrate being stalked into my daily life. I felt more confident, more in charge than I had for almost four years.

In preparation for moving, Tim and I did everything we could to conceal our destination. The office staff in Tucson was given strict instructions that any former patients who wanted to contact either of us were to leave a message, which the staff would then relay to us in our new city. Because the post office was still giving out forwarding addresses to anyone who paid a dollar (a practice that soon ended, specifically to thwart potential stalkers), we had our mail forwarded to our office in Tucson, since Fran already knew that address all too well. Our former office staff would then send it to us in Colorado.

Our home was put up for sale without our names on the listing, and our agent knew not to tell prospective buyers where we were. I even gave her Fran's name and description. Actually, we were doubly protected; before Tim got the new job offer, but while Fran was safely ensconced in another state, we happened to have moved to a different home in Tucson, anyway. I remember thinking with satisfaction, "That should keep her busy for a while."

The only stumbling block seemed to be the Arizona Board of Medical Examiners, who informed me that it was state law that anyone who asked could receive the information they had on file about us. There was no way to block its release. To practice in Colorado, that state's board had to request records from the Arizona Board, so Fran might very well be able to discern where we had moved just for the asking. Tim and I were unwilling to give up the life's work we loved and had gone through eight years of postgraduate training to study; besides, we were simply unqualified to do anything else. I hoped it would take Fran awhile to even figure out we *had* moved. Perhaps that would buy enough time for her to fixate on someone else. For all I knew, she might already be convinced some prison guard was in love with her.

Once we moved to Colorado, we rented a home for a year while our new one was being built. I had our rental agreement listed under a friend's name. I had our car and voter registration information blocked immediately because anyone could walk into those offices with either of our names and get our address simply by asking. To stop the information from being so easily disseminated, both of us had to sign a form that stated: "I swear or affirm under penalty of perjury, that I have reason to believe that I, or a member of my immediate family who resides in my household, will be exposed to criminal harassment, or otherwise be in danger of bodily harm, if my address is not kept confidential." The request took ten days to process, and cost five dollars per record blocked and per car. On the other hand, those seeking such information do not have to pay anything to get it.

Still, I did not feel completely secure because even with the block, I was given a list of eighteen exempt persons and agencies, including not only law enforcement, but insurance companies, collection agencies, credit unions, banks, attorneys, and news media. To get our address, all that was required of them was an ID and the signing of an oath that the person whose information was being sought would not be harmed by its dissemination.

Unfortunately, even assuming they tell the truth about who they are, erotomanics would eagerly agree to such an oath because they do not think they are doing any harm, anyway. They believe they are pursuing what is rightfully theirs.

Before we bought the land, I called the county recorder. As with motor vehicle and voter records, anyone could walk into that office and ask if a particular person owned land in that county. If the answer was yes, the address would be provided immediately and at no charge. I was appalled to discover that there was no way to officially block the information. Anyone who requested it was given the address. I explained my situation to the clerk. She replied, "I know, it's terrible. We had another woman who had been stalked call us the other day. But we're limited as to what we can do. It's the law." She suggested we buy the land under the name of a trust so it could not be traced to us. We did so, also listing our utilities under the trust.

We equipped our home-in-progress with dead bolts on all outside doors, dowels in all sliding glass windows, special motion-detector lighting, and an expensive security alarm system, wired directly into a surveillance company. We minimized any shrubbery near the house to discourage Fran's lying in wait, installed a wide-angle viewer in all primary doors, an electric garage door, and a loud exterior alarm that could be manually activated from various locations.

I used a private mailbox service for all our personal mail, including bills, as well as for our checks. For institutions that would not accept a mailbox listing, I gave the mailbox number as an apartment number. I also took several self-defense classes at a nearby karate school.

I varied my route when I returned home from work and frequently looked in my rearview mirror to see if anyone was following me. I, an avowed cat lover, and much to Shula's chagrin, agreed to get a dog, "one of the least expensive but most effective alarm systems."[22] And he is. Our handsome standard poodle, Miles, constantly keeps us informed of any rogue squirrels in the area.

Tim readily agreed to all these precautions. By now he also fully understood, through the research I had shared with him about other erotomanic stalkers, that I—we—were in very real danger. Taking action also helped his own feelings of helplessness, and he rallied to the cause joining in my preparations. He too seemed to have also moved through his own stages of grief to acceptance. We were in sync again.

Other safety precautions advocated by the experts included having co-workers screen all calls and visitors; not accepting packages unless they were personally ordered; removing any name or identification from reserved parking at work; destroying discarded mail; and equipping the gas tank with a locking gas cap that could be unlocked only from inside the car.

The National Victim Center, a nonprofit advocacy and resource center founded in honor of Sunny Von Bulow, advised stalking victims to keep a packed suitcase in the trunk of their car with reserve money, duplicate keys, and medication and to develop a contingency plan in case of an emergency, including quick access to critical telephone numbers, such as police, shelters, and friends. Those who can afford it are also advised to have two telephone lines, one published number with a 'dummy' answering machine connected to it, and a second private, unlisted line, reserved for close friends and family.[23]

The more I learned about steps I could take to protect myself, the stronger I felt. I devoured every bit of advice I could find. Renee Goodale, of SOS, recommended that victims acquaint themselves with all-night stores and other public, highly populated places in their area and never be afraid to sound their car horns to attract attention. To help a victim in a car determine if the stalker is following in another vehicle, Goodale suggested making four left-hand or right-hand turns, and if the car continued following, locking all doors and driving to the nearest police or fire station, but *never* home.

Better yet, she said have a cellular phone in the car to call the police. There had been many times in Tucson that I suspected a car—Fran— was following me, but I had simply pulled off the road, an ill-advised move I would never make again. Goodale also felt that a cellular phone was an important tool if the victim suspected the stalker might attempt a break-in at her home because she could keep it with her to use if the stalker cut her telephone lines.

If a victim suspected her car had been tampered with, she should check for missing hubcaps, loosened lug nuts, slow leaks in the tires as well as check under the hood before starting the engine, looking for anything suspicious or out of the ordinary. Once inside the vehicle, she should pump the brakes, then look under the car for brake fluid. If anything seemed amiss, she should not drive the car or touch any evidence but get to safety and immediately call the police.[24] It had never entered my mind that Fran could tamper with my car. There was certainly much I still needed to learn about stalking safety.

Although my personal information was not easy to hide, at least the decision to do so was relatively simple. Professionally I still faced some difficult decisions. My office number had to be listed in the telephone book. I had always obtained many referrals from the yellow pages, and as a physician, I needed to be listed so my patients could call me in an emergency. I compromised by not listing an office address and was the only doctor who did not. Still, if Fran were to find out what city Tim and I had moved to, it would be easy for her to telephone my office. I went on a strictly voice mail system so I would never have to answer the phone directly and so I could hear every message left with my own ears, deciphering whether or not it sounded like Fran.

In all the time Fran was hospitalized in Michigan, I was never contacted by the hospital or her treatment team, nor was I informed of her discharge. They did not have to. In January 1994, a year after we had left Arizona and ten months after she had completed her sentence, Fran left a message on my voice mail. She had moved to Colorado.

Chapter Seven

STALKING THE STALKERS

WHEN I RECEIVED FRAN'S VOICE
mail, I was at work. I immediately located Tim behind the
nurses' station on one of the units. Silently I accessed Fran's message on
the unit's phone and handed him the receiver. As he listened, he grabbed
my hand under the desk, giving it a reassuring squeeze even as he shook
his head in disbelief:

> *Hi. This is Fran Nightingale calling. I'm having trouble getting my
> medication. I'm with [a Colorado mental health center] and I'm
> having difficulty getting it and I wonder if you can help me in this
> situation. I don't know if you can or not. If you can give me a call
> I will be at my parents' house this evening and tomorrow. You can
> leave word.*

The message confused me. Fran had left a Tucson telephone number but said she was being treated locally.

I went back to my office and immediately contacted the mental
health center she had named and spoke to an appropriate person there,
explaining who I was and why I wanted to verify that Fran was living in
Colorado. This person, of course, was not legally allowed to give out any
information about Fran, and in fact, was not even allowed to acknowledge that she was a patient.

To encourage some bending of the rules, I said "I would consider it
your duty to protect me," invoking a legal obligation that therapists take

seriously, to protect potential victims from their clients. He gave me the information I needed, and no more, mainly as a professional courtesy, although I was sworn not to reveal who had squealed. He said that Fran was indeed being treated at the center and that she had provided them with a home address in Colorado, not far from where I worked. I was also given the name of her therapist, a female social worker. "If I were you," I advised, "I'd see that her care is transferred to a man. Immediately."

After Tim finished with his inpatients, he came to my office. I told him what I had discovered and that I was going to call the police.

"Honey," he asked gently, "weren't all the charges dropped in Tucson after Fran fulfilled her part of the plea agreement? She didn't contact you for six months." Of course, he was right. Fran had no record of charges against her. There wasn't even a restraining order in place. So what if she had moved to Colorado and made one phone call to me. That was not against any law.

Our year in Colorado had been exciting, full of making new friends, starting a new practice, and building a new home. All the precautions I had taken against an old nemesis had by now been seamlessly integrated into our lives. I had allowed myself the luxury of hardly giving Fran a thought. With resignation, I accepted that my ordeal was not yet over and that I still had more work to do.

The next day I was contacted by Fran's new male therapist. I informed him that I considered that he, too, had a duty to protect me by keeping me abreast of any plans Fran might have with regard to me. True to form, Fran had not told her new treatment team of her more pertinent past history. She had told her therapist only that she had left Tucson because she "needed a change." My next step seemed clear, and I discussed it with Tim. I wanted to take immediate action, not wait to see what Fran might do next as I had in Tucson when she first started stalking me. I was not the same person now as I had been then.

"Look, I'm not saying that you don't deserve a restraining order, or that the police shouldn't help you, but you know what they're going to do," he argued.

"I know. Nothing."

"Why would you want to go through all that, again?"

Tim had a point, but I couldn't just think about the effect on me. The effect on Fran was far more important.

"I'm not looking forward to more contact with Fran, or the courts," I explained. Once I had made the decision to get the restraining order four years ago, I was committed. Not getting another one now would be interpreted by Fran as an invitation to follow me. "And if she thinks I want her to follow me, there's no telling what she might do."

Tim finally had to agree, and I went to the county court a few days later, once again dragging my shopping bag full of more than four years of correspondence, telephone messages, and court documentation of my travels with Frannie. The judge was so sympathetic he not only granted a restraining order, but marked it permanent, saying, "The police don't like when I do this, but I think it's warranted in this case." Unfortunately there was little more he could do.

Over the coming months, Fran continued to leave periodic messages, but all of them appeared to be from Tucson, so while dutifully recording them, I did not report them to the police. For example, she had called and left a message saying she was in the emergency room of a Tucson hospital having side effects from her medications, and that I should call her there; that she had been admitted to another Tucson hospital and "refused my [her] medications and I don't know what to do. If I can't get help, please tell me what I should do to get a second opinion."

I wondered if she had moved back to Tucson, yet when I continued to contact her mental health center in Colorado throughout the year after I had first heard from her in my—our—new state, they told me that she was keeping her appointments there. She must have been going back and forth to Tucson. I wondered how the police were ever going to deal with her now.

Even if Fran remained in Colorado, I did not want to go through the same thing I had in Tucson: waiting for Fran's next restraining order violation, hoping the officer would perform a real arrest and the judge would impose a real sentence, but I did not know of any alternatives. What were we to do?

Fran was a professional stalker. That was her job. Just as I spent eight hours a day in my profession, she spent as much time, even more, on hers, rendering her equally proficient. Since the knowledge and expertise my field offered seemed no match for her delusions, I next turned to professionals in *her* field to try to thwart her. I retrieved the literature I had received in Tucson from victims' organizations over a year before, searching for what I vaguely remembered was a special police unit in Los Angeles that dealt solely with stalkers.

I found a "Security Recommendations" brochure I had been sent, stamped with the name Threat Management Unit (TMU), and called to get more information. A detective was kind enough to talk to me. After all, a psychiatrist being followed by some insane, smitten woman from Arizona to Colorado did not exactly fall under his jurisdiction. He suggested that I might want to attend the unit's upcoming conference at the Disneyland Hotel. Conference? At Disneyland? Oh, I could probably arrange that. I had always had a soft spot in my heart for Disneyland. So in August 1995, I attended the Fifth Annual Threat Management Conference sponsored by the Los Angeles Police Department's TMU.

It was hard enough to believe that an entire police unit was devoted to stalking, and even harder to believe there was a yearly conference, attended by hundreds of people from all over the United States and Canada, and as far away as England and Australia, growing in attendance by leaps and bounds every year. Not only were there law enforcement officers from around the country, but also forensic psychologists, district attorneys, security specialists, private investigators, and various victims. Even Mary Kay, Inc., the cosmetics giant, had a director of Protective Services on hand. That such a sophisticated society around stalking should have sprung up, seemingly overnight, really should have come as no surprise. A 1992 article had estimated that up to two hundred thousand people in the United States exhibited a stalker's traits,[1] and another study would later report that 8 percent of all American women have been stalked, 22 percent of them by strangers.[2]

I arrived in Los Angeles late on a Tuesday night and checked into the Disneyland Hotel. I wanted to be fresh and alert for the next morning's proceedings, so I resisted the considerable temptation to take the monorail to the park. Mickey would have to wait. After a fitful night's sleep, excited by the adventure ahead yet wondering what to expect, I walked to the main part of the hotel for the conference. I checked in and was given a name badge and large notebook with a syllabus, various articles, and a brief biography of each of the twenty-plus speakers who would lecture and hold smaller group seminars over the next two-and-a-half days.

Then I followed the throng of people into a huge ballroom, which had been transformed into a conference room, laid out with what appeared to be seemingly endless rows of tables and chairs. I thought I had left enough time to get a good seat, but I would be lucky if I got one at all. I was later to learn that 450 people were crowded into the room. I managed to find a place toward the back, sandwiched between a Canadian Mounted Police officer, who looked very much like he always got his man, and a stocky Hispanic officer from New Mexico who likewise appeared as if he would brook no opposition. I hadn't felt this safe in years.

As a result of my ordeal over the past six years, I had lost some of my natural openness. Even before arriving at the conference, I had decided that I needed to introduce myself to as many people as possible, to force myself to be gregarious, no matter how uncomfortable I felt. I reasoned that there was no telling whom I might meet and what valuable information they would provide.

I could feel some of my resolve lessening because the majority of the participants, about 75 percent I guessed, appeared to be men. This was going to be interesting. What could I possibly have in common with all these protectors of the peace? I gave myself no time to dwell on the discomfort of the situation and in the few moments before the conference began, introduced myself to my neighbors and found we were attending the conference for the same reason: to learn all we could about stalking and stalkers. I realized that if I kept that in mind, my personal challenge of talking to as many of the participants as I could would be much easier.

The program lineup included a California State Police sergeant speaking on assessing threats to public officials; a U.S. marshal on threats to federal judges; representatives from private security firms on executive protection, corporate restraining orders, and workplace threats; "environmental design specialists" on the impact of corporate layout, from parking garages to cubicles, on threats in the workplace; district attorneys on prosecuting stalking cases and the relationship between stalking and domestic violence; and, of course, members of the TMU on managing stalking cases.

The room suddenly became quiet. I was used to lecture halls full of unruly medical students and psychiatrists, but this well-disciplined group had been immediately silenced by the appearance at the podium of Los Angeles Police Chief, Willie Williams. He offered some brief, introductory remarks, welcomed the conference participants, and outlined the scope of the stalking problem, noting that the incidence of such crimes was even increasing among high school students.

Then United States congressman Ed Royce, who had introduced the first antistalking law in the country when he was a California State representative, gave the keynote address. In discussing why there was a need for such legislation, he pointed out that 90 percent of all women killed by their ex-husbands or boyfriends had been stalked.[3] He also reported on his current efforts to craft a federal antistalking law, a law that would go into effect the next year.

Joy Silverman followed with a lecture on "A Victim's Perspective on Stalking." I recalled her case well. She had been stalked for more than a year, beginning in 1991 by Sol Wachtler, the New York State Supreme Court's chief judge, after she ended their relationship for another man. Through his harassment of her with telephone calls, obscene letters to her daughter, and visits to her and her new boyfriend's apartment buildings in disguise, the judge had apparently tried to terrify Silverman into resuming their relationship. Silverman's sixteen-year-old daughter, whom Wachtler had threatened as part of his ploy to win back the socialite, was also there, and Silverman eloquently described the result of this nightmare on her entire family.

When she called stalking an "act of terrorism," likening it to "psychological rape," I understood exactly what she meant. She persuasively argued that even after the stalker is jailed—as Wachtler had been for almost a year—the victim is still left susceptible to the lasting effects of the ordeal. She ended her lecture by quoting former Supreme Court Justice Louis D. Brandeis: "The most basic right a citizen has is to be left alone."[4] The essential truth in that quotation resonated through me.

During the lunch break, I made a point of introducing myself to the TMU detective I had first spoken to on the phone, months before, who had told me about the conference. I could already tell I would learn much and wanted to thank him. To refresh his memory, because I assumed he must have spoken to a hundred stalking victims since then, I briefly reminded him that I was the psychiatrist from Colorado who had been stalked by a former female patient for the past six years.

His face immediately showed sympathy, yet his obviously genuine concern disquieted me. It felt unnatural somehow, even though I had once longed for that very type of consideration from the officers in my hometown police department. The TMU detective was used to dealing with such stories from victims, so was treating me with the same gentle interest he always showed. In that moment, when I found myself unable to accept his consolation, I realized that I no longer considered myself Fran's victim. I had instead become my own advocate.

After lunch, the conference participants gathered again in the ballroom. Lieutenant John Lane, the head of the TMU, began by playing the telephone answering machine tape that one victim recorded of her stalker who said: "I've been wanting to see you with no clothes on, so I took a picture of you into the bedroom and took my clothes off. Now I've seen you with no clothes on."

Other tapes played by the TMU detectives were less humorous. Particularly chilling was the case of a Korean man who stalked the daughter of his landlord, insisting that she should date, even marry a traditional Korean man like himself, rather than her boyfriend. Her repeated refusals to see him and finally her family's insistence that he move out of the guest house on their property, led to his murderous rampage.

When he broke into the family's home one night, the object of his obsession happened to be upstairs on a cordless telephone with her boyfriend. She quickly hung up and called 911. The TMU detective played the entire 911 tape, minute upon interminable minute, as she hysterically ran from room to room, witnessing the carnage that left her mother and brother dead and her father critically wounded. We sat silent, transfixed. A room of 450 people, mostly police officers and prosecutors who had presumably seen and heard it all, without a sound or movement for the entire eighteen minutes. By the time the tape ended, I was teary-eyed and a little embarrassed that I might appear "soft" to my fellow participants until I saw that even some of the hardened veterans had been so moved.

After the conference ended that first day, I was exhausted. I had been bombarded with new information, new understanding, and new hope. I crawled into bed feeling totally spent. Since Fran had started stalking me, I had always had trouble sleeping when Tim was not with me, but alone that night I slept soundly.

The next morning, I awoke early and was rewarded with a seat toward the front of the room. A jovial atmosphere hung in the air, and I readily found myself joining in, making small talk with the people sitting around me. It was as if we all needed to shake off the intensity of the day before.

During this second day of the conference, many issues arose that I had never considered. For example, how do those with limited resources, charged with protecting public officials, sift through the myriad—250 threats a month for the California Highway Patrol—of threats received? The ingeniously obvious answer is to train public officials' staffs in what would be cause for concern.

I also learned that threats to public officials can be issue driven. When a California State congressman named Floyd proposed a motorcycle helmet law, he received an inordinate number of very serious threats. Public safety officials in the state now refer to taking on a high profile issue as "pulling a Floyd" in his honor.

Dr. Reid Meloy, whose many scholarly papers on pathologic attachments I had read since Fran had started stalking me, lectured on "The Psychodynamics of Stalking." He discussed the case of a male erotomanic who posted pictures of news anchorwomen all around his bedroom, masturbating incessantly but never contacting or stalking his objects in any way, prompting one witty participant to call out, "That's because he was too tired."

When we broke for lunch, I sought out a young woman who one of my neighbors had said he had met the day before. She was working on her PhD in psychology—on erotomania. Finding this petite, dark-haired lady in the sea of mostly imposing men was no easy task. But I somehow managed to spot her and we sat together at lunch. While I was thrilled she had decided to do her dissertation on erotomania, because this topic was clearly one that deserved more study, I was alarmed at her research protocol: She was going to interview the erotomanics herself, and most of her subjects, since she worked in a forensic setting, were men.

I gently suggested that she might want to pay some male graduate students to conduct the interviews for her. Her eyes grew wide with horror as she began to understand that as a female authority figure, one who, for probably the first time in these men's lives, was truly taking an interest in them, she was putting herself at risk of becoming a victim, just as surely as she would be if she went walking alone through Central Park at 3 A.M.

I sought out several more of the presenters and participants, experts in the fields of stalking prevention, intervention, and prosecution, who were kind enough to talk to me and give me their professional advice and opinions. Perhaps the most valuable lesson I learned from them over the entire three-day conference was how well victims can be protected when mechanisms are in place to do the protecting. When all the various facets of law enforcement join in solving a particular problem, first arming themselves with the essential knowledge, then implementing those necessary procedures to tackle each critical aspect, the whole can function as a highly impressive, effective, and efficient entity. It was precisely for this reason that the TMU was conceived.

The TMU, the only such unit in the world, was formed in 1990 after Los Angeles experienced an alarming increase in the number of "star stalkings," culminating in July 1989 with the death of Rebecca Schaeffer. After her murder, members of the entertainment community were understandably concerned at the ease with which Robert Bardo had been able to hunt down his prey, and a system was designed to proactively identify potentially dangerous individuals stalking citizens before they had a chance to act.

Thus the TMU was born. But as the first unit of its kind, its detectives had no ready-made manual to follow. So the TMU gathered information from many sources, including the private sector, to develop its unique procedures for attempting to stop crimes before they occurred. Since then the number of cases handled each year by the TMU has grown exponentially, not necessarily because there have been more stalkers, but because the unit has gained recognition in the community as well as in its own department and has thus received more referrals.

Detective Doug Raymond, one of the TMU's original three officers and now the senior detective with the unit, wryly confirmed, "Initially... a lot of the detectives [in the LAPD] didn't know we existed."[5] Now, most of their cases are referrals from other divisions within the LAPD. The unit has expanded to eight detectives and since its inception has handled hundreds of cases, with no deaths or serious injuries to any of its protectees. The TMU has documented hundreds of cases of celebrity stalkers, including erotomanics, who were drawn to Hollywood from as far away as Ecuador, Germany, Guam, Buenos Aires, and the Ukraine. In some instances, the most persistent pursuers had to be deported.

But it is not only the rich and famous who are stalked in star-studded Los Angeles. Celebrities account for just 30 percent of the cases the TMU handles. The other victims are people like me, ordinary citizens without fame or fortune.

Detective Raymond, who has probably investigated more stalking crimes than anyone else on this planet, believes that had the TMU been in place in 1989, Robert Bardo would never have gotten the chance to kill Rebecca Schaeffer.[6] Her case illustrates well the need for proactive measures to thwart stalkers, which have since been implemented by the TMU.

Although it had been reported after Schaeffer's murder that friends doubted she would have sought protection from Bardo,[7] whether she would have on her own might well have been a moot point. "He was somebody who was known to the studios, although unknown to Ms. Schaeffer, and his conduct was ongoing for three years. She had no idea what he looked like. The studios did not liaison with each other," or with the police as they routinely do now, observed Raymond.

Had the TMU existed, those same studios would have been in touch with the detectives about a stalker named Bardo. The result of coordination by the TMU would have been, Raymond asserts, that Schaeffer "would have known what this suspect was, would have known the fact that he had been contacting her for the last three years, that he'd made several attempts to gain entry to the studio. She would have had a Department of Motor Vehicles' photo of the guy, and so she wouldn't have opened the door."[8]

The TMU also contacts other agencies to determine if a suspect has a mental health history, if there have been other police contacts in the past, and if so, if there was a successful intervention. The TMU will determine if there are family members of the suspect who might be able to assist in dissuading him. The family members are also asked to provide names of mental health professionals treating the suspect so they can be made aware of his activities. This information can be crucial. Research by the TMU indicates that at least 50 percent of stalkers suffer from some form of mental illness,[9] with some experts putting the figure between 80 and 90 percent.[10] In all the years Fran had been stalking me, no law enforcement official had ever spoken to any of her psychiatrists or therapists. Although mental health workers cannot generally disclose information about clients to anyone, even the police, without the client's consent, they are allowed to listen to any information provided to them, without actually acknowledging that they are treating the individual in question.

The TMU has found that in the case of erotomanic and other stalkers, contacting therapists can prove extremely valuable, especially when the client has told the therapist that his obsessions are under control but the police know he has just made his fiftieth phone call to his object.

Before inception of the TMU, if a citizen called the LAPD to report harassment by a stalker who had not actually threatened to harm him or her, nothing much could be done. This situation was, of course, familiar to me. I had run across it repeatedly in my dozens of calls to the Tucson Police Department, which, precisely because Fran had never threatened me, only resulted in one arrest, and then only because the officer had himself been stalked.

In Los Angeles, harassment by a stalker, regardless of whether or not any threat has been made, is precisely the situation that now falls under the mandate of the TMU. Since such harassment can take many forms, once the TMU "buys" the case, they "handle anything that may come up in the future. If the next day, she was the victim of a burglary or if she was raped by the suspect or if her car was vandalized, whatever the case may be, short of being murdered by the suspect, we would handle that case," noted Raymond.[11]

This approach allows the victim to tell her story to the same detective for each incident. Before the TMU was formed, a stalking victim had to report a burglary to the burglary division, an assault to the assault division, and vandalism or harassment to yet other divisions, retelling the entire story to officers who were not aware of her prolonged history of being stalked and who had no idea these crimes might, in fact, be related.

When I recalled how tedious and frustrating it had been to tell my own story more than two dozen times to two dozen different police officers, I appreciated how welcome such an approach would be. Because both Fran and I always dealt with different officers, it was that much more difficult for either of us to be taken seriously, she as a perpetrator and I as a victim, illustrating again how vitally important a TMU could be in every large city.

Once a case is "bought," the detective serves as a resource to the victim, educating her on the dynamics of stalking and what can be expected in her case. Again, I found myself wondering how different my life might have been if I had lived in Los Angeles and had immediately been given such information instead of having to laboriously uncover it myself over the years.

A Los Angeles stalking victim is almost always advised to get a restraining order, thus putting the suspect on notice, but also making an arrest that much easier if any subsequent contacts occur. The TMU detective working with a particular victim personally serves the restraining order rather than leaving it up to a sheriff or process server.

The advantages of immediate involvement by the detective handling the case are obvious: The stalker is confronted by the same imposing officer he will be dealing with if he violates the order, giving him the unmistakable message that such violations will be taken seriously. Actually, to the TMU detectives, the most important function of a restraining order is not to stop the stalker, because that often does not happen, but to prove that the stalker intends to stalk.

In my own case, if I had been lucky enough to have been in prac-tice in Los Angeles County when I first met Fran, Detective Raymond believed the TMU would have immediately advised a restraining order: "Even though chances are she's going to violate [it], at least that gives you a violation." A violation that would have been treated very differently in Los Angeles than it had in Tucson, according to Raymond:

The law enforcement agencies, the judicial system, the mental health system have to be on board because it does no good to say, "I'm going to get a restraining order," if she violates it and doesn't get arrested. All this does is send a real bad message to the suspect that she can do these things with impunity. That the police came out, they interviewed her, they said don't come back again and she came back an hour later and two other policemen came out who were totally different and they said don't come back again. . . it just shows that the law cannot control her.

As I listened to Detective Raymond, it was as if he was reading the police case file of Fran's stalking me. A case file that had never, in fact, even been opened. He continued, further illustrating why restraining orders must be taken seriously, "We would only recommend them if you take the posture that you have a protocol, a priority of arresting people for violations of restraining orders, because it is a good tool, but it isn't a tool if you don't know how to use it."[12]

In most jurisdictions, as I had already painfully discovered, a restraining order violation is a low-grade misdemeanor, with bail set at an easily attainable $250. Not so in Los Angeles County. Specific deputy district attorneys working closely with the TMU know better. They typically ask the judge for bail enhancement, usually $25,000–$50,000, or 100–200 times the customary amount, and they almost always get it.

Normally stalking cases are plea bargained with certain mandatory conditions of probation, such as mental health treatment for erotomanics. In fact, Los Angeles Deputy District Attorney Rhonda Saunders told me that because the TMU is so successful in helping victims gather evidence, suspects prefer to plea. "By the time we get into court, there's no way that the suspect can fight it. . . . I've even had stalkers plead open, which was a big mistake," she said.

When a defendant pleads open, he enters a plea of no contest or guilty and is not promised anything in return by the prosecution. Some defense attorneys, faced with overwhelming evidence against their clients courtesy of the TMU, advise them to plead open, hoping the judge will consider that during sentencing. Los Angeles judges have been well educated in stalking cases, however, and are unlikely to do so.

As Saunders observed, stalkers there "get nailed by the judges." In one of her cases in which the defendant pled open, the stalker had kidnapped the victim's dog, threatening to kill it. He refused to tell the victim where it was, even after he had been arrested.

So, on top of sending him to state prison for as long as possible, the judge also ordered him to pay a restitution fine in the amount of $5000 for the dog. . . . The attorney for the defendant jumped up and said, "But, Your Honor! The dog, it's just a mutt. It's not worth $5000." And the judge looked at him and said, "I have a dog. It's a mutt. And he's invaluable." Well, the victim got her dog back.[13]

If Fran had been introduced to law enforcement in Los Angeles, the Mental Evaluation Unit, a round-the-clock emergency unit staffed by specially trained police officers, would have been contacted. It is considered the mental health command post of the Los Angeles Police Department, and it would have kept tabs on whether Fran was taking her medication or thinking about contacting me, gently encouraging her in the former and firmly dissuading her in the latter. It is "the best way to get the most meaningful resources and services for these people," Walter de Cuir, detective-in-charge of the unit, told me.[14]

What I found comforting yet disconcerting, because it illustrated both what could be done and emphasized what should have already happened, was the agreement among the detectives and prosecutors I spoke with that if Fran had violated the protective order in Los Angeles, she would have been arrested promptly for her first violation—instead of her twenty-fourth.

Of all of the people I met at the conference, there were two women whom I found most inspirational. From widely disparate backgrounds, these women were led to the conference by different paths, even from different countries and cultures, but their attendance attested to their convergent goals: to discover how to best use their experiences to help others. Due to ignorance and lack of effort by authorities, both had been left to deal with the terrible consequences of stalking on their own. Both admitted they were forever transformed by their travails.

They are extraordinary women. I have treated many victims of various abuses in my work and never had believed that there was anything particularly courageous about surviving an ordeal. We survive because we have to. The alternative is intolerable. Where a victim becomes courageous is when he or she uses an awful past to better the future for others. These two women are shining examples of this tenet.

I met Evonne von Heussen-Countryman, a medical researcher from England, during a break on the second day of the conference. Someone I had talked with introduced us because he thought I might be interested in meeting another stalking victim from the medical field. Little did he know how thankful I would be. Evonne and I began talking while the rest of the participants went to lunch, and within a few minutes we were alone.

She had come to the TMU conference in her capacity as the director of Great Britain's National Anti-Stalking and Harassment Campaign and Support Association (NASH), but her motives for activism were doubly personal. In 1975, at the age of twenty-seven, when she was just a medical student at the University of London, Evonne, a tall, slender, striking-looking black woman, had a brief chance meeting that would change her life forever: A white, male, visiting professor bumped into her on a university stairwell. She recognized him as a guest lecturer in a course she had briefly attended.

"Excuse me," he said.

"No problem," she replied, and walked away.

Evonne thought nothing more of the encounter, which she later came to believe had been staged. From there, a seventeen-year "relationship" began. It started with three years of repeated silent telephone calls to her home. Then the calls became obscene and threatening, up to hundreds a day.

At the time, Evonne had been recently widowed with two small children, so she felt particularly vulnerable, especially when her stalker began sending her bizarre gifts, like half-eaten boxes of chocolates, or when he left bouquets of dead flowers on her doorstep. He once even poured acid on her car. But most alarming of all were the pictures he had taken of her and her little girls, which he sent her, letting her know he was always watching. Soon after, he started threatening to kidnap her children.

Looking back, she was able to laugh at herself for believing that she could thwart him by sitting at the top of her stairs at night with a bag of flour and a bucket of water, holding a kitchen knife in her hand. If Great Britain had allowed guns at the time, she would have armed herself, but instead, she had improvised with this strange concoction, thinking that she could throw the flour and water on him to render him immobile, then stab him with the knife.

But she was not at the top of the stairs one Sunday morning in 1978 when he talked his way into her apartment. He convinced her elderly stepfather, who was visiting and had answered the door, that he was her boyfriend. Evonne asked her stalker to leave. Although she expressed her fears to her stepfather, he inexplicably left the apartment. Thus she found herself captive to her stalker in her very own home.

The stalker held her hostage for the next eight hours, during which he threatened to rape and murder her in front of her girls, then ages six and four. As her children's terror grew, he turned his rage on them, threatening to hang them before their mother's eyes. Evonne finally managed to diminish the danger to them by ushering the girls into the main bedroom and shutting the door. He then attempted to rape her and when she successfully fought him off, he tried to strangle her. A neighbor had heard the children's screams, but ignored them until there was no mistaking the distress of an adult woman's cries and the rending sounds of a struggle. She called the police, probably saving her young neighbor's life.

When the bobbies arrived, the attacker was calmly sitting on the couch, smoking a cigarette. Partly due to the times and, I suspect, although Evonne did not so contend, to racism, the police told her that since it was her word against his that they were in a relationship and that he had stalked and attacked her, the matter would have to be treated as a domestic dispute. The police advised him that if he left right away, they would ignore the incident. He, of course, readily agreed and rode off down the block on his bicycle. Within minutes after the police left, the stalker was standing across the street, staring at her under the lamplight. She did not leave her apartment for thirteen weeks.

As Evonne's story filled the cavernous ballroom, I found myself riveted by her every word, yet the contrast between her composed, even muted recitation and the real horror of the events she had endured had, at first, discomfited me. It was only when she shared what she had written, much later, about her stalker's siege, that I realized her subdued stance was a result of the terrible ordeal that had haunted her ever after:

After the attack, I suffered intense fear and distress, finding it difficult to leave my home. Once out of my door, I found difficulty in going back. I became withdrawn, suspicious of others, preoccupied with my safety and even more preoccupied with that of the children. I felt trapped in a world that only included my home, my children's school, and my work. Sleep patterns were very badly interrupted as I spent the nights patrolling my home, as I watched over the children. My eating habits changed, and I became thinner than normal. For many years I experienced panic attacks, anger, and frustration at the thought of feeling so powerless. My ordeal made me into a strict and overprotective mother.

After the attack, I began to have terrifying nightmares and to scream out in the night. I still do. I find it difficult to sleep in strange beds, and it takes very little to trigger a replay of the events of that day. I do not like confined spaces. . . . I find it quite unpleasant when people stand or walk behind me. I find it difficult to be alone in the company of a man, especially someone I do not know. I find eye contact with men difficult. . . . I still panic at one-to-one meetings with men—even bank managers and dentists. During my university career, I feared my male teachers. . . . [A]s an employee, I have feared male employers.

For years, I've felt effectively a prisoner in my own home. I rarely go out for pleasure. I am always looking over my shoulders. I use a taxi or a car to go everywhere, even a mile away from my home.

The letters and telephone calls, often obscene and threatening, continued after the attack. Her young daughters were even exposed to the calls when they answered the phone. The strange gifts also continued, and finally, with no help from the authorities in sight, she left London and moved to a different city, hoping to escape this bizarre and dangerous stalker. As she recalled:

I moved from London specifically to get away from the situation and to start life afresh. I had no idea that my hell was only beginning to start. I left behind my family, friends, and job and all that I held dear, except for the girls.

The man stalking Evonne was somehow able to follow her to her new locale, just as Fran had done to me. Once there, he managed to induce her helpful neighbors to pinpoint her apartment, by showing them the pictures he had taken of Evonne and her daughters, and claiming that she was his wife and had stolen his children. Thus the hunter was able to garner more sympathy and more aide than was the hunted.

Evonne moved twice more. Twice more he found her. Hearing that, I wished that every "expert" who ever said, "go to the police," every unresponsive police officer who had ever chosen not to jail a stalker, every indifferent prosecutor who had ever said dismiss the charges, and every other person who had ever told a victim that she encouraged the stalking, could be made to listen to the story of this traumatized woman and witness her quiet dignity.

Evonne's stalker never spent a day in jail, nor was he ever charged with any crime, despite the horrors he inflicted on her over the course of seventeen years. Until 1992, she still heard from him occasionally, but tragically, even as the stalker seemed to be withdrawing from her life, her ordeal was not yet over. For that year, it began anew when her younger daughter, then seventeen, was approached by a different man who had, unbeknownst to her, already been stalking her for two years.

One day as the young woman left school and was walking to her car, she noticed a man in his mid-twenties running toward her, waving. Perhaps remembering her mother's ordeal, she quickly got into the car, locked the doors, and rolled up the windows. He immediately came right up to the driver's side, motioning to her to roll the window down. Chastising herself that she had overreacted to a man who probably just needed directions, she complied.

He told her that he was in love with her and had been following her for two years. As proof, he told her the details of her life that only someone who had truly been stalking her could have known. If she did not agree to live in his house and to marry him, he said, he would kidnap her right there. When she resisted, he attempted to carjack her vehicle, but she managed to get away.

He continued to follow her for months, going to her school and telling authorities there that he was her boyfriend. Up to that point, she had been a bright, attractive, straight-A student, but the stress of the stalker's constant presence took its toll. She did poorly on her final examinations, which in Great Britain completely determine the rest of a student's life by dictating which schools he or she can get into. Although accepted to a university, she lost her confidence and deferred admission for a year. Regaining her will, she finally attended a school in Scotland, hoping to get as far away from her stalker as possible. She succeeded in that instance, but ran right into a situation far worse.

A thirty-year-old fellow student she had met through friends began pursuing her. Although she consistently rejected his advances, like most stalkers, he did not take no for an answer. Finally, he resorted to violence, raping his prey on campus. Evonne told me:

> *The administration of the university where she was studying absolutely refused to give her protection against her stalker-rapist and threatened her with the probability of getting a bad degree if she went public with the matter. He is still a student and I believe that he is a serial rapist.*[15]

One might think that seventeen years of dealing with your own stalker, only to have the situation repeated with your child, would be more than anyone could bear. Not Evonne von Heussen-Countryman. "Neither of [my daughter's stalkers] was ever arrested or punished; it was the self-professed inability of the police to act against the first that led to my involvement in this issue," she says.[16]

When she and her daughter met with their local member of Parliament in July 1993, his response to her daughter's story was "I'm not surprised you're being stalked, my dear. You're a very attractive young woman." He further told them that "laws cannot be changed just because we want them to be changed."

Really? Evonne and her daughter founded NASH (the National Anti-Stalking and Harassment Campaign and Support Association) two days later. Since then, NASH has campaigned for effective antistalking legislation in Great Britain; worked to establish regional stalking victim support groups; provided public and professional education on stalking; encouraged more effective treatment of stalkers; and established a victim help line that provides emotional support and guidance for victims of stalking and for their families, as well as legal and psychotherapeutic referrals.

Since the launching of NASH, it has dealt with more than seven thousand stalking victims (95 percent women) and almost three thousand victims of other forms of harassment. Through her position as director of NASH, Evonne, working closely with the home office, also drafted Great Britain's first antistalking legislation. NASH has lobbied virtually every member of the House of Commons in preparation for the bill that came before Parliament in October 1996, and in March 1997, stalking became a crime in Great Britain for the first time.

When I met Evonne at the conference in 1995, she told me her daughter, who could barely remember a time in her life without a stalker's presence, was withdrawn, isolated, depressed, and had gained an enormous amount of weight in order to avoid further unwanted attention from men. She concluded her story with the resignation of someone who had been through it all, saying, "I don't know what will happen to her."

In a conversation a year later, she told me that her daughter was slowly recovering, losing weight, and had started a new degree course at a different university. Evonne still finds it difficult to talk about the tribulations she has endured over the last twenty years, especially with regard to her daughter. Yet in order to promote her bill, she has had to retell her story many times to legislators and to the media in Great Britain.

Although she told me recently, "I'm still quite traumatized by it all,"[17] I found it hard to believe her. Someone truly traumatized would not have had the strength and courage to continue the fight to protect her daughter and others for the last four years. Even more extraordinary, after seeing her efforts finally rewarded with the legislation she has fought so long for, Evonne is still hard at work, traveling around her country, teaching the police, court officials, and volunteer organizations about the new law and how to apply it.

After I spoke with Evonne, I could barely register the rest of that day's schedule. Her story had consumed me, particularly the way in which the authorities' indifference and assignment of blame first to her and then to her daughter, mirrored what I had experienced on another continent and what I now knew was being experienced by stalking victims the world over. I could almost sense the oppressive pain and struggle of thousands upon thousands of innocent men and women, just like me, Evonne, and her daughter, fighting alone, receiving scorn instead of aide, futilely attempting to escape their tormentors in a never-ending stalking cycle worthy of an Escher drawing. The scope of the problem overwhelmed me, and I did not think I could find any recesses left in my brain with which to process more information.

Lunch over, the conference participants began filling the hall. Tempted by the promise of a freshly made bed in my room, I considered skipping the afternoon's agenda so I could nap and not think at all for a few hours. Fortunately my good study habits from long ago prevailed, and I will be forever grateful. Because if I had not finished that afternoon's agenda, I never would have encountered Margie L.

I happened to have met, at various points in the conference, several members of Margie's local police department who were in attendance. I had told them a little about myself and why I was there, and each one had said, in tones that could only be described as reverential, "You've got to talk to Margie." After hearing this enough times, my curiosity was piqued, and during a break in the schedule that afternoon, I spotted one of the officers and asked him if he could point her out to me.

Margie, a tall, vivacious woman in her fifties, whose short, stylishly cut blond hair was just beginning to turn gray, said, with just a trace of a Southern accent, that she would be pleased to talk to me, and we arranged to meet that evening in her room. I found Margie an inspiration, and am extremely grateful that she graciously agreed to let me repeat her story, in the hope that it would help other victims thwart their pursuers.

One winter's evening in November 1990, Margie's seventeen-year-old daughter, Julie, was having a slumber party with a group of her girlfriends while her parents and younger brother were away for the weekend. The first snow had already fallen in their suburban Midwestern town, but the skies were clear that night, so the girls decided to go for a snack at a neighborhood diner. Returning with her friends a few hours later, Julie made her way around the sprawling four thousand square-foot home, locking it up for the night as she had watched her parents do many times before, while her friends got ready for bed in her room. When changing into her nightgown, one of the guests noticed that her wallet with one hundred dollars in it was missing. Thinking she had misplaced it, she began searching Julie's bedroom, where the group was gathered.

Meanwhile, Julie was turning out the lights in the kitchen when she noticed a Post-It note on the bulletin board. It said, "I love you, Julie, baby. Eric!" She read it and laughed, thinking that one of her friends was playing a girlish prank. She did not have a boyfriend, let alone know an Eric. But at that moment, one of her friends found her and with an ashen look on her face, handed Julie a note she had just spotted on Julie's desk. This note was more explicit. It said, "I love you, Julie. I love your blond wavy hair. I want to make love to you. Love you forever, Eric." Positive that the notes had not been there when they had left for the diner, the now terrified girls quickly surmised that someone had been on the premises, leaving the notes and stealing the wallet.

They immediately called the police. While they were waiting, Julie recalled that she, too, had recently "lost" one hundred dollars and that her mother had been missing some inexpensive jewelry. The girls' horror grew as they speculated that whoever had been in the house that night must have been there before. The police came, searched the house, and found that a patio door had been forced open. They confiscated the notes as evidence and fingerprinted the house, thinking that it was probably the work of a high school prankster since no items of real value had been taken. On their return to town, Margie and her husband immediately installed a burglar alarm.

Over the next nine months, the family experienced a series of incidents in which the alarm would go off soon after they left the house. There was never any further sign of forced entry, although, strangely, small things seemed to disappear from outside their home: a can of paint, a lawn ornament, a potted plant. Several cars parked overnight in front of their house came up with flat tires by morning. Most distressing, however, were the notes to Julie from Eric, professing his love, that continued to appear at the house, albeit in different forms, sometimes spray-painted on the sidewalk or written in the snow, sometimes put directly into the mailbox or under the doormat.

Like Fran, Eric had an unsettling, uncanny knack for knowing just when to leave his messages so he would never be seen. One of these notes was written on a scrap of paper that appeared to have been torn out of a brochure for a car show. Its tattered edges showed the faintest trace of primer paint and on the back was a Corvette logo. The note asked Julie to meet Eric at the car show the next Sunday. It was signed, "I love making love to you, baby. Eric W."

Margie and her husband had been keeping the police informed of all the strange goings-on at their home, so when they brought this latest note to the station, it was taken very seriously. Julie's parents and the police even discussed letting her go to the car show in order to trap the stalker, the detectives assuring Margie and her husband that they would follow their daughter closely in plain clothes. After much agonizing, Margie finally vetoed the plan, reasoning it was much too dangerous for her daughter because no one still had any clue about who this Eric might be.

A few weeks later, Julie and a friend were sitting on the patio of a restaurant having lunch when they noticed a man in a vintage, bright red Corvette in the parking lot, staring at Julie. They tried to ignore him, but finally, her friend, offended at the stranger's rudeness, shrugged her shoulders at him and extended her hands with her palms upward, in the universal signal for "What's up?" He yelled back, "I don't want you. I want Julie." The girls knew immediately that this must be "Eric" and ran into the restaurant to call the police. By the time they arrived, Eric was long gone, but Julie discovered a note on her windshield that said, "I still love you, baby. I thought you should know I got a mustache, now. Eric."

Margie's blood ran cold when she heard this latest installment. Intuitively, Margie realized that by finally showing his face, Eric was upping the ante. There was no telling what he might do next. Even though the police believed the stalker was using his real name, Eric W., they still had no idea who he might be, let alone how to apprehend him. Fortunately Margie did.

Remembering the note with the trace of paint left a few weeks earlier, Margie guessed that Eric might be involved in automobile repair of some sort, perhaps even working at a Chevrolet dealership. The police assured her that their investigation had turned up no Corvette clubs in their town nor in any town nearby. Margie was undaunted. Hunkering down with a large pot of coffee, she began with her local yellow pages, fervently hoping her search would not be in vain.

Methodically, she started with the first Chevy dealership listed, called, and asked for the parts department. When a man picked up the phone, she asked if there was a Corvette club in the area. He said there was and that he, in fact, was a member. "Great, I'd like to join," Margie told him. The mechanic said he would be happy to send her an application and that the membership fee was twenty-five dollars.

"Better yet," Margie responded, "I'll jump in my car and come there right now. I'll pay you twenty-five dollars, and I'd like a copy of your membership roster right away."

"I'm thrilled that you're so enthusiastic about joining the club, but I'm very reluctant to give you a list of the members so quickly. Why do you need it?" he asked, suspicion creeping into his voice.

"Do you have a few minutes?" Margie replied. He did and she told him that her daughter was being stalked by a man who drove a Corvette and who had only recently showed his face. She then gave him the description of Eric that Julie had provided from the restaurant.

After a long pause the mechanic said slowly, "I think I know who is stalking your daughter."

Margie's immediate reaction was disbelief. "No," she thought, "it doesn't happen quite this easily. The police have assured me. . .they've been taking fingerprints, they have all these databases and they can't find the guy. I can't find him with just one phone call." As calmly as she could, she said, "Well, I haven't told you that he signs his notes, 'Eric.'"

"The guy I'm thinking of, his name is Eric," the man answered.

Margie swallowed hard and felt her heart beating faster. Could this really be? She continued, "I didn't tell you that in one of the notes, he signed his last initial, 'W.'" Margie heard the man take a deep breath.

"His last name does begin with a W." he said. "When your daughter saw him, was he driving an old red Corvette?"

Margie was elated. In that instant, she knew they had the right man. She drove immediately to her daughter's school and took her to the Chevy dealership to meet the mechanic. He had told Margie he would be standing behind the parts counter. When they arrived, they noticed that the man behind the counter had on a name tag that seemed to say, "Eric West." Had they been set up? Was he the stalker? On closer inspection, they saw that the mechanic's first name was Eddie, not Eric, but the doubt and fear still lingered, especially when he said he did not want to talk to them in the shop.

When Eddie took them out into the parking lot, the women's suspicions dissolved at his obvious distress. "Look," he told them, "I'm going to help you. I'm going to give you the guy's name and tell you where he is, but you have to swear never to let the police or anyone else know where you got this information." The two women swore, elated, but their elation again turned to fear.

Eddie told them that the man they were dealing with was "absolutely crazed," had a "volatile temper," and carried a gun. The members of the car club believed he was stealing them blind, pilfering parts and even some cars. They suspected that he was part of a car theft ring that spanned several states. Eddie told Margie and Julie, "We are so afraid of this guy, that even though he's been ripping us off, we haven't kicked him out of the club. A couple of the guys have confronted him and he's threatened to blow them away. We take his threats very seriously because we've seen him when he loses his temper. This guy is capable of anything."

As if to underscore his fear, and theirs, he implored the two women again. "I don't want this to get back to me. You have to promise you won't tell anyone where this came from." Again, Margie and Julie promised.

Driving directly to the police station, Margie regained her composure, allowing herself to marvel, "Within seventeen minutes, I found the man the police had been looking for for nine months." She breathed a sigh of relief, confident that her family's ordeal would soon be over.

Margie gave the police the name of Julie's stalker and the name of the motel where he was staying. She told them that since he always carried a large wad of cash, usually a thousand dollars, but was unemployed, he probably was up to no good. Finding his name in their files, the police discovered Eric was on parole but, concerned about violating his civil rights, would give her no more information. Margie had learned more about her daughter's stalker from an auto mechanic.

The next day, a detective went out to interview the ex-con and started by asking if Eric knew why he was there. When Eric said that he did not, the detective told him, "You've been writing notes."

Eric casually volunteered, "Oh, you mean my letters to Julie."

"Yes, and I'm going to arrest you for stalking her and breaking into her house over the last year," the detective replied.

Eric demurred. "I've never broken into that house. I'm a guest there. She loves me and I love her. I met her at a party last year. She invited me home and we got loaded in her bedroom. She asked me to screw her that night, and I've been doing it ever since."

Margie was informed of the visit and told by the detective that there was not enough hard evidence to arrest Eric, let alone convict him. Crestfallen, Margie insisted that at the least, Eric be served with a restraining order, barring him from coming near Julie or the house. Eric's parole officer served the order himself, telling Eric that it was his idea, hoping to divert the stalker's wrath away from Margie.

But the restraining order would be no deterrent. Eric readily admitted to his parole officer that he could not end a relationship that had been so important to him for such a long time. He did not understand why Julie, who obviously loved him as much as he loved her, would want a restraining order, so he surmised that the resistance to the relationship must have come from Margie, whom, he said, had never liked him.

The police told the family that they were unable to do anything else until there was hard evidence that Eric violated the restraining order, even though they had a parolee who admitted being in their house, writing their daughter letters, and whose fingerprints matched those on the letters that had been written.

This reticence of the police to act was all too familiar to me. I wanted to finish hearing Margie's story, but at the same time, the anger welled up in my brain and I was finding it hard to concentrate. I could almost feel the blood pounding through the capillaries behind my eyes. A massive headache was coming on. Trying to force myself to focus, I asked Margie, "How did you feel when the police told you that they weren't going to do anything?"

"I was dumbfounded," Margie replied, her tone matching my own anger. Regardless of how I felt, I had to hear the rest and I asked Margie to continue.

Now concerned for her own safety, as well as that of her daughter's, Margie did some more checking. She found an informant in the police department who told her that the detective had quietly closed the case, believing Eric's story that he and Julie were lovers. Margie was devastated by the indifference of the police, a feeling that was so close to my own experience that it was obviously responsible for my current physical distress and the pain that had seized my head. Margie could not comprehend how the detective could take the word of a convicted felon with an eleven-page rap sheet against that of her teenage daughter, an honors student who had never been in trouble.

Even worse, she could not confront the detective with the source of her information because she had promised the informant she would protect his privacy. It was then that Margie really had to dig in her heels and get to work. As she put it, "This is the scary part. It's up to the victims to start researching their stalkers just as deeply as they can." What she did was what every victim must learn to do—to rely on themselves and no one else for their own protection.

Margie traced Eric's name through her county court's archives and got lucky, finding a copy of his voluminous rap sheet tucked away among the court papers, something she had not been allowed to see before. When the police had looked at those eleven pages, all they had seen was an assortment of unrelated crimes: arsons, assaults with a deadly weapon, vandalism, malicious conduct, violations of restraining orders. But Margie saw something else.

Instead of the list of random events noted by the police, Margie realized that Eric's violations were clustered; all the addresses at which these incidents occurred were the same for one, two, even three years at a time. Margie took the list of addresses from the rap sheet and consulted back issues of the Cole Directory at her local library, a reverse telephone directory that lists by addresses the names of people living in a given area. Up to this point in her story, I had been so terribly impressed with Margie that I had just accepted her courage and keen intellect without comment. But now, I couldn't help exclaiming in wonder, "How did you ever hear about the Cole Directory?"

Margie shrugged, offering that she read a lot of mystery novels, as though that should explain not only her knowledge of the Cole Directory, but everything else she had done to find Eric. I remained speechless marveling at the supersleuth before me as she continued.

In discovering that all the addresses belonged to women, Margie surmised they were dealing with a serial stalker, one whose predatory activities had been concealed for years by the absence of a stalking law. But that wasn't enough for this intrepid housewife and mother. As she described it, "through sheer tenacity and dogged determination" she set out to find the women who had been stalked by Eric, to learn all that she could about this dangerous man who was stalking her daughter. At this point in her story, Margie's genteel upbringing took over, and as she paused to get a drink of bottled water from her hotel room's minibar, she asked if I wanted anything or if I might like her to order something from room service. I'm afraid I was rather rude at her Southern hospitality, answering a curt, "No thanks." I was too eager for her to continue her tale, but I also realized that

I need not concern myself with her potential hurt feelings. This Southern belle had balls. Sensing my impatience, Margie resumed her story.

Using the Cole Directories that covered the years of Eric's numerous illegal acts, Margie made a list of all the neighbors who had lived in the blocks surrounding Eric's previous victims. Through months of telephone calls and letter writing she painstakingly tracked down every single lead, each neighbor who might remember another neighbor who might remember the victim in question, perhaps even recalling where she had moved. The work was tedious and time-consuming, but Margie persisted, knowing the information could save her daughter's life.

She prevailed in tracking down all but one of Eric's seven previous victims, and that frightened her even more. "I never found the last victim. I don't know if she's dead. She could have just disappeared, or she could have hidden herself very well. But, the thing that's scary is, that if someone is determined enough, I believe there is a way to find anyone."

Many of Eric's previous victims were understandably reluctant to talk to Margie. All the women had purposely covered their tracks and were horrified that Margie had found them, fearing then that Eric could, too. Every single one of them had always expected Eric would look for her some day, believing that he would probably employ some ruse to find her through family or friends. So when Margie found them, the women were suspicious of her motives.

One woman's family even insisted on prescreening Margie and Julie by meeting them for lunch at a busy fast-food restaurant before revealing the whereabouts of their daughter. One by one, though, Margie met the previous victims, and through her conversations with them, she pieced together the petrifying puzzle of Eric's predatory past.

Eric W., she learned, had been stalking various young girls and women since he was seventeen, when he had fixated on a twelve-year-old. All described him as an extremely dangerous, unstable individual. He had a long psychiatric history of stalking women he believed loved him, and had been diagnosed with paranoid schizophrenia with erotomanic delusions.

He was relentless in his pursuit, and when spurned, had resorted to several incidents of violent assault, arson, and attempted murder against his victims and their families. He had also been charged with three separate counts of rape of minor girls, each of whom he was convinced was in love with him, although each time, the charges were dropped when the victims' families decided they did not want their daughters to endure a trial.

On hearing all this, Margie realized Eric had created yet another delusional relationship, this time with Julie. Margie hoped that Eric's family might be enlisted to get their son some help, thereby keeping him away from her daughter, until she learned from one of the victims that Eric's father was long since dead and his mother as delusional as her son.

From a court-ordered psychiatric report one of the victims provided her with, Margie learned that Eric had slept in the same bed with his mother until he was in his twenties, and on several occasions, she seemed to share his delusions: a *folie à deux* all in the family.

Once, Eric's mother even delivered flowers from her son to one of his victims, and when the delusional lover declined to accept them, she screamed angrily at her that she was toying with her son and had better stop. Soon after, Eric made good on his mother's threat by breaking into this woman's apartment, tossing all her clothes on her bed, then setting them afire.

I recalled how sickened I had felt when Fran had simply left her instruments in my garage. I could not imagine how violated and devastated I would have been if she had actually made it into our house, let alone maliciously destroyed our property.

By the time Margie found Eric's previous victims it had been over a year since he had begun stalking Julie. Margie passed along all the information she had gathered to the police, once again naively expecting that her family's ordeal would finally be over. She was shocked when they told her that, on the contrary, her information was virtually useless. They still needed hard evidence that Eric had violated the restraining order before they could arrest him.

Although Margie knew who the stalker was and presented the police with all he had done, he still could not be taken in. I could feel my wrath growing because I had experienced the same thing. But I should have expected that my frustration on hearing this ingenious and resourceful woman's story would not last long—and it did not. Margie continued,

As my devastation turned to outrage, I recalled what the auto parts man had said about all the thefts they believed Eric had

committed. So I went back to the car club and made a list of all the stolen auto parts, with detailed description, year and part number, and the vehicles that the club members thought Eric had stolen. While writing this list on my computer at home, it suddenly dawned on me that our block had had a series of random burglaries for roughly the same amount of time that Julie was being stalked.

We then called a neighborhood watch meeting to determine how many burglaries had occurred, if police reports had been filed, and if anyone had been a witness to the break-ins. Two-thirds of the people who attended had been hit by a burglar within the year, so I made a list of all the stolen merchandise. I felt a growing certainty, as I heard about each break-in and the M.O. (Modus Operandi) in each case, that they were all related. Finally, I knew we were dealing with the same guy.

Margie went back to the police and with all the calm she could muster handed them a three-page list of the items that had been stolen from the car club, her neighbors, and her own home.

She told them that if they would not arrest Eric for stalking her daughter, perhaps someday when they arrested him for something else and found any one item from her list in his possession, they would also be able to charge him with burglary. She also politely suggested they find out if he had access to a storage shed where he might be keeping his ill-gotten goods, because he lived in a series of ever-changing motel rooms and Corvettes do not have trunks. Although filled with disdain at their inaction and ineffectiveness, Margie reasoned, as had I, that she should not alienate the police department that she might have to depend on in the future.

Two weeks later, Margie got a call from the police informing her that Eric had been caught burglarizing another home in a neighboring city. They had found various items from Margie's list in his motel room, including a piece of paper with Julie's name, address, and the name of her school written on it. They also found keys to two storage sheds that contained a stolen car and even more items from Margie's list. Eric was charged with burglary and receiving stolen property, but not with stalking.

Margie explained that the district attorney remarkably did not press the stalking charge precisely because he feared that if he did, Eric would simply walk away, with no jail sentence. The district attorney believed that juries today, when confronted with multiple charges against the criminal, tend to throw the book at the perpetrator for what they consider the most egregious act. Then, he told her, "It's like the good cop/bad cop routine." They would want to let Eric off on the lesser charges.

In this case, Margie explained, the district attorney worried that the jury would find Eric guilty of the stalking charge, and rightly so, feeling that stalking was the worst of all the crimes, but that they would exonerate him of some of the charges of burglary and receiving stolen property. Since juries are not informed of potential sentences, Margie recalled:

> *If they had charged Eric with stalking, they would have unwittingly set this guy free, because the stalking statute at that time only provided for a year in jail and he had long since served most of that [awaiting trial]. He would have been out on the street almost the day they gave him the verdict, whereas each burglary charge carried a maximum sentence of six years.*

At that point in the story, I was truly speechless. After all Margie's hard work to catch her daughter's stalker, he would never be charged with stalking. In a further wrenching twist, as if the family hadn't already suffered enough, Eric's attorney used an appalling ploy to keep Eric out of jail. He argued before the jury that his client *was* a stalker, but not a burglar, and that Margie had framed Eric to keep him away from Julie.

The attorney maintained that by inciting sympathy for their plight, Margie had gotten everyone else to lie about the burglaries. The attorney's outrageous claims were bolstered because several of the burglary victims—including all the car club members who were fearful of retribution at the hands of this volatile predator—backed out of testifying at the last minute. But even without access to any of Eric's prior offenses, the jury managed to see the truth beyond the defense's contemptible claims. Eric was found guilty on all counts and given the stiffest sentence possible: fourteen years in the state prison.

But the bizarre twists of this stalking saga did not end with the verdict. Just as Fran's family had seemed to perpetuate her ability to stalk me, Eric's mother continued to delusionally press his suit. After the sentencing, Eric's mother (who had maintained throughout the proceedings that all the stolen items were, in fact, hers and not stolen at all) approached Julie in the courtroom, screaming at her that she had framed her son. "Why don't you admit you love him?" she yelled, charging, "This is your fault."

Throughout the trial, in fact, Eric's mother had worn a long, blond, wavy wig, in a grotesque Oedipal mockery of Julie's hair. Other victims had told Margie that Eric's mother often appeared in the courtroom wearing a wig that matched the coiffure of his current fixation, but even so, Margie said, the first time she saw the older woman, the effect was even more hideous than she could have imagined. Despite Margie's rousing victory, she and her family did not have much time to celebrate; the authorities told her to count on Eric's serving less than half his sentence.

At the time Margie told me her story, she said Eric would be out of prison in about a year. Margie and her family have since moved to another state. Julie has graduated from college and is studying international finance abroad, where she intends to stay, undoubtedly to keep as much distance as possible between herself and Eric. Margie and her husband plan to move again before Eric is released, possibly joining Julie abroad. In the meantime, Margie has turned to activism:

> *Word got out within our little neighborhood of what had happened. People started calling me with problems, asking me if they qualified as stalking. I would direct them to who to talk to at the city, who to avoid, how to deal with the police. This is what was amazing to me. I don't think people are aware of how prevalent this really is in society, because most people don't want to talk about it. For business or social reasons, it's almost like you're stigmatized because this is happening to you and it's almost as if people think they'll be caught up in it by extension if they're too close to you. We had a lot of supporters, but I also had friends who were afraid to go to the trial because they were afraid that the guy would then start stalking them.*[18]

I found Margie's words stirring as I remembered all the times I had also experienced confusingly mixed reactions from others: sympathy for my plight, yes, but also blame that I had brought it on myself, a reassurance against its ever happening to them.

Margie started working within her state, developing protocols for stalking victims to help themselves and founding a hot line. She became a member of a task force headed by her city's district attorney to look into the legislative, law enforcement, and public education aspects of stalking. She also hopes to soon staff an 800 number from her home at night to help stalking victims when they're most vulnerable—until she has to move again—but you can be sure when she does, she will take her activism with her.

I left Margie's room late that night, after we had shared our stories. She was as appalled by mine as I had been impressed with hers. I think I even embarrassed her a bit by positively gushing at the guts, grit, and incredible guile she had shown in saving her daughter.

By the next morning, the last one of the conference, I felt buoyed by Evonne's and Margie's stories. While I did not imagine that I could ever match their courage, I think it was then that I was inspired to write about my experiences, to publicize the havoc wreaked by stalkers, particularly erotomanics, on their victims—so others would not have to endure the years of shame, self-doubt, and police inaction that I had. As a psychiatrist, I hoped I could also educate other health care professionals through lecturing about my own experiences. Perhaps if more people were made aware of how devastating a problem stalking is not only for the individual victims, but society as a whole, better laws could be passed and police would be compelled to treat the problem seriously.

When Tim arrived later that afternoon, we immediately caught the monorail into the park as I told him about the conference and my renewed strength and determination. With my obvious excitement as I related all that I had learned over the previous two days and what I was planning to do with that knowledge, Tim could not help but fully support me, matching my excitement and my resolve. Although I was still concerned that Fran could be following me around in a Goofy or Pinocchio suit, I was able to thoroughly enjoy Disneyland as Tim and I discussed the conference and made other plans. For when we returned home, I had another project awaiting me, one that would make me a good deal happier.

Tim and I were soon to be married. We had waited until our home was built because it was important to us to have the wedding there. We planned a small, intimate gathering with only close friends and family to witness our vows, and wanted to fill our new home with the memories of the ceremony and reception that would hold such meaning for us.

One memory I was not looking forward to having was that of Fran's showing up as an uninvited guest. The precautions we had taken with our home address in Colorado seemed to be working thus far, but I feared that given her devotion to her work, Fran would someday overcome the many obstacles we had placed in her path. I told everyone associated with the wedding, from the caterer to the rabbi, not to tell anyone where we lived.

Still, I panicked when, a few weeks before the ceremony, I happened to go into the local store we had registered at only to find a large board with the names of every couple getting married that month. I quickly asked the manager to remove our names. Even though so many of the precautions I took with our home address and telephone number were so well integrated into my life, such a "security breach" only reinforced to me how tenuous our safety really was. Like Margie's search for Eric's other victims, I knew that anyone could be found if someone looked hard enough.

As the ceremony approached, I found myself nearly obsessed with Bill Lennon, the father of the singing Lennon Sisters, murdered by an erotomanic who viewed him as an obstacle to attaining his object's love. How would my marriage to Tim affect Fran? "Maybe we should just keep living together," I thought. I could not share my fears with Tim. He was as happy outwardly as I should have been inwardly. I did not want him to know that I was questioning the wisdom of our getting married while Fran was still in our lives.

Thankfully, the wedding came off without a hitch. But I continued to wonder if Fran would view Tim as a threat, an obstacle to getting what she wanted—me. That was exactly how Chet Young had perceived Bill Lennon before murdering him. Would Fran also believe that Tim was an obstacle she had to remove?

Chapter Eight

NOWHERE TO HIDE

THAT SUMMER OF 1995, THE SUMMER OF the conference as well as our wedding, was the busiest of my life. For her part, Fran also kept busy, continuing to leave periodic messages with Tucson telephone numbers on my voice mail at work. Yet every time I called my contact at the mental health center in Colorado, I was told that Fran was keeping her appointments there. Not even knowing which state she was in was somehow more unnerving than the knowledge that she could be right outside my front door.

The TMU conference had galvanized me, particularly meeting other erotomanic "victims." I began writing about my experiences, unsure of where it would lead me. I shared my story with friends and other professionals and was contacted informally by a number of stalking victims seeking my advice. It became a privilege to counsel and help other victims when I could. I no longer, in fact, felt like a victim at all, but like a budding activist, and in my new role, I wondered if I could somehow manage to induce Fran to remain in Tucson.

I recalled that she lied to her new therapist, telling him that she had moved because she needed a change, but I doubted she could afford to make such a move on her own. Her parents must have helped her financially. She must also have lied to them about her true reason for leaving. Surely, they would not have willingly helped her get closer to me. They probably thought I still lived in Tucson. As a victim, I might have resigned myself to the reality of living in the same state as Fran. As an activist, I sought to change that reality.

The potential solution came to me from the most unlikely of sources—Fran herself—after a series of messages on my voice mail in which she left her parents' number. One evening in the autumn of 1995, after telling Tim of her latest communication, I exclaimed in exasperation, "I think I'll just call her parents and tell them to keep her there." Tim, believing I might be serious, said, "I think you should have someone else do that for you." What a brilliant idea, I thought. If I had lived in Los Angeles, a detective from the TMU would have contacted Fran's parents on my behalf. In Colorado, there was not even a specific police officer or prosecutor assigned to my case since Fran had not yet been arrested, let alone charged with any crime in the state. So I hired an attorney, told him what I wanted him to do, and gave him Fran's parents' number in Tucson.

My suspicions about what Fran had told her parents were confirmed when he spoke to her mother. She was shocked to learn that I was in Colorado. At the time of his call, Fran happened to be visiting her parents. She quickly got on the extension and denied that she had contacted me at all since her move. The attorney told her mother that she and Fran's father should know that they had unwittingly contributed to Fran's criminal acts and that unlike Arizona, Colorado had an antistalking statute and that such cases were taken seriously. He informed Fran's mother that I had already gotten a restraining order against Fran, and if she attempted any further contacts, the police would take her to jail, whether or not she was in Colorado. Finally he asked for her help in keeping her daughter in Tucson, for all our sakes.

That brief conversation cost me nearly two hundred dollars in legal fees, but it seemed to be well worth it. It also illustrates the main point I had taken away from the TMU conference: In cases of erotomanic and other stalkers, it is up to the victim to actively spend her own money and time in the pursuit of her own protection. In an ideal society, where victims' rights were at the fore, a victim might not be responsible for managing her own case.

But even the TMU treats the victim as a client, and she is expected to assume an active role precisely because, as Lieutenant John Lane, the head of the unit observed, "The stalking problem belongs to the victim. Not to law enforcement, not to the private psychiatrist, not to mental health, and not to the criminal justice field."[1] I had finally learned that victims need to see themselves as clients, and if they feel they are not getting the best service possible, they need to look elsewhere, starting with themselves.

Months went by and I did not hear from Fran. Still, even if her erotomania was truly idling, I wanted to be prepared for the inevitable re-ignition of her pursuit. When Fran had first started to stalk me, I truly hoped my actions (calling the police, getting restraining orders, keeping in touch with Dr. Trottle) would make her stop. Now any actions I took (concealing our home address and telephone number, not advertising my office address, and varying our routes home) were only to make it more difficult for Fran to stalk me.

This was an important distinction and one I shared with the stalking victims I counseled. False expectations for any safety precaution could be deadly. Although it was true that Fran had followed us to Colorado and knew my office telephone number, she did not yet know where we lived and she might not even know where we worked.

This was not a victory, but only a stalemate and a temporary one at that. Our precautions had been not just to diminish Fran's constant, yet almost spectral presence in our lives, but to protect Tim and me from the very real danger she posed. But what exactly was that danger? I decided that if I were going to be a resource for victims, I had to learn more about predicting that which I and other victims feared most: a stalker's violence. I was about to learn that even for the experts, predicting, let alone preventing, violence was a formidable task.

On the surface, it might have appeared that Tim and I did not have much to fear from Fran. Still, I always had felt that we were in jeopardy in spite of the fact that Fran had never once threatened to harm either one of us, our family, friends, or co-workers. When she started stalking me in 1989, the Threat Management Unit and antistalking laws were only incipient ideas. As I learned at the TMU's conference, the field of threat management had since flourished. And the experts I met there as well as others they referred me to, had some very distinct theories about what made erotomanic and other stalkers dangerous. Theories that were in dark contrast to what I had learned in my psychiatric training about the prediction of violent behavior—theories that only enhanced my fear of Fran, my erotomanic stalker.

Psychiatrists have traditionally relied on no more precise techniques than those of gamblers at a horse race to predict aggressive behavior, examining a patient's past track record of violence to determine its likelihood in the future. Unfortunately the consequences of error for misjudging the potential for violence are infinitely more profound than those for betting poorly on a horse. Professional gamblers, in fact, seem to be more adept at assessing future performance than are mental health professionals, who according to a well-respected study are accurate in no more than one out of three predictions of violent behavior.[2]

A gambler would soon go broke with odds like that: Would-be presidential assassin, John Hinckley, Jr.; Charles Whitman, who from his perch in the University of Texas tower shot forty-four people in 1966, killing thirteen; and Samuel Byck, who shot several people and then killed himself following a failed attempt to crash-dive a jetliner into the Nixon White House in 1974 all were seeing psychiatrists before their attacks. None of these specialists in human behavior considered their clients—Hinckley, Whitman, or Byck—dangerous.[3] I had never once been contacted by any of Fran's psychiatrists or therapists, leading me to believe that they were gambling she was not dangerous, either. But that, I was learning, was the wrong bet to make.

Unfortunately, mental health professionals are not the only ones who are poor at predicting the potential for violence. Law enforcement agencies, including the FBI, Secret Service, and local police, have questioned and released five of the last eight persons who have attacked American presidents.[4] Obviously, whatever thresholds for potential violence used by the experts in those cases were not low enough.

Several security specialists at the TMU conference had referred to work by Dr. Robert Fein, a consulting psychologist for the U. S. Secret Service, and I managed to track him down at his Cambridge office, where we spoke by telephone. He was conducting research with Special Agent Bryan Vossekuil of the Secret Service, which looked at all persons in the last half century who selected a target of prominent public status and either attacked or came close to attacking them. Their findings were that "a very small percentage of these people had a history of arrest for a violent offense."[5]

John Hinckley, Jr., Lynette "Squeaky" Fromme, Sarah Jane Moore, Lee Harvey Oswald, Sirhan Sirhan, and John Wilkes Booth, while perhaps having troubling backgrounds, never perpetrated an act of criminal violence on another person before the attacks that made them famous.[6] That is also true of two of the most recent celebrity stalker-murderers, Robert Bardo, who killed Rebecca Schaeffer, and Mark David Chapman, who killed John Lennon. While a past history of violence, therefore, is an important factor in increasing the risk of future violence, the absence of such a history is completely meaningless. After all, a history of violence is notably lacking before the first time anyone perpetrates a violent act.

Fran's attempt to strangle a prior object—as reported by one of the court-appointed psychiatrists in Tucson—not to mention her struggle with the guards in court that I myself witnessed, certainly strongly suggest that she could become violent again. But I soon discovered that several other factors also increased that risk, when I read a new study that examined how erotomanics with more than one object fit into the assessment of violent potential. Fran had stalked several women before me, I recalled, and this study found that having multiple objects as well as having antisocial behavior unrelated to the erotomania were both significantly correlated with dangerousness in erotomanics. In their sample, substance abuse also seemed to increase the risk.[7]

That antisocial behavior was correlated with dangerousness seemed self-explanatory, but I just did not remember enough about Fran's past to know if she had engaged in such activities. I did know she had several objects before me and used marijuana. I wondered if having more than one love object or using drugs raised the chance of violence because of the threat either one posed to the delusion itself.

Multiple objects may inherently weaken the delusional conviction of being loved by any particular one. Further, if the erotomanic projects her own delusional infidelity onto her object, assuming therefore that her object also has other lovers, she may become enraged, thus predisposing to violence.

In erotomanics who use drugs, the continued delusional rationalizations needed to explain the seemingly avoidant behavior of the object may be undermined by mind-altering substances, again predisposing to violence.

For erotomanics, then, drug and alcohol abuse becomes a double-edged sword, increasing the risk of violence and reinforcing the erotomanic delusions themselves. I had treated many patients who had severe substance abuse since adolescence. When they quit, ten, twenty, or even thirty years later, they found themselves in an emotional state most akin to the one before they started—that of an adolescent. Because of the drug abuse, they had completely missed the period of emotional growth that normally accompanies young adulthood, leaving them perplexed in their relationships with others.

Since erotomanics appear to be stunted already at an adolescent stage of relating, perhaps substance-abusing erotomanics are exceptionally vulnerable to forever remaining erotomanically and only erotomanically attached to others. The drug use may further compound the problem by contributing to their viewing relationships with such an immaturity that they are even more likely to act out violently on the inevitable disappointments these "relationships" bring. I wondered if Fran's marijuana use contributed not only to her adolescent belief in our perfect love, but also to her seeming inability to ever have any other type of relationship. This lonely, isolated state, in turn only compounded her erotomanic delusions.

For all the precautions Tim and I took to prevent Fran's discovery of our move to Colorado, she was still able to follow us there. Although I desperately wanted to learn how she managed such a feat, I soon understood that the move itself, not how she found us, was the greater cause for concern. Dr. Fein, who has extensively studied threat assessment and threat management under grants from the National Institute of Justice, confirmed my worst fears. He said:

> *The kinds of situations I worry about are people who are in a position where someone appears to be following them or appears to be maintaining an unusual interest in them and in what they do. . . . In my experience, in cases of stalking where somebody engages in travel related to a potential target, that's. . . more worrisome.*[8]

Travel exemplified by Fran's move to Colorado.

His warning was very much in line with opinions I was encountering elsewhere in my research on stalker violence. As a National Institute of Justice report asserted, although stalking may temporarily subside, as Fran's pursuit had since my attorney's call to her parents, it almost always progresses:

Over time a stalker's behavior typically becomes more and more threatening, serious, and violent. The stalking activity generally escalates from what initially may be bothersome and annoying but legal behavior, to the level of obsessive, dangerous, violent, and potentially fatal acts.[9]

Fran had already moved beyond the "bothersome and annoying" into the illegal and "obsessive." Just where was she as far as the "dangerous, violent, and potentially fatal" was concerned, I still needed to learn.

Dr. Fein, again, provided me with a framework with which to view and better understand Fran's and other stalkers' potential for violence. He said that the important factors in assessing the dangerousness of stalkers are "unusual or inappropriate interest coupled with behavior." His view of potential perpetrators, including erotomanics like Fran, is that they are:

. . . following a path which might result in actual violence toward a particular target. Obviously, there are many people who spend too much of their lives having unusual or inappropriate interest in all kinds of people. But when somebody like Robert Bardo. . . began to visit studios to try to personally meet Rebecca Schaeffer, and then when he determined that she was wrong in not responding to his letters and not meeting him, and so he was going to kill her, and then when he got a weapon, when he went back a third time, each time is a step by step process [along the path leading to violence].

Dr. Fein's research with Special Agent Vossekuil has focused on the behaviors that occur along that path rather than on the diagnoses of the potential perpetrators who walk along it. They are continuing to study which interventions might encourage these potential perpetrators to change paths, backtrack along the same path, or get off altogether.[10] I could not help wondering how far down the path to violence Fran had wandered, in addition to the six-and-a-half years and hundreds of miles she had already traveled.

Many experts I spoke with, both at the TMU conference and later, felt that the longer Fran stalked me, the higher the risk that she would become violent. It seemed to me that a long period of erotomanic stalking increased the chance of violence because of the increased risk to the delusion itself. If there were more opportunities for perceived threats to the "relationship," such as an object's new love interest, announced betrothal, or as in my case, wedding, the erotomanic might be presented with more delusional "reasons" to become angry at the love object. Robert Bardo, for example, became disillusioned with Rebecca Schaeffer after seeing her in bed with an actor in a movie. Just before his final, deadly journey to Los Angeles, he wrote to his sister: "I have an obsession with the unattainable and I have to eliminate [something] that I cannot attain."[11]

In one of the last letters I received from her before her arrest in Tucson, Fran had angrily demanded, "Are you and redbeard getting serious?" If she knew that Tim and I were now married, would she be more likely to come after me or him? I read that Dr. Park Dietz, a psychiatrist who runs a private threat assessment firm near Los Angeles has observed that the seriously mentally ill often fail to reach this "approach" stage. Instead of being able to put a coherent, viable plan together, they are easily distracted or get arrested for other behaviors along the way. It is the higher functioning mentally ill patients, like erotomanics, who possess the ability to effectively stalk their objects. Fran had clearly shown through her relentless, determined, and at times even cunning pursuit of me that she was higher functioning, indeed.

My concern only grew as I read about similar cases where erotomanics felt they were being victimized by their victims. Erotomanics narcissistically disregard the pain they have caused their objects, instead viewing themselves as the true victims by projecting their own rage onto others.

A twenty-three-year-old engineer became erotomanically convinced that his older sister-in-law had fallen in love with him and was performing fellatio in the middle of the night while he slept. He projected his own anger and aggressive feelings onto her, believing that her nocturnal visits were causing genital lesions that could lead to impotence. He indirectly warned the unsuspecting woman several times to stop, finally assaulting her in a rage, gouging out one of her eyes. Later, he maintained that she continued her sexual offenses against him, even in his jail cell.[12]

Similarly, Robert Bardo projected his anger at Rebecca Schaeffer's unresponsiveness onto Schaeffer herself, seeing himself as her potential victim. He wrote in one of his many letters to her, "I'm harmless. You could hurt me."[13] Arthur Jackson's prison psychiatrist noted that Jackson believed Theresa Saldana "bewitched him and cursed him."[14] In an interview before his trial for his attempt on her life, Jackson remarked, "[W]hat if it was the other way around? She was the victim and I was the assailant?"[15] As one erotomanic finally sentenced to prison incredulously exclaimed about the married object she had tormented incessantly for years in the belief that she was his mistress, "Marla Maples ended up being engaged, and I ended up in maximum security."[16]

I had learned, up to this point, that Fran exhibited several important potential predictors of erotomanic aggression: a past history of violence, directed travel, home visits, prolonged stalking time, a continuous obsession, substance abuse, multiple objects, and the ability to carry out a plan. Despite all this, I was heartened to learn that Dr. Dietz had estimated that the incidence of violence in erotomania was only 5 percent.[17] Dr. Michael Zona, the forensic psychiatrist who works with the TMU, explained to me that this low incidence is probably due to the fact that "the erotomanics like their person."[18]

However, it is this same affection that encourages the erotomanic to displace anger onto a third party, leading her to believe that a spouse or other family member forced her object to be so rejecting, preserving the fantasy of an ideal relationship. Fran had often signed her letters to me with, "I love you," and often referred to me as her "friend"; a friend who had done marvelous things for her, like paid for her hospital stay, tried to give her money and jewels, even attempted to get her into show business. Those who are erotomanically obsessed may be more likely to kill themselves, family members, or friends than they are to kill their objects. "More deaths are related to this phenomenon than the few publicized celebrity murders," Dr. Dietz noted.[19] So while I might be relatively safe, Tim was likely in greater danger.

It was not until months after our wedding that I read about the increased risk to family members, providing concrete confirmation of my fears before the ceremony. When I shared this information with Tim, he shrugged, as if to ask, "What does that have to do with me?" My retort, however, was neither silent nor subtle. "You need to be careful," I said, adding that even though I still had not heard from Fran since my attorney's call to her mother, the erotomanic impasse was in all likelihood far from over. I knew Fran would resurface, and I wanted both of us to be prepared.

"Sure, I'll be careful," he answered, matter-of-factly. I sensed that Tim was placating me.

"What are you going to do to be more careful?" I demanded. Realizing that I had called his bluff, his psychiatric training leapt to the fore, and he answered my question with a question of his own.

"What do you want me to do?"

I reviewed with him the precautions for victims that we had both taken in Tucson and that I continued to take, although I assumed he was not nearly as vigilant as he should have been. After all, Fran could just as easily follow Tim home as she could me, and I reminded him to scan the parking lot before going to his car, to glance frequently in his rearview mirror on his way home, and to be alert and aware in general of Fran's ever-possible presence. Despite all the research and discussions with experts that I shared with him, I could not seem to convince Tim that he was in any real danger. I was frustrated that he did not take the risk to himself seriously, even though I knew that he now fully appreciated the risk to me.

As medical director of our local psychiatric hospital, Tim dealt with violent patients all the time. When we had first moved to Colorado, I too did inpatient work at the same facility, but gave it up soon after, once my outpatient practice was established. I had always enjoyed inpatient work, but unlike seeing outpatients, inpatients are randomly assigned to the on-call psychiatrist who usually has little information about them before accepting the case. I just did not want to risk getting saddled with another Fran—or worse.

Part of Tim's job, in fact, was to train the staff to deal with difficult, even violent patients. Whenever a *code green*—a patient becoming out of control—was called at the hospital, he rushed there to help and ran the intervention on his own patients. Since the code green would, in a matter of seconds, bring a crush of well-trained staff members from all over the hospital to deal with the emergency, this adroit show of force almost always guaranteed that no one, including the patient, got hurt. I wondered if Tim's nonchalance about Fran's potential threat to his own safety reflected the fact that since he dealt with violence all the time, he had become almost desensitized to it.

As a psychiatrist, Tim also knew that women, in general, are less likely to act violently than are men. Finally, even if Fran did become violent toward him, I'm sure Tim believed that as a man, he could easily defend himself. I was not as certain. What if she used a weapon? What if she came at him from behind? What if she came at him in her car?

As I continued to run down the endless list of possibilities in my mind, I feared the staff might have to call a code green on me. I was able, however, to quiet my anxiety without intervention, but I remained frustrated and concerned for Tim's safety. Although he had agreed to take the precautions I had requested, I doubted he took them seriously.

The more I learned, the more it seemed to me that the chance Tim would become a target of Fran's jealous enmity was very real. From the erotomanic's point of view, there is probably little emotional conflict over attacking an object's spouse, lover, sibling, or parent, since such people are viewed simply as blocking access to the object or poisoning the object's mind against him. Madonna's stalker, Robert Hoskins, threatened Madonna's assistant and tried to kill her bodyguard "because," according to Deputy District Attorney Rhonda Saunders, who prosecuted the case, "he saw them as obstacles in his quest to reach Madonna."[20] Even people with no relationship at all to the victim seemed to be at risk. One erotomanic, convinced that his object was being kept prisoner at the television station where she worked, attempted an armed "rescue" with a rifle, discharging the weapon in a crowded street.[21] Another attacked the postman he was convinced was stealing his object's letters to him.[22]

In a perverse kind of Karmic equilibrium, erotomanic delusions can backfire, and the erotomanics themselves may become the objects of violence, as in the case of a mentally ill woman who was charged with a minor offense and sent to jail. When she developed erotomanic delusions toward a senior police officer and boasted of her "relationship" to the other prisoners, they took her at her word and attacked her for fraternizing with the enemy. She had to be placed in protective custody.[23]

Regardless of how the erotomanic views those surrounding his object, his pathological attachment to the object seems to follow a typical progression, according to Dr. Reid Meloy, the forensic psychologist I had met at the TMU conference and an expert on stalking and erotomania: First, the initial contact, much like a crush, resulting in the love object being placed on a pedestal; second, the approach behavior by the erotomanic, leading to the inevitable rejection.

At this point, most individuals would feel the rejection and hurt, perhaps topple the love object from her exalted status, mourn the loss of what could have been, and move on. In erotomania, however, there is a third stage, in which the delusion comes into play and the erotomanic projects his own feelings onto the object, convincing himself that *she* loves *me*. Dr. Meloy believes the erotomanic's shame at being rejected:

> ... *is defended against with very intense anger. The anger fuels the pursuit of the person to rectify the situation, and that pursuit can be motivated by a desire to injure, to control, to dominate or in some cases to kill the victim. If successful, the narcissistic fantasy is restored.*[24]

He feels that erotomanic violence is most likely to occur when the erotomanic begins to devalue the love object, the polar opposite to the previous idealization, leading to a wish for some event, or retribution, to correct the perceived rejection and abandonment. In a landmark legal case for mental health professionals, the parents of a young college student, the object of an erotomanic, discovered just how deadly such a desire for retribution could be when inaction by those who should have protected her led to tragedy.

Over twenty years ago, Prosenjit Poddar developed erotomania toward fellow University of California at Berkeley student, Tatiana Tarasoff, after becoming acquainted with her from folk dance lessons at the University's International House. When she kissed him at a New Year's Eve party, his delusional embellishment of their "relationship" took off logarithmically. Despite her consistent, active discouragement of his advances, he maintained the unshakable belief that she loved him, and by splicing together their audiotaped conversations, which he surreptitiously recorded, manufactured the false professions of her love that were his "proof." To finally force Tarasoff to acknowledge her love for him, Poddar devised a disaster from which he would rescue her, but the confusion of his plan coupled with Tarasoff's reaction of terror, not the love or gratitude he expected, resulted in his becoming her slayer, not savior.

Sadly, tragedy could have been avoided at several points along this particular path to violence. First, Poddar had been seeing a campus psychologist, who, fearful of his client's potential for agression, had unsuccessfully attempted to have him involuntarily committed. Second, although the psychologist notified campus police, who even detained the deluded graduate student, they released him from custody after deciding he posed no danger. He had not actually threatened Tarasoff. Finally, the psychologist did not, in compliance with therapist-patient confidentiality, warn Tarasoff herself. She was murdered after returning from a vacation she had taken precisely to get away from Poddar.

The court case resulting from her parents' lawsuit against the therapist, the campus police, and the university for contributing to the wrongful death of their daughter, was ultimately appealed to the California Supreme Court, giving rise to what clinicians and attorneys have referred to ever after as the Tarasoff Decision. The justices, holding that "The protective privilege ends where public peril begins," ruled that clinicians are obliged to use reasonable care to *protect* the intended victim of a patient's violence, care which at times may include warning the victim.[25]

Since then, the Tarasoff ruling, born out of an erotomanic's deluded rage, has become a national standard of care for therapists of every persuasion. In fact, it was this Tarasoff "duty to protect" that I frequently invoked when confronting Fran's therapists' reticence to talk to me. The same duty to protect that I believed Dr. Trottle had failed to perform when I had first informed him that Fran was under my care. His comment a few weeks later, when he said, "I was afraid this would happen," only underscored that belief.

In erotomania, of course, the "rejections" or abandonments themselves can be delusional, even as the rejection rage itself is all too real. One middle-aged woman assaulted a neighbor with a broken bottle as he entered their apartment building. The victim was rushed to the hospital in shock, with deep abdominal wounds and slashes of his face and limbs. He subsequently lost the use of his left arm. Although he barely recognized his assailant and had never spoken to her before the attack, she was completely convinced that he loved her and that they would be wed. She had been certain that he was not really married and, therefore, held onto her delusion, until she learned that his wife was pregnant and the couple would be moving to the opposite Coast.

Feeling betrayed, she started hating him, ruminating about his duplicity, and hearing voices telling her that he deserved to die. One night, fueled by alcohol and her sense of abandonment, she finally assaulted him with a whiskey bottle.[26]

As I read the paper the treating psychiatrist had written about this incident, it seemed even more hopeless to think that Fran's actions, including her violent ones, could ever be understood, let alone predicted: Once the integrity of the delusion is threatened, it may take only one insignificant event for the rejection to ignite into uncontrollable rage, exploding toward its violent denouement, threatening the object's life.

Ironically, as Dr. Meloy observed, it is the perpetration of that act of violence by the erotomanic on his object that restores his emotional equilibrium and with it, the object's idealization. This restoration may have severe consequences for the object, however:

> *The irony is that if the devaluation of the person in real life leads to that person actually being hurt, injured or somehow damaged, or in extreme cases killed, then that event in real life allows the perpetrator to restore his narcissistic fantasy of having this idealized relationship with the victim.*[27]

Thus, in an interview after his murder of Rebecca Schaeffer, Robert Bardo asked his examining psychiatrist if Schaeffer was still alive: He had seen a picture of a woman in a magazine who resembled her and wondered if she was secretly sequestered somewhere as a security precaution. The integrity of his delusion had been so wholly restored that he even asked to see Schaeffer's autopsy results as proof of her death.

In another case, Dr. Meloy examined an erotomanic man whose rejection rage led him to crash his car into that of his object, forcing it to a stop. He then threw sulfuric acid and a flammable liquid on her, immolating his victim. Later, at the scene, he asked the police if she had died. Here, too, was an erotomanic who had his delusion restored through a violent act in which he killed the object of his affection.

In Dr. Meloy's evaluation of the stalker for the defense, he commented on this erotomanic's dreams in prison, in which he and the victim he murdered were united and happy:

Paradoxically, his relationship with the victim has been renewed through her death. He now experiences her, once again, as an idealized object in his mind, when in sleep he can suspend the "reality-tested" knowledge of her death and can be with her in a pleasant, isolated place. He has intrapsychically come full circle: he initially idealized her, she rejected him, he devalued her and killed her, and now, once again, he can idealize her.[28]

This only reinforced what I had already experienced through Fran all along: Erotomania has nothing to do with the object and everything to do with the objectifier. The delusion about the object is more important than any reality—even the reality of death.

Yet I had more to worry about from Fran than actual physical assault with the intent to cause harm. Erotomanic violence toward objects or others can take many forms. Their violent acts may even seem bizarre to the casual observer but are possessed of their own logic when viewed in their delusional context: For example, the erotomanic who tried touching the genitals of young girls who reminded him of his love object.[29] Or the erotomanic who threw himself on top of his object as she was walking in front of her home, shielding her from imagined gunfire.[30] Violence can even be purely metaphorical, as in the woman stalker who sent the assistant director of a popular television show a GI Joe doll with red paint smeared all over it and little cocktail swords stuck in strategic places.[31]

Although rare, sexual assaults by erotomanics against their victims have also been reported. Given the inherently delusional view of the "relationship," the sexual attacks themselves are often fraught with fantasy. One man thought he was destined to sire a race of rulers with his "beloved," and thus he needed to have intercourse with her. He broke into the woman's home and entered her bedroom naked, informing her that he had come "to make babies." He was only prevented from raping her by neighbors drawn to his victim's screams.[32]

In cases such as this, the stalker-rapist delusionally reinterprets his love object's fear and refusals of intercourse as eager invitations. Erotomanic aggression can even be taken out on property. I knew Fran had damaged the car of one object who ignored her advances. Other erotomanics have not only vandalized their victims' cars, but broken into and damaged their homes, and otherwise maliciously destroyed property after evidence of rejection.

And aggression can take the form of lawsuits: I came across the case of a Singapore doctor who had treated a woman who developed erotomania toward him. When the patient filed a complaint that he had acted inappropriately by seducing her, his medical board charged him with "taking advantage of the mental and emotional state of a patient and committing adultery with her."[33] Although there was no independent corroborative evidence of any misconduct on the doctor's part and the only witness was the complainant herself, a woman who was under a psychiatrist's care—for erotomania—the doctor was found guilty. The conviction was eventually overturned on appeal.

For once, I considered myself fortunate. At least Fran had not gone to my medical board with all her claims about my involvement in her life, let alone our "relationship."

As I learned more about what might lead an erotomanic to violence, I kept trying to reassure myself that Fran had never threatened me until I discovered that all the experts agreed that threats don't count.

For law enforcement, private security, and others in the field of threat management, the most critical and challenging aspect of their work has become distinguishing between those who make a threat and those who pose a threat. As Dr. Fein and his colleagues have noted, "Postponing action until a threat has been made can detract attention from investigation of factors more relevant to the risk of violence."[34] Those who actually threaten violence generally appear *less* likely to act violently than those who do not. One study found that only 3 percent of those who threatened to kill someone actually did.[35]

According to Gavin de Becker, head of Gavin de Becker, Inc., Studio City, California, who is widely regarded as the country's leading security expert, threats are not the best indication of future violence: "In letters from someone who is potentially dangerous, you are more likely to find expressions of shared destiny than of hatred. Ironically, someone who

says 'I'm going to kill you on Tuesday' may be less likely to act than someone who says 'You and I must be united on Tuesday.'"[36] Fran, while occasionally expressing anger at my not responding to her, had never once
said she hated me. On the contrary, her poems and songs were filled with
references to our eventual happiness together: "The mysteries untold will
unfold to us as we open up our lives to each other;" and "We could take
the highs and lift the lows if we should want to grow to love each other"
were typical declarations. When I had originally read these sentiments, they seemed juvenile and harmless, certainly not threatening, but
now I wondered if something sinister lurked beneath their impassioned
facade.

As Dr. Park Dietz, a psychiatrist who has researched the relationship
between incidents of stalking and threatening letters[37] concluded:

> *We have disproved the myth that only threats count. Nearly every-*
> *one makes the mistake of assuming that unless there is a threat,*
> *you can safely ignore "nut mail," "kook calls," and weird visitors.*
> *This false assumption is the source of more misguided policy and*
> *decision-making than any other error in this field.*[38]

I wish I had been aware of this nonrelationship between threats and
violence all the times the police had asked if Fran threatened me before
deciding that she was not dangerous enough to arrest. I could have told
them they were mistaken and cited the research to prove it.

Still, some useful information can be obtained from erotomanic
threats. When assessing the potential for an erotomanic to become
violent, Dr. Meloy looks at the patient's mobility, the chronicity of the
obsession, previous reactions to restraining orders, and the nature of
the delusion.[39] He feels that the "sensible approach would suggest the
subject's history of threat and his or her relationship to subsequent violence is the best source of data for assessing future risk subsequent to a
threat." As "threats may inhibit, disinhibit, or have no relationship to
actual violence in any one subject," he encourages a "*periodic* violence
risk assessment of the patient."[40]

As far as I knew, Fran had not threatened the attorney before she
put her hands around her neck. She certainly had not threatened the
guards. That meant that the absence of threats toward me now was

completely irrelevant. Ironically, I found myself wishing Fran *had* threatened me. At least the police and courts might have taken her more seriously.

I had sought the restraining orders to avoid the many possible ways that Fran might further invade or even threaten my life—and Tim's. But now I wished that I had known that restraining orders were almost always routinely ignored by persons obsessed with pursuing another. One study that followed stalkers over seven years found that almost half violated restraining orders. The percentage was even higher for erotomanic stalkers. In many cases, restraining orders only increased the resolve fueling a stalker's pursuit and were even less likely to be heeded if the pursuer perceived passion rather than persecution from the victim.[41]

This certainly seemed to have been the case with Fran. She must have thought I was passionate about her indeed if she believed I tried to send her one hundred thousand dollars, jewels, and cars. She began coming to my home only after I had gotten the restraining order, and only then did she move to my neighborhood. It is as if, when faced with even more firm, objective evidence of rejection, she needed to bolster her delusions by coveting closer contact.

Victims of erotomanic and other stalkers need to be educated that such people will seldom behave rationally. While a victim may assume that her stalker will respond to a restraining order the way she herself would, such an assumption is, at best, terribly foolish; at worst, deadly.

A retired New York City Police Department homicide detective has said that court orders were only effective deterrents in a few instances involving "normal and rational respondents who remain away from the petitioners in order to avoid any further legal problems." In other words, people unlike erotomanic and most other stalkers who have something to lose. The same detective noted that he had "personally investigated hundreds of cases where women who had obtained orders of protection were beaten, knifed, sexually assaulted, and killed." He cited the case of one man who stabbed his estranged wife to death, knifing the court order to her chest.

He maintained that police detectives, in fact, have been known to refer to orders of protection as "orders of illusion" as they give victims only the appearance of security.[42] Even a National Institute of Justice study stated that restraining orders in and of themselves don't do anything, that it is up to the police and courts to enforce the orders: "Enforcement is the Achilles' heel of the civil protection order,"[43] the report said. Restraining orders can even worsen the potential for erotomanic and other stalkers to become violent. According to Dr. Fein: "In certain cases. . .the stalker says, 'Geez, they got a restraining order. I've got one chance or I'm gonna get locked up. I'd better get her now.'"[44]

One of the worst mass murders in California history, in fact, took place in 1988 after the object of a former co-worker's erotomanic obsession obtained a temporary restraining order against him after four years of stalking. Sixteen days later, seven of her colleagues lay dead and she and three others were critically wounded after his murderous rampage at her workplace. The day after the shooting, "a San Jose court commissioner cried as she finalized the restraining order. . . . 'Pieces of paper do not stop bullets,' she said."[45]

I had not heard from Fran for several months since my attorney's call to her mother, but when I did toward the end of 1995, her message was simple and to the point. She said only, "This is Fran Nightingale" but she did not leave a telephone number. I, too, responded simply. I called the police. Since I had not made such a call in quite some time, I was a little taken aback at what should have been familiar questions: "Did she threaten you? Have you had a relationship with her?" I explained my story, yet again, feeling all the old, familiar frustration that nothing was about to be done. This time, however, I tried to enlighten the officer.

"As a psychiatrist and because of my experience with the perpetrator, I have extensively studied stalking. The fact that she has never threatened me has absolutely no bearing on whether or not she will become violent, and actually, she exhibits almost all of the risk factors for someone with erotomanic delusions to act violently," I told him.

The officer surprised me by assuring me he would arrest Fran for the restraining order violation. Had my newfound knowledge, born of activism really paid off so soon? Or had my attorney been right when he had informed Fran's mother that stalking cases were treated differently in Colorado? It turned out that neither hypothesis proved to be correct.

When the officer called me the next day, he said he had not been able to find Fran, even with the telephone number and address I provided. I told him that I did not even know if Fran had called from Colorado or Arizona. With that, it was clear that he intended to spend little additional time tracking down Fran, despite my pleas that he continue.

So much for the power of knowledge or the wrath of Colorado law against stalkers. I was left alone again in my attempts to arrest Fran's behavior, alone except for several disturbing questions: Had Fran moved again? Had she not even been in the state when she made the call? Was she toying with me, showing me how powerful she was, purposely heightening my fear before coming in for the kill?

The TMU conference had been replete with stories of dangerous stalkers, erotomanic and otherwise, who had never threatened their victims, yet went on to commit vicious, even murderous acts against them and their families. I knew feeling that Fran was deliberately tormenting me before executing some final, violent assault was ridiculous. Or was it? I had been completely honest with the officer about Fran's exhibiting almost every risk factor for erotomanic violence. The only risk factors she lacked were previous unrelated antisocial behavior (and I wasn't even sure about that), and she was not a man.

Fran had never proven so elusive before. She had always let me know that she was right there for the taking. I only wished the police had been the ones to take her. Instead, all law enforcement and court interventions seemed to do was escalate her behavior: After the first restraining order, Fran shifted her visits from my office to my home. The morning after she was finally arrested, more than a year later and after nearly two dozen restraining order violations, she called my house—collect—from jail. When Tim and I moved to Colorado, while she was undergoing court-ordered treatment in Michagan, she followed us. Had I been taking the wrong approach all along? Unfortunately my research seemed to confirm that painful conclusion.

Dr. Meloy refers to "dramatic moments," those instances in which a stalker's intense rage and humiliation are triggered by some event. During these dramatic moments the stalker's victim is at the greatest risk of violence. I learned that Fran and I had engaged in many such dramatic moments over the years, including confrontations by the police, service with court documents, arrests, orders to seek treatment, and warnings of civil commitment or jail if her behavior did not stop. According to Dr. Meloy, "Risk escalates right after those particular humiliations." In the Madonna stalking case, for example,

Dr. Meloy, the consultant to the prosecution, told me that when her stalker:

> . . . *was rejected by her, immediately after that rebuff, he threatened to kill her and kill the people surrounding her. . . . At one point, following being told that she did not want to have contact with him, did not want to see him, and wasn't available, that was when he said that he wanted to slit her throat from ear to ear.*[46]

I felt as if I was in a catch-22 situation: Dramatic moments that enraged and humiliated Fran increased her potential to be violent, yet there did not seem to be any way to protect myself without engaging in the very behavior that caused those dramatic moments. As I continued my education in approaches to dealing with stalkers, however, I realized there could have been steps to take to better protect myself, and that those steps did not necessarily involve what the police might recommend.

The TMU conference had been geared toward law enforcement personnel and the legal community. Their philosophy demanded action, but I discovered that those in the private security field seemed to advise a different tack. Perhaps that was because the two schools of thought had different goals: for law enforcement, the capture and punishment of stalkers; for private security firms, client safety. Although these goals might appear to be the same, capturing and punishing stalkers does not necessarily equate with the permanent safety of their victims. Gavin de Becker has a reminder of this to clients on his desk, a sign that reads, "Do not come here for justice."

De Becker believes that whether or not to intervene with stalkers is one of the most complicated and challenging questions that case managers and victims face.

His study of pools of possible attackers led him to observe that there was an "overwhelming majority who would not act violently regardless of intervention, some who would decide not to act because of intervention, some who would decide to act because of intervention, and some who would act out violently in either situation." His work has focused on devising crucial methods of determining which potential attackers fall into each group. While most experts agree that there are no common characteristics for all "stalkers," de Becker has identified four motivational categories of stalkers:

1. *Attachment-seekers.* Stalkers in this group want a relationship with their victims but recognize that none exists. John Hinckley, Jr.'s fixation on Jodie Foster leading to his assassination attempt on President Ronald Reagan to win her love is an example.

2. *Identity-seekers.* Stalkers who pursue their targets as a means to achieve some other end. Mark David Chapman's murder of John Lennon in order to become famous himself is an example of this group.

3. *Rejection-based.* Stalkers who pursue victims who spurned them, either to reverse or avenge the rejection. For example: Robert Bardo's murder of Rebecca Schaeffer after he saw her in a movie in bed with another actor and was refused access to her studio lot.

4. *Delusion-based.* Stalkers who have major mental illnesses, including erotomania, in which delusions about their victims drive their pursuit. For example: Arthur Jackson, whose near-lethal stabbing of Theresa Saldana was motivated by the delusional belief that Saldana's death was the only way for him to be united with her. Fran is also in this category because her pursuit is motivated by the delusional belief that I love her.

In general, de Becker believes that the type of stalkers most likely to attack are the rejection-based and identity-seekers, although the other two groups can also attack if they are moved into the rejection-based group, as Robert Bardo was. He notes that few stalkers start out as rejection-based and adds, "We are wise not to move them there," because this is the group most likely to kill.

De Becker feels *identity-seekers* are the best candidates for interventions because the attention provided in the intervention itself will somewhat assuage their need for recognition. Identity-seekers are also the most likely to transfer their attention to other targets because their victims are used as a means to end, such as fame, rather than as an end in and of itself, such as a relationship with a particular person.

Rejection-based pursuers are least likely to transfer targets because their emotional investment in the pursuit is focused on harming the specific victim who rejected them. De Becker notes that when a victim or someone acting on the victim's behalf continually restates the rejection in the hope that the pursuer will finally "get it," that person is simply aggravating the emotional investment by the pursuer. When the intensity of the rejection is increased by getting a restraining order or by having the police warn the potential attacker, that is simply "taking a rejection that was intolerable when private, and can only be worse when public."

According to de Becker, *delusion-based* pursuers such as Fran are less threatened by interventions because the nature of delusions dictates that not much will sway them from their beliefs. Still, as in all other categories, care must be taken not to move them into the rejection-based group.

De Becker observed that before coming to professional attention, pursuers in every category have already been subjected to many interventions by their own friends and family, understandably alarmed at their obsessions. Further attempts at persuasion by professionals is likely doomed to failure. De Becker noted, "Straight talk does not work with crooked people."

Deciding which types of pursuers are most amenable to interventions is not enough for de Becker. As one charged with the protection of others, he feels he must also know when to intervene and equally important, when not to. De Becker believes that most cases that drag on for years result from an emotional "war" between victim and pursuer and that if this can be avoided, the pursuer will likely become bored and lose interest, turning his or her attention to someone else. Interventions, he feels, generally worsen more cases than they improve.

For pursuers of any group romantically interested in a public figure, the situation is almost never improved by intervention because the pursuer views the intervention *itself* as progress, having gained the attention and emotional involvement of the celebrity. The importance of the pursuit is, therefore, validated. Dr. Becker notes that "Expert evaluators at the U.S. Supreme Court Police have monitored some pursuers with romantic fixations for several years. They have elected not to apply direct or intrusive intervention, because the risks of worsening the situation outweigh the benefits, and because monitoring is practical." He feels that police interventions:

> are best applied when a pursuer has committed a crime. When police get involved, it should be swift and effective; it should be to arrest and charge the pursuer, not to chat. When police come and warn someone, and then they leave without arrest, they hope to deter, but they may get the opposite result. As the officers leave, the pursuer just faced the single greatest weapon in his victim's arsenal: the police. And what happened? They talked to him and he survived without a scratch, and he is back to normal. Who got stronger, the victim or the pursuer?

Since my first restraining order against Fran, that is exactly what had happened: With every police visit that did not result in an arrest, she became stronger and more emboldened while I become weaker and more afraid. The police, after all, had only put her in jail once during the entire time she had stalked me. The nearly two dozen other times they had gone to see her because of her restraining order violations, had resulted in paper citations. With odds like that against incarceration, it was no wonder she persisted, even intensifying her pursuit. In fact, for private citizens and public figures alike, de Becker found that cases that escalated to the point of violent attacks overwhelmingly shared one factor: intervention.

It is common, he believes, for restraining orders to precede violence in stalking cases, noting that the restraining order itself is often cited by the attacker as the trigger. He calls this dynamic, "engage and enrage," noting that it was usually possible to try a safer plan of management instead, such as "detach and watch." In this latter approach, he said, "The victim makes one explicit, unconditional rejection, and then stops all contact."

Before even considering an intervention, de Becker and his staff use MOSAIC, a computerized screening program he designed for threat assessment to determine whether a particular case contains what he terms "pre-incident indicators," including various references to obsessive love, a shared destiny, weapons, death, suicide, religious themes or, traveling a great distance to see the object. When de Becker's office does recommend a restraining order, it is usually only after all safer interventions have been tried, especially "detach and watch," and after making certain that the victim completely understands all the issues involved, particularly that he or she is adequately prepared for an escalation of the pursuit. Recognizing that the period immediately following the issuance of a restraining order is highly charged for the pursuer, de Becker and his staff do everything possible to make the victim unavailable during that time.

Without knowing it, without ever having heard of de Becker, I had managed to stumble on his "detach and watch" policy, employing it for almost the first two years of Fran's pursuit. It was only when she seemed to become more menacing, that I obtained my first restraining order. That, I had come to believe, was perhaps my first mistake because we did seem to become engaged in a "war" of sorts after that; certainly, at least, a contest in which my determination to be rid of her, buttressed by all the force of law the courts could muster, proved no match for her delusions.

Fran clearly believed I had come to the courts to do battle; when she was granted unsupervised probation in her first sentencing in Tucson for multiple restraining order violations, she immediately came to my house and left a note with a large feather attached, claiming, "Here's a feather for your cap." Her note would seem to indicate she thought I had "won" when, in fact, this was probably a projection, because she was the one who had become stronger.

While de Becker will not reveal exactly what his pre-incident indicators are for fear of tipping off stalkers, Fran had certainly traveled a great distance to be near me and had often referred to her love for me as well as to her spiritual beliefs. The *I Ching,* for example, told her "not to hold back" where I was concerned. I had not held back as far as the legal system was concerned. Unfortunately, the system itself was impotent to stop her.

De Becker's personnel also focus on what victims can do to reduce the effect of pursuit on their lives. He notes that the most harassed people in society are public officials such as governors, congressmen, and mayors, yet he is unaware of a single instance in which any one of them has gotten a restraining order. Since most of these public officials do not have security details, it cannot be that they feel safer than anyone else similarly harassed. "Since interventions are often victim-driven, could it be that these people have an expectation of some harassment, so their threshold is higher?" he asks. While restraining orders appeal to our sense of justice as well as to victims who feel they must *do* something, de Becker believes "The desire to change the pursuer is almost irresistible, but changing the victim's conduct is often more practical."

As a society, however, de Becker understands that interventions make sense, because most pursuers never really stop, but move on to other victims. I wondered if this further illuminated the difference in philosophy between law enforcement and private security: The police have more responsibility to society than to a particular victim; security firms are only concerned with the welfare of their clients. Thus, the two different approaches. Frequently the best threat management for an *individual* is not to intervene directly with the pursuer, but rather to use the "detach and watch" philosophy, to encourage the pursuer to look elsewhere. For the police, having a perpetrator look elsewhere may not be an acceptable outcome.

De Becker feels that the "detach and watch" approach proves particularly challenging for victims who are public figures, because most successful people got where they are by *doing* something, by taking action, *not* by detaching and watching. For example, if a victim is bothered by a series of disturbing letters from a pursuer, a common problem with stalkers, de Becker might argue that those very disquieting letters are actually performing a critical service by allowing the pursuer an outlet for his passions. What might happen if the letters are made to stop before the pursuer is ready to stop them? While others might argue that forcing the pursuer to stop writing the letters will focus his mind elsewhere, de Becker points out the fallacy in assuming that if one stops the letters, the thoughts will stop as well.

An intervention to stop the letters could instead be interpreted by the pursuer as a sign that his messages are getting through and that he is being taken seriously; in reality exactly what has happened. Stopping the letters could also be taken by any category of pursuer as a rebuff, moving him to the dreaded rejection-based group. So what does one do to stop the letters? Perhaps nothing at all. Letters by themselves are not harmful, it is the impact the letters have on the victim that is damaging, but that impact rather than the letters themselves is much easier to control.

"Often, victims of threats or unwanted pursuit believe it will be simpler to modify the pursuer's behavior, rather than their own, but that is rarely the case," de Becker says. He recommends that victims consider hiring a third party to screen their mail, so they do not continuously anticipate disturbing letters, let alone read them. If the third party is trained in what to look for, the letters may provide important information about the pursuer that security firms and the police might rather not cut off, such as his mobility and whereabouts, via postmarks and continuing indications of his condition, feelings, and plans.[47]

When I had been bombarded with Fran's series of more threatening letters, in which she wrote it was "Okedokey [sic] to steal me," and "If you don't come back to me soon. . . I'll have to come get you," rather than getting a restraining order that would be neither needed nor enforced, perhaps I should have continued to monitor the letters. De Becker was probably right: The letters were a needed outlet for Fran's passions. By involving the police, I both threatened that outlet and validated that she was having an effect on me, leading her to intensify her pursuit by frequenting my home. In fairness to myself, if I could have imagined at the time that the police had no intention of arresting her, I probably would not have bothered getting the restraining order, anyway.

At times, security firms may find themselves in the seemingly awkward position of playing therapist to a would-be lover of one of their protectees if doing so means becoming privy to otherwise difficult-to-get information. One security specialist told me of a situation in which a male construction worker developed erotomania toward a wealthy socialite who was about to be married. She was very concerned about a promised disruption to her wedding:

> Up until the time the security company became involved, the subject knew the rules better than the referee [the law] did. The security company changed this as they had their own private set of rules. This was clearly explained to him as were the penalties for trying to cheat. It was also emphasized that the urge to transgress was expected, but that the security company was there to talk to. The security company clearly helped the subject to cope.

In one instance, they even managed to intercept the erotomanic enroute to a prenuptial celebration, based entirely on his confiding to someone from the firm what he "had" to do.[48]

Security specialists are also more likely to circumvent legal restrictions that the police are sworn to uphold. Another expert told me about a ballerina who for some years had been the focus of a mentally ill fan with erotomanic delusions. To elude him, she always managed to perform away from the city in which they both lived and even to plant a story in her community that she had died. This seemed to have been working until the telephone company accidentally published her home phone number and address in its new directory. The ballerina discovered the mistake after receiving a call from the stalker on her home phone, claiming that she had purposely published her number to taunt him.

She initially involved the police, but they told her there was little they could do. He was not threatening her and could circumvent the law on harassment by hiding behind his mental illness. The police could legally do nothing, "hamstrung by the fact that [he] was a certified schizophrenic and when he was under pressure would retire to the local institution."

The security firm, however, was not hamstrung by the law. They enlisted the help of the dancer's neighbors to report sightings of the stalker. Most important, however, they were able to establish an off-the-record contact with the local psychiatric institution where he "hid between events," and that advised them of when the stalker was back on the streets. This was, of course, a violation of his privacy and confidentiality, something the police could never do, but in this way, the security firm was able to alert the dancer and her company to times of potential danger. The dancer finally sold her home and is now dancing exclusively in Europe. The stalker continues to haunt her former American ballet company.[49]

Most stalking victims, unlike socialites and prima ballerinas, cannot afford to hire a private security firm. Even if they could, the experts provide varied and often conflicting advice. One expert advised me that the "best form of defense is attack," and that "those who have not got the cash to hire a security company" should "attack the stalker verbally, emotionally, chase his friends, family, workmates, in other words, stalk him."[50]

Another security specialist agreed:

. . . tactically, our rationale is referred to as "Push Back." An early step is letting the stalker, we call them 'villains,' because that's what they are, know we are involved. This can be a phone call, the worst option [for the security company, that is, as it is less threatening to the stalker] or a surprise interview when the villain is eating out. A visit to the place of work is very effective as well. There are never any threats, in fact the nicer we are the better the effect, we refer to this as "risk assessment."[51]

This declaration of war is a far cry from Gavin de Becker's policy of "detach and watch." It seemed to me that once one made contact with a stalker, let alone began to stalk him, one was well beyond assessing risk. Any direct contact by the victim was bound to be construed by the stalker as a successful outcome, only encouraging further stalking.

It had never occurred to me that I had actually perpetuated contact from Fran, but I realized now that the restraining orders themselves only reinforced her delusions; the more I pushed away, the harder she pulled herself toward me. After all I had learned, if I had it to do over again, I reluctantly concluded that I would not have gotten the restraining order in the first place. It had been a dismal failure. Rather than stopping her, with the help of police and courts, the restraining order had emboldened her.

In fact, as there was little face-to-face contact with Fran over the years, the most frustrating situations became those instigated by the restraining order itself, situations in which I was forced to rely on the legal system. And the legal system seemed to have no idea how to deal with her.

Chapter Nine

THE EVOLUTION OF
ANTISTALKING
LEGISLATION

B Y EARLY 1996, SEVERAL MONTHS after my attorney had spoken to her mother, Fran began to step up the frequency of her calls. She never left a telephone number, just her name. I still did not know where she was, and so began to feel more and more threatened. I contacted my local police department again, hoping that a series of calls so close together—three in as many weeks—would prove to them that she should be taken seriously and charged as a stalker.

I had saved all of these messages on my voice mail and played them back for the officer—yet another one I had never met who came to see me at the hospital. I explained my situation one more time. There was no question it was Fran on the tapes; she had, after all, left her name. But it was not my stalker's identity that concerned the officer. Instead, he asked, as so many others had before him, if Fran had ever threatened me.

Once again I patiently explained the research showing that the presence of threats was irrelevant to the potential violence of stalkers like Fran. When I last contacted the police, they hadn't wanted to spend any time looking for her on a misdemeanor restraining order violation, especially since they didn't know where to find her. Her one telephone call did not a stalker make. But now she had made repeated contacts. I tried to impress upon the officer that the danger Fran posed could be heightening, and concluded by asking him to arrest her for stalking. He told me the Colorado law did not consider Fran a stalker.

"You're kidding," I blurted out.

"Are you sure she hasn't threatened you?" He asked again. Hadn't he been listening? What difference did it make if she threatened me?

"Her whole behavior is threatening," I exclaimed in exasperation.

"She's got to make a direct verbal or written threat to you. She has to say she's going to kill you or harm you or your family in some way to be considered a stalker. That's the law." I had never heard that before. I remembered that some experts from the TMU conference told me that it had taken some time before local police, prosecutors, and judges had learned how to apply the new antistalking laws in California. Surely, this officer was misinformed.

I went to the public library immediately after work to look up Colorado's antistalking law myself. I could not believe what I saw. The officer was correct. Fran was, apparently, a stalker by anyone's definition except the law's. According to CO 18-9-111, which I reread three times to be sure there was no mistake, Fran was not a stalker. In Colorado, a stalker was a person who "directly. . . makes a credible threat to another person and, in connection with such threat, repeatedly follows that person. . . or repeatedly makes any form of communication with that person. . . whether or not a conversation ensues."

Although Fran had never directly threatened me in her telephone calls, I considered the messages themselves extremely threatening: Through them, she let me know just how far she was willing to go, over a thousand miles, to be near me. But the law disagreed; none of her messages contained the direct, "credible threat" its language required.

I returned home that night thoroughly frustrated. Tim was already there and heard me slam the front door on my way in. While Shula, our cat, scurried away in fear, Tim and our dog, Miles, came to greet me, their furry faces reflecting the same concern, as if to ask, "Had a bad day?" I had to laugh at their identical expressions.

"What's wrong?" Tim asked as he and Miles comforted me, each in his own way, Tim with a hug and Miles by thrusting his muzzle against my leg in the canine code for "Pet me!" My head remained buried in Tim's shoulder as I answered with my own question: "What good is an antistalking law if someone like Fran can't be charged under it?"

Tim silently led me to the couch with Miles following close behind. Shula kept a wary eye on us from the top of a cabinet. Tim took my shoes off and began rubbing my feet one by one. Miles did his part by attempting to give my free foot his version of a hot soak—a big wet poodle tongue. Shula did nothing but fend for herself.

It felt so good to be home where life was predictable and calm, where everyone (well, maybe not Shula) acted rationally. How different from the outside world, where stalkers roamed free, where nothing, not the powers of the police, not even the force of law, was as it should be. I sank down into the couch while the men in my life worked their magic.

I closed my eyes, but I could not relax. My mind was racing. There had to be a way for the law to control Fran. I had not come this far in the evolution of my thoughts and feelings, the development of my knowledge and expertise, to be thwarted by a few ill-advised words in some statute. There had to be a way to change the law. Change the law. I recalled the Member of Parliament's condescending words to Evonne von Heussen-Countryman after she told him about the horrific ordeal that she and her daughter had endured: "Laws cannot be changed just because we want them to be changed," he had said.

Then I remembered the California legislator I had also met at the TMU conference who had written the first antistalking law in the nation. He had discussed why his state had been moved to pass the law in the first place. Would it take a series of catastrophes, such as those that had galvanized California legislators, to spur the state of Colorado out of its stalking stupor?

Just two years before the California law was passed in 1990, the state had been shaken by one of the largest mass murders in its history, when in February 1988, Richard Farley blasted his way into the Sunnyvale electronics firm that had fired him. This deadly erotomanic attack, on a very public scale, demonstrated how ineffective restraining orders could be.

Farley was looking for Laura Black, the twenty-six-year-old engineer he had pursued for four years beginning shortly after she was hired by the same firm. Although the petite, athletic Black had consistently rebuffed his advances, Farley, a forty-year-old computer technician, had been secretly photographing her at her aerobics class, showing his friends pictures of his pretty young "girlfriend." He sent Black over two hundred letters, breached confidential personnel files at work to obtain her home address and phone number, and broke into her desk to copy her home and office keys, all the while following her everywhere.

In one letter to her, Farley explained his philosophy, writing, "it's my option to make your life miserable." Black moved three times to escape him. Three times he found her. For Farley, it had become a game. "He won if Black went out with him; she won if she got rid of him," one observer noted. After being warned about his behavior, he was finally fired from the company in 1986, but that did not put an end to his pursuit.

On the contrary, his letters became even more menacing as he projected his own personal rage onto Black and his former employer, perceiving them as threats to his own safety. Farley wrote Black months before his murderous rampage: "I feel capable of killing to protect myself and to hell with the consequences." When his latest threatening letter contained a key to Black's apartment, she obtained a temporary restraining order. In doing so, she confided to a friend her relief that her ordeal might be over at last.

Just sixteen days later, on the day before the hearing to make the restraining order permanent, Farley, armed with close to a hundred pounds of guns and ammunition, drove to his former place of employment to demonstrate to Black "the end result of what I felt she had done to me." Within a matter of minutes, seven of her co-workers lay dead and four others, including Black, were critically wounded.

Farley surrendered to police after a five-and-a-half hour standoff. He was sentenced to death.[1] Game over. A 1993 television movie, *I Can Make You Love Me: The Stalking of Laura Black*, dramatized the events leading up to the tragic shoot-out; within hours of its being aired, the National Victim Center was deluged by three thousand calls from targets of obsessed stalkers.[2]

In 1989, the year after Farley's erotomanic bloodbath, the slaying of Rebecca Schaeffer in Los Angeles again thrust stalking into the limelight, this time on a national level. Lawmakers and law enforcers from around the state were finally compelled to examine ways to protect citizens from stalkers. On the enforcement end, the Threat Management Unit was soon created. On the legislative end, then State Senator Ed Royce sponsored the new antistalking law in the California legislature after his Orange County district experienced a series of deadly attacks in a six-week period, only six months after Schaeffer had been gunned down.

Four women, all of whom had obtained temporary restraining orders, were murdered by the ex-lovers stalking them. One of the victims, a nineteen-year-old, implored police, "What does he have to do, shoot me?" only days before her ex-boyfriend did just that, then set himself on fire.[3] When police found the body of another victim, a former Olympic skier, they also discovered a restraining order against her assailant, her estranged husband, in her purse.

After reading about the slayings, Royce "talked to one law enforcement officer who said that the hardest thing he had ever had to do in his life was tell one of these four victims that there was nothing he could do until she was attacked physically. . . . These were victims who told their family members or told their friends that they thought they were going to die."[4]

Representatives of the Conference on Personal Managers, Inc. testified at the California hearings on the new legislation, maintaining that the government's lack of response to the threat of stalking against their clients had created a "free for all" environment that encouraged "deranged people to stalk their human prey."[5] But it was the testimony of one stalking victim in particular, Kathleen Gallagher Baty, that Royce believed finally spurred the legislature to pass the nation's first antistalking law. He recalled that:

> *Half-way through her testimony, the chairman of the committee motioned for me to come up and he said, "Originally there weren't the votes, we were not going to pass this bill out, but based upon what she's telling the members of this committee, this bill is going to go."*

Her testimony "turned the tide in terms of convincing those that otherwise did not want to create a new crime of stalking."[6]

Baty herself believed she was asked by Royce to testify because, "I was the only stalking victim he knew who was alive."[7] Wife of now-retired Miami Dolphins' tight end Greg Baty, she was first noticed by Larry Stagner in high school where they were both on the track team. Although they had never spoken, Stagner apparently remembered Baty well and several years later, called the pretty blond cheerleader when she came home in 1982 for Thanksgiving break during her junior year at

UCLA. The telephone calls were anything but cordial; Stagner threatened to abduct Baty and kill her boyfriend. When the police found the unemployed auto mechanic, he was circling her parents' house in his truck with 180 rounds of ammunition and a semi-automatic rifle. He was detained for 48 hours pending a psychiatric evaluation and then released. Within a few months, he was again caught circling the house, this time with not only the rifle, but with more ammunition, a knife, handcuffs, and a police radio scanner.

After each arrest, even in spite of restraining order violations, Stagner was given a brief jail sentence on misdemeanor charges plus probation with the requirement that he attend outpatient mental health treatment. Each time his probation ended, he continued stalking Baty, methodically calling, writing, and following her for nearly eight years. One afternoon in 1990, a few months after Stagner's fourth release from custody and two weeks after her honeymoon, Baty returned home from work:

> I turned around and he was standing behind me with a knife. It was very natural for me to say, "Sit down. I knew you'd come. Sit down, I've been expecting you. We need to talk." So, we stood there and bantered back and forth and the phone rang. He let me answer it, and it was my mother. She would ask me a question and I would answer something completely different, hoping that she would catch on. She did because she knew that he was out and she was calling to check on me. So, she called the police.

Because Baty had already informed local law enforcement of Stagner's stalking her, they reacted swiftly:

> They saved my life. He took me out in the garage and he tied my hands up and it was at that point that he pulled out a gun and said, "Don't run and don't scream." We went out the side garage door and that was probably the most scared that I ever was because I knew the police were out there and I truly thought that I would be shot in the crossfire. I thought that this was it. We went out the side gate and he had my car keys and I looked and I saw no one and I thought, "Great. They're not here yet." He put the keys in the car

door and I kind of stepped back. Suddenly, from everywhere, the
police, with their guns, "Freeze!"[8]

At that moment, Baty jumped over her yard's fence—into the comforting arms of her distraught father. Stagner's ensuing standoff with the local SWAT team lasted ten hours. Because he had taken his victim only 242 feet, the charges were lowered from kidnapping to attempted kidnapping. He was sentenced to eight years and ten months in the state prison.

Despite well-publicized executions by stalkers, first the massacre of Laura Black's co-workers by Richard Farley, and then the killing of Rebecca Schaeffer by Robert Bardo, incredibly it was only after the four other women in Los Angeles County were murdered by their stalkers, and then, only thanks to Baty's testimony, that the California bill was signed into law in the Fall of 1990. When it became effective the following January, stalking was for the first time anywhere a criminal act.

As I lay on the couch, I recalled in one unbearable instant, all the horrible events that had conspired to create the first antistalking law in America. When I opened my eyes, Miles had turned his considerable lingual talents on himself and Tim was looking at me expectantly.

"I thought you'd fallen asleep," he said.

"No," I quietly replied, surprising myself at the calm I felt. "I was just thinking. I have a lot of work to do."

The next morning, I went to the local library to obtain a list of attorneys general in other states. When I got to my office later that day, I began telephoning them, sandwiching the calls in between my normal routine of seeing patients.

"I'm a stalking victim in Colorado," I began each call. "I'm trying to research if your state requires a direct threat in order to prosecute a stalker." I was usually referred to the State Capitol's law library, whose clerk frequently offered to fax me a copy of the state's antistalking statute. Over the next several days, the faxes poured in and I pored over them, without really knowing what I was looking for. Buried somewhere in the legal jargon had to be a clue. But a clue to what?

I found that many of the statutes had language similar to Colorado's and required a direct threat. Many more did not. If stalkers like Fran who never threatened their victims could be charged with stalking in other states, perhaps there was hope in my own.

One clerk I spoke to happened to know of studies and seminars on stalking sponsored by the National Institute of Justice in Washington. I called the Institute's research arm, the Bureau of Justice Assistance, and ordered every material on their list pertaining to stalking. The booklets and monographs I received the next week outlined the evolution of antistalking legislation throughout the country.

It was in this mountain of paper that I began to understand that states vary widely in their antistalking laws: Some charged stalkers with misdemeanors, some with felonies. Some, like Colorado, required a direct threat, most did not. Several more originally had such a requirement, but later amended their law.

This meant that following California's lead, states no longer had to prosecute stalkers under a hodgepodge of dissimilar statutes directed at each separate illegal stalking behavior, whether menacing, loitering, trespassing, or terrorist threatening.

No longer could stalkers could rack up a series of seemingly unrelated misdemeanor offenses that allowed their outrageous acts to continue, sometimes for years. Opponents of the antistalking legislation had argued that antistalking laws were simply not needed because stalking could be prosecuted under other, already existing statutes. Nonetheless through the wrenching testimony of victims, legislators in state after state were moved to pass specific laws prohibiting stalking, providing prosecutors and law enforcement officials with a framework linking distinct stalking behaviors, allowing them to build a case for a pattern of willful harassment and to press more serious charges.

Inspired by California's example, victims across the nation had been galvanized into advocacy, and by 1993, every state except Maine (which took until 1996) had passed its own antistalking legislation. I discovered that these antistalking laws are unique in several respects: By definition, they criminalize behavior that would not normally be criminal if it occurred only once, but becomes so when it takes place repeatedly, over a period of time.

Because they group seemingly disparate and normally Constitutionally protected activities, such as following, telephoning, and letter writing, into a "course of conduct," antistalking laws also make it possible to press the identical charge for a series of different activities, and to increase the penalties for each subsequent stalking conviction.

Yet, despite all the laws were accomplishing, much work remained to be done; as one Justice Department study stated, "Although there is a common purpose underlying all State antistalking statutes, there is little uniformity in how they define and address the problem."[9] This seemed to be exemplified by the glitch in Colorado's law that had inspired my recent foray into government documents in the first place; many states, including my own, continued to require that a stalker directly threaten a victim in order to be charged with stalking. In these jurisdictions, further legal evolution was still desperately needed to recognize stalking behavior as threatening in and of itself.

I now understood what the antistalking laws had sought to address and how many continued to fall short of providing better protection for everyone against stalkers like Fran. But I needed to take that general information and somehow apply it specifically to my own state, to figure out how Fran might eventually be charged as a stalker.

Over the following weeks, I continued to sift through the materials to learn how the laws had evolved in other states, reasoning that if I understood what had and had not worked elsewhere, I would be better equipped to make a case for changing the law in Colorado. Gradually, I came to understand the elements that comprised the laws. In most states, for a stalking conviction, three components had to be proven beyond a reasonable doubt:

- A course of conduct: The stalker must exhibit a pattern of behavior based on a series of acts, in most states defined as approaching, pursuing, or following; lying in wait; surveillance; harassing; trespassing; and nonconsensually communicating.

- The presence of threats. Although the defendant must pose some threat to the victim, the majority of states, unlike Colorado, did not require that the threat be direct or explicit, but could be implied by word or deed as long as it would cause a reasonable person fear.

- The criminal intent to cause fear in the victim. To get around the fact that an erotomanic like Fran would certainly assert that her intention was to pursue a recalcitrant lover, not to cause that lover fear, in most states, the stalker did not have to intend to cause the fear itself, just the act that resulted in that fear.[10]

I was heartened to learn that a few states that had once required a "credible" or explicit threat, had amended their laws to include threats implied by conduct, and several more were considering doing so. I began to wonder if the same could occur in Colorado, so that stalking behavior alone would be recognized as the terrible threat it was.

Detective Raymond of the Threat Management Unit confirmed how difficult if not impossible it was for the police to intervene in stalking cases if there had been no threat in states that required one to arrest a stalker. Although he had indeed dealt with many stalking victims like me who were justifiably fearful even though the stalker made no direct threat, there really wasn't much even the TMU could do before California dropped its "credible threat" requirement. He, too, thought such language needed to change to reflect the fact that "abnormal behavior, obsessive behavior, is in fact a 'credible threat,' is in fact alarming to a lot of people."

As one well-versed in the "vocabulary" of stalkers, Detective Raymond observed:

> Leaving a dozen roses on your doorstep every day for a week or a note that says, "I loved that blue dress you wore yesterday and I was so close I could've touched you," are very alarming statements to victims and their fear level goes up, but for filing purposes, that's probably not going to fly.[11]

Since its inception, there had been several changes in California's antistalking law that resulted from the inability to prosecute clearly dangerous stalkers who had not made threats. And it was Los Angeles Deputy District Attorney Deputy Rhonda Saunders whom I had met at the TMU conference, who was responsible for most of these changes.

Saunders traced her interest in crimes of stalking to an outrageous case of erotomania in which the glaring inadequacies in the existing law culminated in an eleven-hour SWAT team standoff. Although this erotomanic's exploits were devastating to the victim, the police had been unable to act due to the absence of a threat. As I listened to this story unfold, I hoped that other states, including my own, could learn from California's efforts in crafting improved antistalking laws and avoid the potential for such flagrantly destructive sagas to drag on and on.

Toward the end of 1991, Saunders was working night court. "I pick up a file and it's the weirdest scenario I've ever seen in my life," she recalled. The victim, Jane, a fairly well-known fashion designer, was a mature, sophisticated woman in her late forties. The defendant, Susan, nearly twenty years her junior, was the daughter of one of Jane's prior employers.

Saunders noted Susan "looked somewhat like a Manson girl—very young, unattractive, kind of a loner." She had developed erotomania toward Jane during the several years the older woman had been employed by Susan's father, although according to Saunders, Jane "never knew it. . . there was no relationship whatsoever, nothing more than perhaps a passing in the hall for a couple of years."

That changed. A few years after Jane left her job, she and her boyfriend happened to run into Susan at a movie theater. The younger woman approached Jane, saying that she was going through a difficult time and needed someone to talk to: In a tragic twist, Susan's own sister had just been murdered on her prom night by a stalker. Jane agreed to lend an ear, little knowing she was about to relinquish her entire life.

Jane and Susan started meeting for lunch and soon began a brief lesbian affair that lasted only a week, because Jane quickly recognized that Susan was "so obviously disturbed," Saunders recalled. Jane tried to break it off. Susan would not hear of it. She relentlessly stalked Jane for almost a year, even quitting her job to devote more time her amorous pursuit.

Susan was convinced that the victim was simply playing hard to get. She "looked at third parties, such as the victim's boyfriend and the victim's friends, as obstacles to her getting to the victim. . . she believed that the victim truly loved her, and were it not for all of these obstacles, they would be together." Once Susan even shattered a window in Jane's bathroom, stuck her head through and screamed obscenities while Jane was in the shower.

Then Susan started showing up at Jane's workplace, screaming similar obscenities. Saunders marveled:

In fact, Jane was working for another company when the suspect broke in and caused such a ruckus that the victim's employer. . . suggested that she start looking for another job, because he was afraid there would be a post-office-massacre–type situation. So, [Jane] was just being victimized over and over and over again.

Although Jane "was just devastated by what was going on. . . we couldn't prosecute the case under the stalking law," Saunders lamented, because there had been no direct threat. Even though Jane "had gone to the police over and over, they kept telling her, 'Sorry, there's nothing we can do.' And, under the stalking law as it existed, there wasn't anything they could do. Finally, the TMU stepped in."

Susan had stolen Jane's Rolodex® from her house and proceeded to write angry letters to all of Jane's business associates, friends, and relatives. "So," Saunders continued, "They arrested [Susan] on residential burglary charges. She got out, though." Susan's father made bail for her and on release, she immediately went to his house, looking for the gun she knew he kept there. She found it.

Meanwhile, Jane was not informed of her stalker's release. In fact, Jane "felt safe for the first time in a year and sure enough, [Susan] shows up with this loaded gun," Saunders remembered. Susan broke into Jane's home where she and a couple of friends were having lunch. At first she threatened to kill herself, and then threatened Jane and her guests. The SWAT team was called in. After an eleven-hour stand-off, Susan was arrested.

About a week later, Jane hired a security company to install an alarm system in her home. In the process, they stumbled upon a veritable bunker the stalker had set up in a four-foot crawl space under the floorboards. The contents included a pillow, clothing, and a stockpile of dried food. It appeared the stalker had been living under her victim's home for at least six months. The security firm also discovered scratches on the telephone box in the crawl space, explaining Susan's uncanny knack for always being aware of Jane's whereabouts: She had been tapping into all of her victim's telephone calls.

Saunders told me:

Whenever the victim had friends over at the house, she'd hear these horrible noises coming from the crawl space, banging on pipes, and scratching noises, and she thought it was a raccoon or a squirrel or something. She had even hired an exterminator who came and threw some poison bait in the basement, which obviously did no good.

The stalker was convicted of several charges, including assault on a SWAT officer and attempting to inflict great bodily injury for pointing her gun at one of the women at the luncheon. But she could not be charged with stalking because there had been no threat associated with her stalking behavior. It was this failure of the law that motivated Saunders to take action herself: "That's what made me so determined to change the law so that victims of stalkers wouldn't have to go through years of stalking activities before the police could actually step in and do something." Stalking, Saunders emphasized, is a crime of deeds, not words.

When Saunders initially proposed amending California's antistalking law in 1992, she sought to change the direct threat requirement to allow threats implied by conduct. During her testimony, she was actually asked by the chairman of the State Senate's Judiciary Committee, "Why should we put someone in prison for being a pest?" He quickly changed his tune when stalking slithered its way into Sacramento, right to the State Capitol where a State Senate secretary was shot in the parking lot by the ex-boyfriend who had been stalking her. Saunders' bill was passed the next year.

But that was only the beginning. Shortly thereafter, she was called by several of the legislators who had initially tried to block her proposed changes. They were now proposing two changes of their own, which were also rapidly signed into law: 1) At the victim's request, he or she must be notified of the stalker's release from prison, and 2) incarceration could not be used as a defense against a stalking charge. Saunders explained:

> *We really needed this one because the conduct doesn't stop just because they're in prison. I've had a lot of cases where the stalker continues to write letters, and even to make threats from prison [that often begin with such remarks as] "When I get out. . ." or "I'm getting out in a few months. . ." or "I can hire someone to kill you."*

Under changes in the law, such threats by incarcerated stalkers can affect their good time/work time credits. In California, as in many states, any prison sentence can be reduced by as much as half by good time/work time credits, and if stalkers continue their activities in prison, according to Saunders, "We can get a lot of those credits revoked and keep them in longer. Plus, we can bring subsequent charges." Fortuitously, Susan was affected by these subsequent amendments to the law. Although sentenced to seven and a half years in prison, she could have gotten out much sooner if her good time/work time credits had not been revoked after she sent a stream of threatening letters not only to Jane, but also to her public defender, arresting officer, and Saunders.[12]

Saunders' crusade to change the law was precisely what I now faced in Colorado, and what many other stalking victims continue to face in other jurisdictions where the "credible threat" requirement remains an impediment to filing charges against stalkers. That such language is irrelevant to the crime of stalking is proven again and again by cases like Jane's and mine and thousands of others. The case of David Letterman for example: Although Connecticut's antistalking law was, in part, inspired by Margaret Ray, Letterman's perennially persistent and resourceful erotomanic, she cannot be prosecuted under the statute because she has never directly threatened him. Instead, she has been arrested for trespassing and stealing Letterman's car. Only last year, she was picked up for shoplifting at a store in Indiana near his parents' home. Even if Ray had traveled there as part of her stalking of Letterman, it made no difference, for in both Connecticut and Indiana, Ray could not be considered a stalker since she had never made a "credible threat."

In Colorado, Stephen, the "tunnel stalker" who followed Mona all the way from Arizona and burrowed his way into her bathroom from his apartment down the hall, was convicted on ten misdemeanor counts, including restraining order violations and third-degree sexual assault, yet could not be charged with stalking because he had not made a direct verbal or physical threat. This loophole allowed Stephen to serve only one year in prison. He will serve the rest of his five-year term under house arrest. With a felony stalking conviction, Stephen would have received a stiffer sentence.

After weeks of talking to experts, reading laws, and sifting through government documents, I was lead back to what I already knew, that passing antistalking legislation was not enough; the laws themselves had to become more effective in order to protect victims from stalkers. A National Institute of Justice report, the *Project to Develop a Model Anti-Stalking Code for States*, had been completed in 1993 specifically to help states meet those goals.

This report addressed several of the issues in charging, punishing, and rehabilitating stalkers, by encouraging states to 1) make stalking a felony, 2) establish penalties for stalking commensurate with the serious-ness of the crime, and 3) provide criminal justice officials with the authority and legal tools to arrest, prosecute, and sentence stalkers.

Specifically recognizing the limitations in requiring a "credible threat," the *Model Code* asserted, "Stalking defendants often will not threaten their victims verbally or in writing but will instead engage in conduct which, taken in context, would cause a reasonable person fear." It termed such behavior "threats implied by conduct" and recommended against the use of the term "credible threat" altogether.[13]

Dr. Fein, the consulting psychologist for the United States Secret Service, participated in the meetings that led to the adoption of this report and pointedly told me, "We worked so hard to get the credible threat requirement taken out. It doesn't make sense. If somebody really wants to kill somebody, why would they make a threat before-hand?"[14] The *Model Code* has already met with some success: seventeen states have amended their stalking laws in alignment with the *Code*'s recommendations.[15]

Even if perfect state laws existed, when a victim moved to escape her stalker and was followed, as I had been, the process of obtaining a re-straining order and building a case for stalking began all over again. To address this problem, Representative Ed Royce, now a United States Congressman, introduced federal antistalking legislation. To illustrate the need for this law, he again called upon Kathleen Gallagher Baty, the same victim whose testimony had been so instrumental in the passage of the antistalking law he had authored while in the California State legislature.

Although Baty's stalker had been sentenced to almost nine years in prison, "after good time and work time credit, he was released after only serving four years. Seven short days after being released, he cut off his electric monitor bracelet and jumped parole," she said. Baty was warned that her stalker was on his way to Florida where she had moved with her family to get away from him.

For the next seven days, my husband, myself, and my three-year-old little boy were held in protective custody by the Fort Lauderdale police department. He was arrested in Nevada, trying to make a withdrawal from his bank account. . . In so many instances stalking is not just contained in one city or state. The need for a National Law is imperative.[16]

In August 1996, Congress would unanimously vote to make stalking a Federal crime. The law prohibits crossing state lines to stalk, stalking on federal property, and makes a restraining order in one state valid in another. As Congressman Royce told me; "If we're going to give the advice to stalking victims to stay away from their stalker, then at least we should make certain that the protections [of a restraining order] are extended across state lines."[17]

Unfortunately in 1994 when Fran followed me over a thousand miles and across three state lines to Colorado, there was no such federal law in place. Once she and I were living in the same state, it would apply to Fran only if Tim and I moved again. Or, if she stalked me at the post office. As I wondered what to do next, I thought about the lie Fran had told her new therapist: that she had moved to the state because she needed a change. In reality, the change she sought was to be "reunited" with me after almost two years of separation. What further changes would her move mean for Tim and me? We loved our new home and our new community. We did not want to move again.

It did not appear that Fran as yet knew where we lived, only where we worked, since her latest restraining order violation, like all the others since she had moved to Colorado, had been a telephone call to my office's voice mail. In this one she said, "I'm trying to make sense of my life and perhaps you can be of some help if you're in Colorado or maybe you're in Tucson. Anyway, I have a plane ticket for you that I bought."

The police officer I called had again been unable to locate her. Had she given the mental health center a false address, attempting to conceal her whereabouts just as I had done? Did this mean she was getting even better at eluding the law, and if so, might she also be able to get herself together to finally retaliate against the object who had caused her so much grief?

If only she could be charged with stalking, I mused. But what if she could? Colorado like many other states only provided minimal penalties for this heinous crime. Even when stalking is taken seriously by the police and the courts, antistalking laws serve no deterrent effect when the penalties imposed are insufficient.

I had been amazed to discover that in the majority of states, a first stalking offense remains a misdemeanor on a par with spitting in public, littering, or loitering, punishable by up to only a year in jail and a $1,000 fine. Most of these states impose felony counts and stiffer penalties for repeat offenders, yet several states still consider even a second stalking offense merely a misdemeanor.[18]

Charging stalking as a felony, a serious crime, gives stalkers the message that their criminal acts will be taken seriously, with serious consequences. Sentences of a year or less often lead to the intolerable situation in which stalkers are imprisoned for far less time than they have emotionally incarcerated their victims. Given that the crime of stalking is progressive and chronic, sentences should be long enough to both deter and punish.

As I completed sifting through government papers on antistalking legislation, I remained without a federal or state law to protect me from my stalker. With all I had learned, I kept returning to the inevitable conclusion that my state's antistalking law needed to change. It seemed to me that the best way to go about changing it was to publicize my case. I had to get legislators interested in the issue by laying a groundwork of support.

I continued counseling stalking victims, but I also began lecturing about stalking with the ultimate goal to increase public awareness and change the law. As the agenda for the 1996 legislative session had already been fixed, I set my sights on 1997. Now I could feel myself truly moving beyond the acceptance of my erotomanic ordeal, to the next stage that I had only first become aware of at the TMU conference—activism.

For Evonne von Heussen-Countryman, activism meant establishing a national organization, for Margie it meant starting a local task force, for me it seemed to mean educating others as I had educated myself, hoping to eventually change a law. In each case, activism meant making the going easier for those thousands of victims whose stalking ordeal had yet to begin.

By now, I had accepted almost seven years of being stalked. I had no choice. While I could even accept that stalking would always be a part of my life, I could not accept that it had to be a part of life for so many others.

I had started working on this book and even had an article on erotomania published in a national medical magazine when Fran made what appeared to be her final call from Colorado in February 1996. She said only, "Well, I hope you had a good Valentine's Day" and did not leave her name or number. As usual, when I heard her message on my voice mail, sandwiched in between my regular, legitimate patient calls, it was as if I had been struck in the face. I felt myself flush with fear and frustration.

Fran could still assault me, invade my privacy even while miles away. The normal routine of my day, the routine I so enjoyed of responding to and treating patients was again interrupted. Would I never be rid of her? I called the police. They were again unable to locate Fran, but my usual follow-up call to her mental health center revealed that she was no longer active in their system.

Given this information, I decided to speak to her therapist myself, something I had resisted in the knowledge that he would have to tell Fran of my contacting him. But I had to find out exactly what "inactive" meant. She could have transferred to a different center, one closer to my home or office. Or, she could have simply dropped out of therapy altogether, possibly placing Tim and me in even more danger.

The truth behind her inactive status was, as always, stranger than Fran's psychotic fiction. Her therapist told me that he had finally convinced her to move back to Tucson. I cannot even remember exactly what he said, I was so overwhelmed with joy and gratitude. I thanked him profusely and immediately sent him the largest gift basket the local candy company produced, with the note, "Thanks for your help. No offense, but I hope I never speak to you again."

I literally ran out of my office and found Tim on one of the hospital's units. "It's over!" I gleefully exclaimed, knowing even as I did, that I was probably overstating the meaning of Fran's move. Tim immediately knew who I was referring to, although he too, could not imagine that she had simply given up.

"Did they arrest her?" He asked.

"No. But, the next best thing happened," and I told him of my call to Fran's therapist. "I don't know if she called me from out of state, or if she made one last attempt to contact me before she left. And I really don't care. As long as I know she's not in Colorado, I can live with her telephone calls." Tim agreed and took me to the nurses' break room to give me a quick, celebratory hug.

The pressure from her parents as well as her therapist had finally seemed to pay off. It appeared that Fran and I were happily never after, at last.

Chapter Ten

FOREVER EROTOMANIC

ALMOST EIGHT YEARS AGO, IN ONE OF those seemingly benign quirks of fate, I performed the duties of my job and treated a patient who could not let go, forever changing my life. After Fran left Colorado, I continued to receive periodic telephone calls from her for several months on my voice mail at work. I documented them but did nothing more. The Colorado police were hardly going to travel out of state to arrest a woman on misdemeanor charges when they had done nothing for the two years she had violated the restraining order in their own backyard. Fran even tried, on occasion, to appeal to my professional persona, by asking me for a second opinion on her medications or a recommendation for a psychiatrist. In one of her more imaginative attempts, she left a message as the representative of a management company, saying, "We have a junket trip to offer you to Tucson. Please call if you're interested."

Even if the police had shown any inclination to arrest Fran, I did not want her brought back to Colorado. I felt safer knowing she was a thousand miles away. With that distance between us, her telephone calls from Tucson became no more than occasional minor annoyances, bringing with them only the tiniest twinge of my former terror. The moment would quickly pass. I kept a record of the calls in case I would ever need them as evidence, and allowed myself to promptly forget about them. Knowing that she was several states away seemed to have made all the difference.

Then, in July 1996, five months after it seemed she had left the Rocky Mountain State for good, a member of the staff at the psychiatric hospital that had brought Tim and me to Colorado in the first place, the hospital at which Tim was medical director and at which I continued to maintain my office, left me a message.

"Doreen, this is Kitty. I don't know how to tell you this, but Fran Nightingale was here last night for an evaluation. Call me when you get this."

I was still at home when I picked up that message, but I returned the call, immediately. Kitty told me that Fran had come to the hospital seeking an evaluation so she could obtain a referral to a psychiatrist to fight the power of attorney her brother had over her. Fran had told Kitty that both of her parents had recently died and she wanted to prove she was competent to handle her own affairs.

I realized then that it must have been the death of her parents that led to her abrupt departure to Arizona and subsequent physical absence from me in Colorado, not anything I, my attorney, or her own therapist had done. Perhaps her parents' illnesses even accounted for her seeming to waiver between the two states during the two years after she initially called me in Colorado. For the first time, I understood why Fran had confined her stalking of me to telephone calls and made no visits to my home or work. Until now.

One of the precautions I had taken when we moved over three years before, had been to give Fran's name to the admissions department at our hospital and ask that they notify me if they heard from her. In the ensuing years, the staff had changed. The memories of those who were left became understandably hazy. I had become complacent once Fran had returned to Tucson, and I had neither given the new staff members her name nor filled them in. Yet, at the end of the standard interview when Kitty asked nearly the last question on her printed list, "Do you have any legal charges against you?" and Fran dutifully answered, "Well, Dr. Orion has a restraining order against me," Kitty vaguely recalled hearing something about this a long time before.

As she finished up her evaluation, Kitty struggled to remember the details she knew were important, and finally did, but not before giving Fran the name of a psychiatrist who practiced in the same suite of offices I did. Kitty then called to warn me. As soon as she and I hung up,

I called the psychiatrist to whom Kitty had referred Fran for the second opinion. I asked him not to see her, and after I explained the situation, he readily agreed to my request. I did not want to encounter Fran in the waiting room we shared, nor take a chance that some judge would make an exception to the restraining order by allowing her to be there.

My office-mate agreed that if Fran called, he would refer her to some other male psychiatrist in another part of town. While he and I spoke, Kitty faxed me the evaluation form that Kitty had filled out during her interview with Fran. Luckily, Fran had provided her home and work telephone numbers and addresses. I would need them to let the police know where they could find her. I glanced at the form and was overcome with horror: Fran worked only a few miles from my office, in the same small town. How could she have been so close to me while I had allowed myself to believe that she was a thousand miles away? How long had she lived here? How long had we been breathing the same Colorado air, no longer crisp, but chilling, how long had we been gazing at the same Rocky Mountains, no longer majestic but menacing? How long?

The realization that at the very moments I had felt safe, I was probably in the most danger began to suffocate me. I went to the front door and peered anxiously outside. No Fran. I took a few moments to catch my breath and went back to phone the police. It took some time to connect with an officer because I was loathe to give the dispatcher my home telephone number, despite assurances that it would not go any further. I had heard those same assurances in Tucson, heard them in fact just the day before Fran called me at home for the first time.

When I finally spoke to a police officer, I gave him the short version of the almost seven years of events I had recited many times before. I added that I had a permanent restraining order in the state of Colorado against Fran, and provided him with her current address. He told me he would go arrest her. I foolishly allowed myself to feel some relief, forgetting that "arrest" did not necessarily mean what I assumed it did. I had been caught off guard by Fran's sudden reappearance and distracted at the thought of all the work that meant I still needed to do.

It felt so unreal. I had let myself believe, finally, really believe that Fran was gone forever. In an instant, it seemed, she had returned. I remembered all my false hopes in Tucson, when I thought Dr. Trottle could stop her, when Fran would herself write that if I did not respond she would understand, when the police finally arrested her, when her attorney promised there would be no more contacts, when she was sentenced to a psychiatric institution out of state, and when Tim and I left Arizona. I had finally learned not to hope. How could I have let myself hope again? How could I have believed she had left Colorado for good? Hadn't I learned anything after all these years? With Fran, was I always going to blame myself for something?

When I still had not heard from the police by the next day, I called them, but the officer I had dealt with was off duty. His partner thought Fran had been arrested, but I would have to talk to the specific officer to be sure. I called the county jail. Fran was not being held there. Finally I spoke to the original officer the following day and was told that Fran had, indeed, been at the address I provided. She was even at her apartment when he arrived.

"Did you arrest her?" I asked, cutting to my only concern.

"Oh, yes," he asserted.

"Then why isn't she in the jail?" I asked. I don't even remember what he said, just how I felt at his answer: first astonishment, then disappointment, and finally rage. He had merely given her a piece of paper with an arraignment date a month away. Tucson toujours.

It had been so long, I had forgotten that "arrest" could merely mean issuing a summons—adding still another piece of paper to Fran's permanent collection. He knew this woman had been relentlessly stalking me for years, knew she had been violent in the past, knew she continued to obsess about me and yet not only did he not take her to jail, but he did not even inform me that she was still on the streets.

Did he think she would be happy with me for contacting the police? Rather than pose these excellent questions, (for I was afraid to alienate an officer in this small police department it appeared I would need to depend on heavily in the future), I inquired if he had gotten a description of her vehicle as I had requested. I wanted to be able to easily spot Fran in the hospital parking lot. I was determined that with all the precautions Tim and I continued to take with our home address, Fran was at least not going to follow us there.

The officer told me Fran said she did not own a car and indeed, his check of DMV records bore this out. At least he had some good news for me, since without a car, it would be far more difficult for Fran to physically stalk me, even though she had already shown how adept she was at hunting me down by telephone.

A few days later, I received notice in the mail of Fran's arraignment date, as well as the name of the assistant district attorney (ADA) who would be prosecuting the case. I called immediately to fill him in, as I was afraid that on the face of it, Fran's misdemeanor violation of a restraining order by simply coming to my place of work when I wasn't there would seem trivial. The ADA informed me the statute of limitations on her telephone calls from Tucson, which I had not reported, was 18 months. This meant that she could still be charged with those restraining order violations. Since I had documented the calls meticulously, he told me I could now report them to the police.

I could not imagine what good that might do. Fran could theoretically amass quite a collection of citations, as she had in Tucson. In my exasperation, I envisioned her wallpapering her apartment with her assortment of police paperwork, gathered over the years, not just from me but her other objects. A sort of Veterans of Erotomania Memorial, dedicated to the victims of her deluded war. I snapped myself out of this frustrating reverie to finish talking to the ADA.

"Look, I don't care how it's done," I said. "I just want her to leave me alone. If the best way is to make her leave the state, that's fine with me. I don't really care if she gets a brief jail sentence. It's not much of a deterrent to her, anyway." He told me he thought that was "doable," explaining that demanding she leave the state was a violation of her Constitutional rights, but that compelling her to leave, by letting her know she faced a more severe punishment if she stayed, was not.

"Can it be forever?" I asked, hopefully. The ADA laughed, mistakenly thinking I was joking, and told me the longest the judge could compel her to remain out of state was two years. He said he would offer that if Fran pled guilty and left the state, she would remain on probation during that time. If she contacted me while on her two years probation, she would be brought back to Colorado and jailed. If, on the other hand, she decided not to leave the state, he would ask the judge for the maximum allowable jail time on the restraining order violations: a whopping 60 days.

"Well, at least I'll have two years," I answered. "Maybe she'll use that time to fixate on someone else. I've done my time."

He went on to explain that I did not have to be at the arraignment, for Fran would only be asked what her plea was. I felt relieved that I would not have to face her. The thought of seeing her again after nearly four years was horribly disturbing. I did not want to see her smile at me, to know that she delusionally believed she was being rewarded for her pursuit by being with me—even in court.

When I hung up the phone, I called the police as the ADA had instructed, to report Fran's previous telephone violations, the transcripts of which I kept in a separate folder in the same large shopping bag in which I carried the evidence of the rest of her many contacts over the years. "Fran—Colorado" was, of course, separated from the folders marked, "Fran—Tucson—pre-restraining order," and "Fran—Tucson—post-restraining order." By keeping these items thus "filed" in a large paper bag instead of in my desk or file cabinet, I was seeking to set them apart, refusing to lend them any permanence or intimacy by incorporating them into the rest of my personal effects.

Within a few weeks the ADA's deal was rejected and he explained to me that despite this, the case was still unlikely to go to trial. Although somewhat relieved, I was still apprehensive.

"I really don't want to see her," I told him.

In the years since I had last seen Fran, her stalking of me had taken on an almost surreal tone. Although I had never seen her when she visited our home in Tucson, I witnessed the end results—her cards, notes, and instruments—and I knew she had been watching the house, making the anguish of the intrusion almost as acute as if I *had* seen her.

Whenever I walked out to my front yard, or down the driveway to my mailbox, it was entirely possible that Fran had just been there, that I was breathing the same air, getting the same grains of dust on my clothes, and walking over the same gravel that she must have, if not moments, than at least hours before. The same molecules that had been a part of her were thus a part of me. I could not shake the feeling of being constantly contaminated by her presence.

In Colorado, she had "only" been stalking me through the telephone wires, leaving messages on my voice mail, meaning that I had listened to them hours, sometimes days after she had left them. This had lulled me into feeling safer, more removed from her erotomania.

The ADA said he understood I did not want to see Fran, but that he still needed my input. He explained that Fran's attorney would have agreed that she leave the state in exchange for a deferred sentence. In other words, that if Fran did not violate her probation and had no contact with me for its two-year term, all charges would be dropped.

Instead, the ADA had insisted Fran plead guilty before she departed, leaving a permanent record of her crimes. He reasoned that a deferred sentence had already been tried in Tucson and had obviously failed miserably; Fran had spent six months in a psychiatric institution, deferring the possibility of future jail time pending her abidance by the court's condition that she not contact me for those six months. Since she had not, in fact, contacted me, the charges were subsequently dropped. And Fran, of course, then followed me to Colorado.

While it was obvious to me, as well, that a deferred sentence would not deter Fran, I was concerned with the practical aspects of the ADA's plan. Whether Fran pled guilty or not, she would remain on probation for two years. Even assuming she left Colorado and really did not contact me during that time, the only advantage of a guilty plea was that if (when?) she returned to Colorado after her probation was up, her next contact with me would result in a higher order of violation.

On the other hand, if she refused to plead guilty, I had to take my chances at trial where she could be found not guilty, or even guilty, but given no jail time and remain in the state, anyway. I told him my priority was to be rid of her. My chances of her fixating on someone else were much greater the farther away she was from me. I'd take the deferred sentence, as long as she left the state.

After we hung up, I was bothered all day. Something just was not sitting right. I recalled cases of stalkers far worse than mine, in which their victims stood up to them, regardless of their fear. I remembered Margie's fortitude in facing her daughter's stalker in court. She had even tracked this dangerous predator down herself when the police hadn't a clue how to find him.

I remembered Evonne von Heussen–Countryman's resolve as she very publicly lobbied for Britain's first antistalking law, despite her stalker's continued freedom. Katarina Witt, the two-time Olympic figure skating gold medalist, I recalled, was even cross-examined by her erotomanic stalker, who represented himself at his trial. She had managed to face him even though he had written her, "Don't be afraid when God allows me to pull you out of your body to hold you tight. Then you'll know that there is life beyond the flesh."[1]

I felt ashamed as I remembered the courage of these women. I was taking the coward's way out. I might get two years of peace with no contacts from Fran, but so what?

Fran had stalked at least two other women in Tucson who had also obtained restraining orders, but she had no record of convictions there, either. I could only surmise that the other women had also opted for deferred sentences, further proof, as if I needed any, that this type of punishment was not effective. Even if Fran left the state, I had no doubt that after two years, she would move back to Colorado, unless she had begun to stalk someone else.

But in either case, without a record, the victim, whether myself or another woman, would be starting from scratch. I was struck by how unfair I was being, not only to myself, but to her future victims, as there were sure to be many more. How could I even think of saving myself at their expense? All of us needed a permanent record of Fran's illegal acts, and it fell to me to initiate it.

Perhaps if someone had done this years ago, her stalking of me would not have been allowed to escalate to its current level. With prior convictions, she might have gotten tougher sentences, or prolonged mandatory treatment. I might never have met her in the first place. Still, I did not blame her previous victims. I could understand how easy it was to let Fran off the legal hook. The system itself encouraged it by plea bargaining and deferred sentencing. I had done it myself in Tucson and was seriously considering doing it again.

I discussed my decision with Tim, and while saying that he would support whatever I chose to do, he agreed that after nearly seven years, two years Fran-free was pretty meaningless. That night, I called the ADA's voice mail and left him a message. I said, "I've given it a lot of thought and I've changed my mind. My priority is no longer the amount of time I can get away from Fran. I want to get her violations on record."

Fran rejected the deal. She wanted her record to remain clear. Unfortunately, if we did not accept, the most Fran could get was 60 days in jail plus two years probation but the ADA doubted that the particular judge assigned to the case would give Fran anywhere near the maximum.

"Is the judge a man or woman?" I asked.

"A woman," he replied.

"Good," I said, as I recalled the case of a prominent New York physician, chairman of the surgery department at Memorial Sloan-Kettering, who was stalked for years by an erotomanic woman. She had never been his patient, but instead had chosen him for his position, as she had also erotomanically stalked his predecessor. I told the ADA that this erotomanic's delusions had been so capricious, they had grasped at any male authority figure who had the misfortune to cross her path.

She even latched onto the judge and prosecuting attorney, finally forcing the courtroom to be staffed with all female personnel, down to the bailiff.[2] Perhaps, I mused, if Fran fixated on the judge, her honor would be persuaded to mete out a tougher sentence. The ADA laughed, not realizing, again, that I was serious.

"No offense," I told him, "I haven't had any experience with you or with how the Colorado courts handle such cases, but I've been made promises before and nothing happens. It just seems inherently unfair that she can stalk me for seven years and yet come out with no record to show for it." He agreed and asked if I were ready for a fight.

The ADA had suggested I complete a Victim's Impact Statement for the judge to read prior to sentencing. I knew I had to word it carefully, because Fran would be allowed to see it. I detailed her seven-year history of stalking me since September, 1989, including her numerous restraining order violations and I tried to impress upon the court the impact the stalking had had on my life, even though there had been no physical injuries or direct threats.

I tried to strike the proper balance between sounding concerned and fearful, but not angry toward Fran. I did not want her to feel threatened. I did not want her to become violent as she had in the past.

I could not seem to let go of the ADA's comment about being ready for a fight. While that might be the proper stance for an attorney, I knew that for Fran, an erotomanic, a fight, even a legal one, would only enhance the possibility of her becoming violent toward me or Tim. While there was probably no way for her not to perceive the upcoming hearing as a conflict, there still might be a way to convince Fran to leave the state and take the charges with her. Maybe, I reasoned, I could have her taken off the battlefield altogether.

I recalled that when she came to the hospital, it was to seek a second opinion because of her brother's power of attorney over her. Fran had wanted to find a psychiatrist who would agree with her that she was capable of handling her own affairs. That meant her brother controlled her finances. If this really had been a war, the most likely way to put an end to hostilities would have been to petition Congress to cut off funding rather than engage in further indecisive skirmishes along the front line. So, too, perhaps I could appeal to the brother who now might unwittingly be funding Fran's aggression.

I had never met nor spoken to Fran's brother before and I did not know anything about him. When her parents were alive, they had been responsible for Fran and her finances and had unintentionally furthered her delusional pursuit of me by hiring private attorneys for her. Might her brother be possessed of the same misplaced concern? It was a gamble; any contact I had with her family was sure to be interpreted by Fran as further evidence of my involvement in her life. Yet that was how she seemed to interpret everything I did and even what I did not do, anyway.

I had to hope that making one real contact with an actual, immediate member of Fran's family would, in her deluded mind, get lost in the sea of hundreds or perhaps thousands of imagined contacts I had never made. I truly believed that unlike the empty threats of the police and courts, the very real ability of a relative to control her finances, might have an impact. All of my hopes were of course based on my ability to get through to her brother and appeal to the sense of reason I was assuming he possessed, a sense that was nevertheless notably absent in his sister.

Next I had to decide how to track him down, and how the contact should best be initiated. I could hire an attorney to do the talking for me again, but I knew the situation better than I could possibly brief anyone else and I did not want to appear threatening to her family by starting off on an adversarial foot, an unavoidable stance with an attorney. I needed their help, not their animosity.

Perhaps there was also valuable reconnaissance I could gather, information that an attorney, unfamiliar with stalking, might not recognize as useful. If I lived in Los Angeles, a detective from the Threat Management Unit would almost certainly have contacted Fran's brother on my behalf. But everywhere else in the world, including my little corner of it, no such unit existed. Whenever I had appealed to the police, they had demonstrated time and again their indifference to Fran's criminal acts by not arresting her when they should have. I could not afford to take the chance that even if the police agreed to call her brother on my behalf, they would treat the telephone call with the same apathy.

Thus I began my search. I had no idea if Fran's brother lived in Tucson. He could just as easily have lived in some other city, even in some other state, but I decided that it was most logical to begin with where her parents had lived before they died. Even if he resided elsewhere, I might find another relative who could direct me to her brother's whereabouts.

I called information over a dozen times to get the numbers of enough Nightingales in the Tucson area before I finally hit paydirt several days later. Right now, there are probably several Nightingale families in Tucson still wondering what the cryptic message, "I'm looking for the brother of Fran Nightingale who lives in Colorado. If this is the correct number, please call me" meant.

Ed, the right Nightingale, called back the night he received my call, leaving a message on my work machine. He sounded matter-of-fact and I realized that he probably did not know who I was. He may have assumed that I was some psychiatrist treating his sister in Colorado. I did not know if that was good or bad. I waited until I got home to return his call, mulling over what I might say to him on the hour-long drive from my office.

"Hello. Is this Ed Nightingale?" I asked. He said it was.

"Just to be sure, you're Fran's brother?" I asked. Again, he answered, yes.

"And, she used to live in Tucson and has had psychiatric problems?" I continued. I thought I heard him chuckle when he said that sounded like his sister.

"My name is Doreen Orion. Do you know who I am?" I asked. He said he did not, so I continued.

"I'm a psychiatrist. I used to practice in Tucson and Fran started stalking me there in 1989." I heard him suck in his breath, stunned, as he asked quietly if I was in Colorado. He managed to say that he knew about me, but never knew my name.

"The reason I'm calling is that I understand you have power of attorney over Fran. I don't know if you realize that many times in the last two years she has violated a restraining order I have here. She has a court date for the violations coming up."

He not only had no idea, he was "flabbergasted" that I was in Colorado. In fact, he said, when she had announced three years before to her parents, another brother in Tucson, and a sister in Michigan, that she was leaving Tucson, they were all relieved, thinking that I was still in Arizona.

Her parents had not included Fran's siblings very much in her legal transgressions or in her admissions to psychiatric facilities. I wondered if this was again part of their misguided attempts to protect her. It certainly appeared that her parents had tried to insulate Fran from the shame they must have felt by never mentioning my attorney's telephone call over a year ago. Since they were now both deceased, I saw no reason to, either.

"I was hoping you could help me by using some financial pressure to persuade your sister to leave the state," I said.

When Ed told me that the power of attorney was not permanent and had actually recently expired, I sank in my chair. I had lost the gamble. Sensing my overwhelming disappointment, he sounded genuinely sorry when he admitted there wasn't much he could do to persuade Fran to stop; the family had been dealing with this for years, well before I came into the picture and expected to be dealing with it well after.

I pulled myself together and tried to salvage something from my mission, all the while praying that he would remain open to helping me. I tried to phrase my next questions carefully. "I know she's done this to other women and that they obtained restraining orders. But it's been almost seven years and I don't know why she just continues to stalk me. Do you know of anything the other women did that might have stopped her?"

Unfortunately, he did not. But I was not going to give up. I had made this call myself to find some answers and just because I had not yet found the ones I wanted did not mean that I would stop asking questions. I just hoped my stalker's brother would continue to answer them.

"She told the police that she doesn't have a car," I continued. "Is this true?" He said that Fran did have a car. I held my breath as I asked for its description, explaining that I wanted to watch for it. In effect, I was asking for his help in trapping his sister, for he must have known that if I saw her car, I would have reported her to the police for violating the restraining order. Would he be willing to give me information that might lead to charges against his sister? I did not have to hold my breath for long, as he was kind enough to give me the make, model, and color of the vehicle she had recently purchased.

As we spoke, Ed did confirm my suspicions about their parents. He told me that after they passed away, Fran seemed to do much better. In fact, he had also believed their parents had inadvertently contributed to Fran's delusions by funding her legal fights.

I recalled the times they had hired private attorneys for her. I understood the instinct to protect one's offspring, the most basic of the animal kingdom. I could not fault them for wanting to defend Fran and to desperately believe that she was over her life-long obsessions. But sometimes safeguarding those we love only hurts them more in the end. By insulating Fran from legal consequences, her parents had only sealed the hold her delusions had on her, confining her to a prison of her own psychotic thinking, where reality was not given so much as a visitor's pass.

I knew that both my telephone call to Ed, as well as the hope that he might be able to stop his sister were at an end. I was a bit disappointed, but by no means crushed. Although I had not obtained the sought-after relief, I was truly grateful for her brother's good will. I do not know if I would have been so forthcoming if it had been my sister.

"My goal is not primarily to punish Fran," I reassured him, "I just want her to stop."

He surprised me, then, astutely observing that punishment might be the only thing that *could* stop her.

Fran's brother promised to consult his other siblings to try to come up with a way to pressure her to leave Colorado. Now I came to my biggest fear in making the call in the first place: that Fran would use it as concrete evidence of my involvement in her life. I told him, "I know I can't ask you not to tell Fran I called. I'll leave that up to you, but my concern if she knows is that she'll interpret this as more interest on my part." He promised to consult his siblings on that issue, as well. When I got off the phone, I told Tim what kind of car to watch for.

I was still concerned that Tim was not taking seriously the potential for Fran to be violent toward him, although I believed that he was even more likely a target than I was. I began repeating to him daily, like a mantra, "white Nissan pick-up truck, white Nissan pick-up truck," urging him to be careful. I was, as well. But stereotypically female, I could barely tell the difference between a pick-up and any other kind of truck.

Trying to discern a Nissan from a Mazda, or even from a Ford for that matter, seemed totally hopeless. I had never realized how many white trucks there were. Coming to work, I slowly drove around the parking lot, pausing before any white truck to see if there was someone waiting inside or if it really fit the make and model of Fran's vehicle.

Days later, I learned there was to be no trial. Fran had decided to forgo a court fight and accept a permanent record of her crimes. She was pleading guilty to the restraining order violations.

"So what exactly does that mean?" I asked the ADA when he called to tell me the seemingly good news. Fran, he explained, could either leave the state with two years probation, or stay in Colorado and serve 60 days in jail, the maximum possible, and still have the two years probation. Either way, there would be a permanent record of her conviction. All that remained was for Fran to formally accept her sentencing in the hearing set for the next month, and decide what she was going to do.

"Great, so she has a lot of incentive to leave the state." I said, "I'm really pleased I won't have to see her in court."

He told me that by law, she had thirty days to make up her mind and that he would contact me as soon as she did.

"O.K." I answered, hesitantly and less pleased. "You should also know that I contacted her brother last week."

He knew. Her attorney had told him. Obviously, that meant Fran knew, as well. By telling Fran that I had spoken to him, her brother had, in the end, acted in neither his sister's nor my best interests. I found myself disappointed in this stranger who as much as I wished otherwise, had no obligation to me. Moreover, I worried what this might do to

Fran, if she would now decide to stay in the belief that I would become even further involved. Or, would she view my contacting her brother as a betrayal, and in her shame that my call had alerted her entire family to her legal difficulties, be driven to violence? She might also feel as if I had gone on the attack by requiring that a guilty plea be placed permanently on her record.

The courts were once again only adding to the danger by giving Fran thirty days to simmer in her inevitable feelings of anger and betrayal at the hands of the woman who was "in love" with her during this "dramatic moment" of deciding whether or not to go to jail. The penalties for her actions, while less than serious, were still quite real. She clearly got the message that this time there was to be no clemency; no deferred sentence.

Now I would have to wait and see if my decision had any adverse effect on Fran's behavior. I anticipated the day of the hearing with dread, knowing that it, too, was another dramatic moment; a time when Fran would have to face the consequences of her illegal behavior and be sentenced by a judge.

My fears only heightened when the ADA called me back a week later. I could immediately tell something was wrong.

"Is this a good time for you?" He asked. He had never asked that before. Was he hoping it wasn't?

"It's fine," I answered, cautiously. He explained that Fran had backed out of the deal, thinking she could prove the restraining order itself was invalid. This meant that she was not pleading guilty, not leaving the state, and not receiving any jail time. Fran would now have even more time to wallow in her anger, humiliation, and shame over whatever betrayals she believed I was responsible for.

Unlike me, the ADA did not sound overly concerned. He was focusing on the legal outcome, on winning a case. I was focusing on mitigating the danger to myself and Tim, since I knew that in erotomania, there are no winners. The ADA confidently asserted that even Fran's own attorney believed that she would lose this motion and would then have no choice but to enter a guilty plea.

"Will I have to be at that hearing?" I asked. There was a long pause. He said I might, but that the date had not yet been set. My heart filled with dread at the thought of seeing her. As empowered as I had felt since the Threat Management Conference, since my decision to make Fran accountable for her actions, and since my contacting her brother, I could feel my resolve starting to ebb at the mere thought of facing her.

If only the possibility robbed me of my strength, what might the reality of seeing her do? I could feel the old doubt and blame creeping back into my psyche, feelings that had been foreign to me for so long. Was this the end result of my contacting her brother? Was Fran now going to ensure that we met face-to-face for the first time in four years? I rather stupidly asked, "Why do you think she changed her mind?"

He hesitated for a second or two, struggling to find the right words, knowing that he was talking to a psychiatrist.

"Because she's mentally ill," he finally replied.

I felt like an idiot. How could I have forgotten? How could I have expected rational behavior from someone who was clearly irrational? But, I knew how. I had set aside my psychiatric knowledge and succumbed to viewing myself as the attacked, and she the attacker, opposing sides in an ongoing battle. I had been deceived by her apparent power, evidenced by the fact that it was she who acted and I who reacted. I had forgotten that her "power" was derived from her delusions and was just as unreal as they were. She was not powerful, but she was dangerous. And I could not afford to get caught up in the "war" again.

Now instead of being proud of my activism on my own behalf, I wondered if I had forced a showdown. Had Fran rejected the deal specifically so that she could see me? And in this respect I thought of Madonna and her widely publicized incident with an erotomanic stalker. Although I had always been a fan of Madonna's, I never imagined I would have anything in common with her. Now I did: She had been forced by the courts to act contrary to what she knew was right, as I now expected to be.

Dr. Meloy, who was a consultant to the prosecution in her case, had told me:

> One of the reasons that she did not want to testify is because she knew that being there in the courtroom would fulfill Hoskins' fantasies. She would be sitting twelve feet from him and testifying and talking about her own personal reaction to him. This is exactly what he wanted.[3]

It had taken a court order to compel her to testify. Madonna herself eloquently expressed the feelings of a stalking victim forced to face her perpetrator when she testified before the jury:

> *I didn't want to be in the same room with a man who threatened my life. I feel sick to my stomach. . . disturbed that the man who threatened my life is sitting across from me. . . I feel it made his fantasies come true. I'm sitting in front of him, and that's what he wants.*[4]

Madonna had confirmed for Hoskins his identity—his self-importance—as her stalker. As Dr. Meloy told me:

> *Subsequent to her appearance in court, three weeks later, on the walls of his LA County Jail cell Hoskins had written, "THE MADONNA STALKER. I LOVE MADONNA. MADONNA LOVES ME," in big letters. He'll do ten years in prison for stalking her. Yet she has legally been forced to contribute through this one event to stimulating his fantasies of being narcissistically linked with her in a special way.*[5]

And even in jail, his link with her is being further solidified. According to Dr. Meloy, Hoskins' fellow inmates refer to him as "the material guy."[6]

If I, like Madonna, had to confront my stalker in court, it would undoubtedly feed Fran's fantasy and would certainly give her exactly what she wanted. Or would it? If Fran really wanted to see me, she had had ample opportunities over the years where she would not have been saddled with a judge as chaperone. Even her most recent excursion to the hospital had been at 8 p.m., a time of day she could have reasonably assumed I would be gone, as I was. I was again left with the premise that if Fran had really wanted to see me, she would have; therefore, she must not want to see me.

I recalled learning years ago that erotomanics are the only type of stalkers who generally seem to avoid direct, face-to-face contact with their victims. It did not make sense that she would force the issue now in court. This was not like the Hoskins/Madonna case where the court itself forced the issue, leaving neither stalker nor victim any choice. My reasoning as a psychiatrist, instead of my fear as a victim, led me to conclude that she would not go through with the hearing. And she did not.

Shortly after my last conversation with the ADA, in October 1996, he called again to tell me that Fran had decided to plead guilty to the restraining order violations and would be leaving the state after all. I allowed myself to be cautiously optimistic, but no more. Tim was even more skeptical, rolling his eyes and saying, "I'll believe it when I see it."

There seemed to be no end to the twists and turns in this erotomanic epic. So it was that a few weeks later, I got a message from a man who asked me to call him regarding Fran Nightingale. Was she setting me up? Yet the voice on my message sounded genuinely distressed. When I returned his call, a man identifying himself as Chris said he knew Fran and was very worried about her attitude, since she still "just doesn't get" that she should not be in the same city, let alone same state as me.

Fran had admitted to Chris that it was no coincidence that she was in Colorado or that she had taken a job in the same little town in which I worked. Chris, who happened to have some mental health experience himself, said that while he had not directly observed Fran to be violent, he believed that she was certainly capable of it.

"You can just tell it's in her," he said.

Fran had told Chris that I had written a "scathing" letter about her to the court, including her potential for violence, and Chris believed that the letter had actually had a "deterrent" effect on Fran, making her view our "relationship" more realistically. Still, Fran told Chris she had no intention of leaving Colorado, and I was stunned to further learn that she was slated to begin her twenty-day sentence in the county jail—on work release—the following day.

"What?" I sputtered, incredulously.

After I concluded my call with Chris, I immediately called the ADA. While I waited for his return call, I marveled at how in the entire seven years of being stalked by Fran, no one, not Dr. Trottle nor any of her numerous subsequent psychiatrists or therapists, had ever seen fit to warn me about her. It had taken an acquaintance of Fran's, with no responsibility to me whatsoever, to perform this most basic duty shirked by all the rest. I was as outraged by their callousness as I was in awe of his conscience.

The ADA told me that Fran had decided not to leave the state, after all. He, too, had been surprised when the judge had, on her own, suspended 40 days of the agreed upon 60-day sentence.

"Why wasn't I told of this?" I asked, barely controlling my anger.

"You should have been," he agreed. "Didn't you get a letter from the court?"

"No, I did not." I answered tersely.

I had apparently fallen through the cracks. Again. His only reply to my astonishment and dismay at Fran's release to go to work every day, was his assurance that inmates were supervised very closely while on work release.

"She works a few miles from my office!" I exclaimed. "It's nearer to where she works than the jail is. How could she possibly be supervised closely?"

He had no reply for that at all.

As I approach almost eight years of erotomanic stalking, I can't help wondering what will happen in the years to come. I think back on all the knowledge I have gained through my reading and talking to experts and other victims. I believe I have learned from my mistakes. Fran does not seem able to learn from hers.

I have begun working with the Colorado legislature to try to change the state's antistalking law. If the law is amended during the 1997 session, as I hope it will be, to include an implied threat as the basis for bringing a stalking charge, a good prosecutor could, for example, make the case that Fran's moving over a thousand miles to be near me and violating restraining orders clearly qualify as implied threats.

But then the punishment must be commensurate with the crime. Stalking is an act of terrorism against an individual, just as organized groups perpetuate terrorist acts against a country, and should be treated as such.

Whereas a terrorist contacts a newspaper warning that a country's policy had better change, the stalker does the same with regard to his victim's attitude. Whereas a terrorist blows up buildings, a stalker vandalizes property and tampers with cars. Whereas terrorist activities are always taken seriously by the authorities, the violation of a restraining order by a stalker is routinely assigned to a low priority. While it is true that one act of terrorism may result in many deaths, the cumulative effects of stalking ravage a far greater number of lives. Stalking has become the most common form of social terrorism and no less devastating than its political counterpart.

Clearly, in many stalking cases, especially in those involving perpetrators with erotomanic delusions, incarceration alone is not the answer. In fact, it probably does nothing to deter erotomanic and other mentally ill offenders. Arthur Jackson wrote Theresa Saldana threatening letters from prison. Margaret Ray's ardor for David Letterman appears undiminished by repeated incarcerations. Fran called me collect from jail.

An erotomanic who has stalked a famous female English entertainer for over two decades has amassed a grand total of ten criminal convictions in the British courts (for mischief and breaches of probation), 54 months in custody—that's four-and-a-half years—plus 24 years of probation, but he never stops, recontacting his victim almost at the very instant of his release from custody.[7]

Remarkably, only a handful of states mandate psychiatric evaluation or treatment for convicted stalkers, either as a condition of parole or while in prison. Yet even the Department of Justice recognizes that for mentally ill stalkers like Fran, "It is unlikely that simply punishing the convicted stalker will resolve the problem." Such a stalker, "who has been convicted and incarcerated, may be embittered and seek retribution for being kept from the victim, especially if the illness was left untreated during incarceration."[8]

Some states have tried to address this need, but the defect seems to have more to do with money than mental illness; mandating psychiatric treatment for stalkers during their incarceration means building more psychiatric facilities attached to prisons and hiring more psychiatrists. Perhaps we will one day come to the realization as a society that the cost of not treating stalkers is far more expensive, both in terms of victim devastation and lengthy prison stays.

Counseling and medications, where prescribed, should also be made a requirement of parole, probation, or early release from prison, and should continue for extended periods. In this way, the courts would still maintain some control over stalkers who were no longer incarcerated, and any mental disorder present would continue to receive attention. Parole or probation should be immediately revoked for any stalker who contacts his victim.

What kind of treatment might be effective with stalkers? When I asked Dr. Fein, the consulting psychologist for the United States Secret Service, for his opinion, he confirmed that current methods employing incarceration only were not enough. He suggests other approaches that might be taken with stalking offenders:

> *We do, in some cases, a relatively good job of locking people up for three days, but I'd like to put them into a cell and give them a television screen with some button they can push and see stories of people who can say, "Listen, I know what it's like to feel so desperate and feel you can't live without her, but let me tell you what happened to me." I wonder what might happen if we tried to get some new images, some new ideas into some of these people.*

An intriguing plan, yet one that Dr. Fein admits would probably not work with erotomanic or other mentally ill offenders because, not being rational, they would not respond to rational arguments:

> *It clearly makes a difference if someone is, shall we say, having a really tough time letting go and is unable to tolerate the depression of a lost relationship, so therefore holds on and starts stalking, or someone who really is quite psychotic and really believes that this person is in love with him or her.*[9]

Perhaps court-mandated treatment that places stalkers in therapy groups could prove useful, especially for nonmentally ill offenders. In such a scenario, group members who have essentially been able to control their obsessions could act as mentors for newer members still struggling.

Stalkers, as is true for all of us, may find it easier to relate to others who have been through similar experiences. Taking a cue from such support groups as alcoholics anonymous, overeaters anonymous, and gamblers anonymous, perhaps stalkers could be encouraged to contact mentors who are themselves "in recovery" from stalking, when the urge to call the victim or drive by her house seems overwhelming.

Such groups would also provide an additional social outlet for stalkers whose entire life frequently revolves solely around their victims.

Any such groups, unlike their addiction counterparts, might have to be facilitated by an experienced therapist to prevent them from becoming training grounds in which members learn better, more efficient methods of stalking, producing only new and improved, rather than controlled, stalkers.

Mandated treatment, therefore, should be long-term and include focusing on ways to expand the stalker's satisfaction in life apart from the obsessive pursuit of unattainable goals.

With all the research I have done for this book, what was most troubling, at times, were the inconsistencies in the stalking literature. True, there is not just one type of stalker: Their motivations for stalking, their behaviors when they stalk, their potentials for violence all depend upon many differing factors. But researchers and other experts in the field cannot seem to agree on a nomenclature. More than a dozen different terms for stalkers are bandied about to describe overlapping behaviors, making comparing the studies nearly impossible.

In any discipline, the utility and credibility of research hinges on researchers speaking the same language. In the case of stalking, some consistent terminology needs to be developed so that we can all better understand which stalkers are more likely to become violent, which are most amenable to treatment, and what types of treatment might work with which stalkers.

If research methodology improved, the discovery of effective treatments for stalking would become more likely. Even with a better-educated, concerned, and well-equipped society, the proliferation of this insidious crime will not stop without such therapies. Fran and erotomanics like her, as well as other stalkers, need help with their connectiveness, their emotional investments in other pursuits. They need to become less isolated. They need to find a purpose in their lives, perhaps through volunteer work, creative outlets, or other activities that bring them success and satisfaction. The only hope for an erotomanic to give up the pursuit of his object is if there is something equally promising to fill the resulting void.

As one expert in the field put it:

> *An abiding problem with managing these cases is the almost total lack of motivation for treatment. Those caught up in pathological*

love do not see themselves as ill, but as blessed with a romance whose only blemish is the tardiness of response in the beloved or the interference of third parties (often including the would-be therapist). The benefits of these disorders for the patient should not be forgotten, for they provide some solace for their loneliness, some support for their damaged self-esteem, and some purpose to their otherwise empty existences.[10]

A knowledgeable therapist with a trusting, long-term relationship with an erotomanic patient could to point out how his single-minded preoccupation is destroying his life, regardless of whether his beloved really loves him. The tragedy of stalking is not soley its effect on victims. With more research on stalking, perhaps better treatment can be found, and perpetrators could transfer their considerable talents and intellect to more contructive pursuits.

Even with adequate stalking laws, sentencing, and treatment, victims need additional legal safeguards to protect them against the chronic, toxic attention of their pursuers. Victims and potential victims—all of us—need to lobby for victim notification of the following:

1. An alleged stalker's release before trial or a stalker's release or escape from prison.

2. The termination of a stalker's mandatory treatment, since mentally ill stalkers who have been noncompliant with their medications in the past will likely become noncompliant in the future, especially when such compliance is no longer court-ordered.

Additionally, there is a clear need for educational materials and resources on stalking. Victims must be taught that stalking is a chronic activity, and not assume that because their stalkers are in treatment, the stalking itself has ceased. Treating clinicians should also be well aware that just because an erotomanic or other stalker asserts he is over his obsession, does not mean he is telling the truth. Since erotomanics in particular tend to be intelligent and well-educated, they may quickly understand that it is in their best interests to conceal their beliefs from their therapists, especially when the therapy itself was foisted upon them.

Victims and therapists are not the only ones who require education about stalking, and this is really why I finally decided to write a book about my experiences: It is crucial to publicize the effects of stalking on victims. It is only in this way that laws will be strengthened, effective treatments will be developed, and tougher sentencing imposed. As my story amply illustrates, police, prosecutors, and judges need to be better educated about the crime of stalking.

Concurs Deputy DA Saunders "What good is having a good law?" she asks. "It's worthless unless people know how to implement it and know how to argue it."[11]

Despite the presence of antistalking laws and the publicity of some particularly egregious stalking crimes, Fran and stalkers like her continue to receive leniency from law enforcement and the courts. This highlights the experiences of thousands of victims across the country. One stalking hotline volunteer who has spoken to 30,000 victims since 1991 says that victims tell him "every day" they are not getting anywhere with prosecuting their stalkers.[12]

Dr. Fein agreed that a unified effort to combat the crime of stalking is essential:

> *Certain principles appear pretty important. First, if you really want to prevent the behavior, you have to have multiple systems working together. That is, the police need to understand what they're doing and need to work both with the prosecutors and the courts who need to work with the mental health professionals because unless you have the systems working together, there is not going to be a coordinated effort to communicate to this person you cannot do that. This kind of system coordination is tough to do.*[13]

Since the criminalization of stalking behavior, many jurisdictions have become overwhelmed by victims filing stalking charges. One police spokesman characterized the explosive number of such arrests as "unbelievable."[14] The crime has, in fact, always been with us, not lurking in the shadows, but out in the open, daring the law to catch up. And while not there yet, the law has at last been trying. There is still a long way to go, however, in educating victims and potential victims, law enforcement, prosecution, and judges, in strengthening the existing laws and penalties, and in discovering improved treatment methods. Until we do, this plague will only spread.

As I wrote and researched this book, I spoke to victims of stalkers and erotomanics from all over the country and was repeatedly dismayed by the expansion of this problem into epidemic proportions. At a recent session on "Women in the Rabbinate" at the 1996 Annual National Meeting for Reform Rabbis, for example, when one woman rabbi, concerned about her ongoing experience with an erotomanic stalker, asked "Has anyone else been stalked?" 25 of the 32 women rabbis present told their stories.[15]

Stalking and erotomania have become almost commonplace in our society, and for this reason, are in danger of being accepted as such. As I speak out and lecture about stalking, I have heard many women excuse the behavior by saying, "All of us have sat in our cars in front of some man's house," but research belies the popular notion that stalking is just an extreme reaction in "normal" individuals. Deputy District Attorney Saunders, in fact, told me that before she took Madonna's stalker, Robert Hoskins, to court, she was contacted by reporters from all over the world asking, "How can you prosecute this poor man, after all, he merely was trespassing and he wound up getting shot."[16] Study after study identifies most stalkers as people with either serious mental illnesses or prior, unrelated criminal acts. Yet, even as the facts about stalking have gained more attention, the fiction surrounding stalking—that it is not a serious problem, or that it is a noble pursuit—remains. Popular culture is replete with portrayals of a relentless pursuer persisting in his noble endeavor despite rejection after rejection, at times even rewarded with the attainment of the elusive object in the end.

We experience this idea most vividly, perhaps, on screen and stage, but it is also a staple of comic books, songs, advertising, and other forms of entertainment we daily encounter. One of our culture's strongest subliminal messages may in fact be that stalking is an appropriate, even expected activity for the lovelorn.

In the world's most performed opera, Bizet's *Carmen*, the obsessive, pathological attachment of a soldier for the woman who spurns him is chronicled. His "love" leads him to stalk and then stab Carmen to death in the final act, but not before asserting the stalker's refrain that even in

1875 was all too familiar: If he can't have her, no one can. By then, her total disregard for his feelings, combined with her slatternly ways, are designed to make us feel sorry for *him* and his ruined career, rather than for her, the slaughtered one.

Stalking victims are sometimes dismissed in comical ways. Charlie Brown's little sister, Sally, has been relentlessly pursuing Linus for decades, narcissistically oblivious to his demands that she stop. Although he has not yet succumbed, we laugh at his futile attempts to get rid of her, juxtaposed against her erotomanic conviction of his love. And stalking is even perceived as sexy. Recently, a well-known jeans company has seemingly mounted a pro-stalking campaign. In the most egregious ad of the series, a car with Ohio plates drives onto a ferry and an attractive young woman gets out, wearing the advertiser's jeans. Seconds later, another car barely makes it to the dock in time, screeching to a halt as the equally attractive young man behind the wheel leaps onto the boat as it departs. He, too, is clad in the same brand. He follows the woman to the top deck, where, holding a locket in his hand, the stranger shyly tells her, "You dropped this." Pleased, as well as terribly attracted to him, she asks, "Where?" He responds with a smile, "Nebraska." As they sail away, the jeans' logo is superimposed onto the sunset.

Is it any wonder then that a stalker can even be perceived as a boost to a waning career? One fading female Hollywood celebrity vandalized her own beautiful black Porsche with nail polish. When the TMU detectives realized it was nonpermanent, a search of her home revealed the same color.[17] And how often have we seen movies, television, and songs portray a man bombarding a woman with telephone calls, flowers, and cards asking her out until her steadfast refusals turn to acceptance?

Stalkers, of course, can also nose around their victims while wearing one of the most popular scents in the world, Calvin Klein's *Obsession*.

Perhaps the tacit sanctioning of obsessional pursuits in the glamorous worlds of entertainment and advertising has contributed to their growing numbers in this country, as well as the increasing boldness with which these pursuits seem to occur. Could this partly explain why a nine-year-old Michigan boy was recently accused of stalking his ten-year-old neighbor, allegedly telephoning her 200 times over several months?[18] One forensic psychiatry clinic in New York City recently reported a threefold increase in the number of stalkers as a percentage of their total referrals.[19]

Advertising and entertainment change in response to societal norms, but they are also responsible for helping to create them. Women's groups have been up in arms, and understandably so, at how the so-called "waif models" have promoted the dangerous view to teenage girls than one can never be thin enough. Some responsible magazines have even refused to run ads with particularly anorexic-looking "beauties."

More awareness of the significant destructive force that stalking has become will lead to its also being viewed as a serious threat to women's (and men's) health. It was not long ago that domestic violence and child abuse were thought to be "family matters" and were treated as such. It was not until widely publicized educational campaigns leading to changes in laws and effective enforcement, that these threats emerged from behind closed doors. That the public remains uninformed about the curse of stalking is apparent by the fact that despite excellent evidence, some stalkers are still being acquitted by juries. One recent article that asked, "Why don't the new laws work?" concluded that "Victims. . .point primarily to leniency in the courts, inadequate sentencing, and a society that fails to appreciate what stalking really is—and the violence it can spawn."[20]

It is, in fact, due to the danger that Fran will always pose in our lives that Tim and I will probably not have children. Although many other considerations went into the decision-making process, when it came right down to it, I knew that I just could not give Fran that kind of hold on me. I still vividly remember the letter she wrote almost five years ago, saying she knew I was pregnant when I was not, and offering to put me in touch with a couple who wanted to adopt. If she would get rid of my delusional child, what might she do with my real one? I could see that any child we had would likely become, in psychiatric parlance, a neurotic mess, even more so than already decreed by having two parents who were psychiatrists. How could I let my child do the simple, everyday things essential to childhood, like play in the front yard, or wait for the schoolbus with the other kids? Would I have to tell every other child's parents whose home my child was playing in to watch for Fran? And if I did, wouldn't my child have no friends? As concerned as I am for our safety, I cannot imagine feeling that way about a child.

When I first read the statistic that erotomanic delusions last an average of 125 months,[21] it seemed like such a long time. Now, it has given me hope; I have little more than two years to go. I have no feelings for Fran. I am weary and frightened by her actions. I can understand when people say they feel sorry for her, just as I can when they say the same about me. In many ways, it is easier to sympathize with Fran than it is to be sympathetic toward me. At least I have a life. I *am* Fran's life. As long as she remains free, she will always remain a threat. If not to me, then to another woman or her husband and children. And while her delusions may end at some time in the future for me, they will probably never end for her. This is perhaps the greatest tragedy of all.

The worst part about erotomania is the not knowing. I could much more easily live with Fran's intrusions if I knew exactly what they would be and when they would occur. This is the most difficult part of the psychotic melodrama I have found myself a player in, for without benefit of audition or script, I simply do not know how, when, or whether it will ever end.

She has already begun contacting Tim.

Epilogue

Less than two months into her probation, in November 1996, Fran left a message on Tim's voice mail:

> *This is Fran Nightingale calling. I'm currently with the [mental health center] and your wife has an injunction, a permanent injunction against me and I don't know whether you are included in that or not. Anyway, I'm having difficulty and if you feel so moved, I would appreciate speaking with you.*

Fran left her telephone number. As soon as Tim heard the message, he called me.

"You're not going to believe this," he began.

But, I did. I knew that Fran could not possibly last the two years of her probation without contacting me. If anything, I was surprised it had taken her as long as two months. Yet I was concerned that she had never called Tim before and I hoped this did not presage her focusing on him as a new way to get to me.

I recorded this message for evidence as I had all the others, and called her probation officer (PO). She surprised me when she said this was not a violation of Fran's probation.

"But the statement I have from the court says she can't contact me directly or indirectly. Isn't this indirect contact?"

"No. It's only indirect if she asks your husband to give you a message for her. Something like this isn't covered. It's also not a violation of the restraining order you have against her." She explained that Tim would have to get his own restraining order against Fran. Otherwise, she could call him all she wanted.

"What can you do about this?" I asked. She replied that she would call Fran and tell her that contacting Tim was inappropriate.

"Will you at least make her come in to discuss it?"

"I just saw her last week," she protested.

"But unless she has consequences for her actions, like having to miss work and make another trip to see her P.O., it will be easier for her to continue to do these things." I explained. "Will you bring her in to talk about it?" I asked again, certain she would see the logic of my argument.

"No," she replied, leaving no doubt in my mind that once again, my stalker was not being taken seriously.

Tim and I discussed the feasibility of his getting a restraining order, but given how little protection such a piece of paper seemed to afford, especially since there was every reason to believe that getting one would only encourage Fran to harass him, we both agreed it would be a waste of time. It was then that I decided to try to change Colorado's antistalking law as soon as possible. With the elections recently over, the legislators could focus on the problems of their constituents. Waiting for more awareness about stalking was no longer an option. If the law could be amended to include people like Fran, Tim, as a family member, would automatically be protected from her contacts. The fact that technically, I had no idea how laws got changed, slowed me down only a little. After all, I hadn't even heard of erotomania almost eight years ago and now I was an expert—albeit a reluctant one—in the field.

I did find myself wishing, however, that I had paid more attention in my high school civics classes. I called the ADA whom I had dealt with most recently on Fran's case and asked him, "How would I go about changing the stalking law?" I could hear a muffled laugh, whether at my ignorance or my impertinence, I did not know, but he was very professional when he replied that I should probably start with my state senator.

I wrote to her, briefly outlining my situation and the absurdity of a law under which someone like Fran could not be classified as a stalker, simply because she had never made a threat. People like Fran *are* threats, I asserted. I also pointed out that most other states did not require a direct threat and that even the federal government recommended against such a requirement. Instead of the form letter from a staff member I expected, she telephoned me herself to say that she happened to be fashioning some victim's rights legislation and wondered if strengthening the antistalking law could fall under that. She promised to have the attorney she was working with in the Division of Criminal Justice contact me.

Meanwhile, of course, having seen that the legal system failed yet another one of her peculiar tests, Fran apparently decided to see how far she could push the probationary envelope and had someone else call me on her behalf a month later. I needed none of my psychiatric training to discern that the man who left the message on my voice mail at 5:30 p.m. on a Saturday evening was about as drunk as one could get and still manage to dial a telephone. Come to think of it, Fran probably dialed the number for him, herself.

"Yes, this is [his name]," he began. "I'm the execative—executive director of the crisis inervention program. I'm calling on behalf of Fran Nightingale and she jus' wanted me to express, ah Merry Christmas— wish Merry Christmas—and she was aware of a restraining order and so this was prob'ly the best that could be done. She was thinking. Merry Christmas."

I would have a Merry Christmas, indeed, if this meant Fran's probation could be revoked. The message had been left the weekend before the holiday and I did not pick it up until first thing that Monday morning. I immediately called Fran's PO who had already heard from her deluded charge. Fran had explained to her that she was trying to work out her obsession with me and that the call had enabled her to do just that.

"You don't really believe her, do you?" I asked.

"No, of course not," the PO replied.

"This does count as a probation violation, doesn't it?" I asked, hesitantly, not quite sure what the answer might be.

"Oh, yes," she said, firmly. The wave of relief I felt was soon washed over by incredulity at her next statement. "And I told Fran that whether or not I would ask the judge to revoke her probation and put her in jail was entirely up to you." I know she meant to reassure me that I finally had some control in this situation, and perhaps even to make up for her past inaction. But instead, the result apparently obvious only to me was that Fran would know exactly where to focus her rage and blame.

"Please don't tell her that," I said. "If she thinks I put her in jail, there's more of a likelihood that she'll hurt me when she gets out. By the way, when will she go to jail?"

"I have to send a letter to the judge to ask for her probation to be revoked. Then a hearing will be set and the judge will decide. She can get up to a year. In the meantime, you might want to call the police to see if they can arrest her on a restraining order violation." The PO insisted that there was no way for her to put Fran in jail immediately on the probation violation. I later found out she could have had Fran arrested if she felt the situation warranted it, but at the time, she told me that the only possibility of Fran's going to jail was if the police arrested her on a restraining order violating. In desperation, I called the police. I knew very well that Fran's indirect contact did not qualify. The officer who responded confirmed my fears, saying he really couldn't do anything, but suggested I petition the court for a "no contact" order, basically an amendment to the restraining order to cover such indirect contacts in the future.

I did not know what to do. Although I now believed that I should have never obtained a restraining order in the first place, once I started down that path, it seemed that any backtracking would be interpreted by Fran as an invitation. I went to the court to see what was involved. I needed to write a letter to the judge, stating the reasons I was seeking the order. He could grant the petition outright or hold a hearing. I could not imagine that there would be any question, so I took a gamble. A gamble I was to lose.

The week after Christmas, I received a call from the judge's clerk, the same judge who initially granted the permanent restraining order against Fran two-and-a-half years earlier. He wanted a hearing. Stunned, but wanting to get it over with, I agreed to his next available opening, two weeks away.

It was only once I recovered from the shock of the judge actually ordering a hearing, that I began to fully appreciate what I had set in motion. I could potentially see Fran for the first time in four years. The thought of actually being close to the woman who had tormented me from afar made me go weak in the knees, but not in the way I was sure Fran would have liked to think. I loathed the thought of facing her, both of seeing her and letting myself be seen by her. She would not have to conceal herself as she observed me, would not have to make do with fleeting glances as I walked to my car. I would be motionless and exposed for her full appreciation.

There was nothing to do but convince myself that she would not show up. I understood erotomania very well now. I knew that Fran would want to avoid face-to-face contact, perhaps even as much as I did. She had probably seen me many times without my knowing it in the last four years, why would she need to reveal herself to me now? Besides, if she did not show up to challenge my request, the judge would grant it on the spot. I let myself believe I had nothing to fear, even as I understood that such a belief was grounded in fear.

Although I did not really think I would see Fran, I knew I still had to plan for every contingency. The courthouse parking lot was a few minutes' walk from the building itself. It was a small lot and I was afraid that if I used it, Fran could easily discern which car I drove. Only cars with drivers in them were permitted to wait in front of the building, and then only for a few minutes. I did not know if Fran would easily recognize Tim and did not want to refresh her memory, so I vetoed his plan of accompanying me to court. I also did not want her to see which car he drove. A close girlfriend also offered to come with me for moral support, but I did not want Fran to start following her or to think that my friend and I were really lovers, thus embellishing her already deluded conviction that I was a lesbian.

I felt as if I was sinking into madness myself as I tried to anticipate my stalker's every possible move. To hold on to my sanity, I gave in to a little fantasy and pretended I was Jane Bond. I was able to devise a plan where I would park at another friend, Jim's, nearby store, get a cab and ask the driver to wait for me outside the courthouse. If Fran did show, she would not be able to follow me after the hearing. Even if she tried to do so, I would be long gone while she was still walking to the parking lot. The cab could then return me to Jim's store. Just in case she had managed to follow me, I would give Jim the keys to my car and have him drive it around the alleyway to the back entrance so that I could leave without her noticing. I congratulated myself that even while shaken, I was definitely not stirred, as I had managed to come up with such an ingenious plan. Too bad I wouldn't need it, for Fran would certainly not show up.

My confidence was belied by several sleepless nights before the court date. Tim, of course, slept soundly, only adding to my agitation. The morning of the hearing, I awoke with my now all too familiar grogginess to a day typical for a Colorado winter; clear skies, crisp mountain air, barely cold enough to jog the memory that it was really winter. I was reminded why I loved living here, and that I was trying to ensure that I could continue to do so, peacefully. Tim asked me again if I wanted him to come with me. I assured him I would be fine, and that I really did not expect Fran to be there. As if to postpone the inevitable, I was a few minutes late arriving at Jim's store. One of his employees told me he'd seen a cab wait and then leave. There was no time to call another one, so I asked Jim if he would drive me the few blocks to the courthouse. He did and I left him reading a book as he sat in his car in front of the entrance. I told him I thought it would only be a few minutes. As I walked toward the building, I looked around, feeling a little foolish. I was taking this clandestine operation thing a little too far. Still, I noticed that I did feel more uneasy than I had expected—tense and a little scared. Up until then, I had been preoccupied by being late, but now, I was free to worry about what I should have all along.

"She won't show," I told myself. "Be cool. Be Bond."

But who was that heavy-set woman with short gray hair walking toward me? She was wearing a lavender, full-length down coat left open over a plain skirt and blouse. She looked to be in her fifties, about ten years older than Fran would be by now, so I knew it couldn't be her. I also did not recall that Fran had gray hair, but it had been four years since I had last seen her. Then I remembered that she had looked quite a bit older than her age when we had first met. Could it really be? I squinted involuntarily in the woman's direction, willing myself to discover that I was mistaken, that it was not she, just some harmless older woman, probably on her way into court to pay a fine for keeping too many cats in her apartment.

But in that instant, the woman smiled right at me, her whole face lighting up, as if seeing a long-lost friend—or lover—and I knew. I felt that same suffocating fear I had experienced all those years before when I had last seen Fran in another parking lot.

I hurried into the building without looking back. The guard was having a problem with the metal detector and I felt someone step in behind me. Without turning around, I knew who it was. I started to panic. I wanted to scream at him, "She's stalking me! Let me through!" but I managed to maintain my "cover"—that of an unconcerned, disinterested citizen going to court. It was only a few moments before the guard indicated I could put my purse on the conveyor belt.

After passing through, I walked quickly into the designated courtroom. It was empty. Remembering the time Fran had sat behind me in a similar setting, I chose a spot all the way in the back against the wall. I sat down still wishing, but without any real hope remaining, that I had been mistaken. In less than a minute, Fran walked right in and sat a few rows ahead of me. We were alone in the courtroom.

I felt my heart race in fear. It was almost surreal that Fran and I were finally alone for the first time in years. I barely had time to ask myself, "How can this be happening?" when the judge's clerk appeared from a passageway behind his bench. She looked right at me, as if it was that easy to tell the hunter from the hunted and said, "Dr. Orion, the defendant's attorney, Mr. Barnes, is finishing up another hearing. The judge is waiting for him to arrive. It should only be a few minutes."

I was glad Fran was looking straight ahead at the clerk, because my jaw dropped open in disbelief, and panic was surely plainly showing in my eyes. The clerk disappeared behind the partition. An attorney! What chance did I stand against an attorney? I needed some air and this was clearly going to take more than a few minutes.

I ran outside and told Jim what had happened. Before I could ask if he would park the car and come in, he offered to do just that, putting his hand on my shoulder and asking if I was O.K. I thanked him and went back inside, realizing that I hadn't answered the question. Even while I had tried to convince myself that Fran would not show, I knew there was a possibility that she would and had tried to prepare myself. But it had never even occurred to me that she would bring an attorney.

When I got back into the courtroom, there was an armed guard standing in the back. I assumed the judge had asked him to wait there to reassure me. A compassionate touch I appreciated, and I did feel a little more secure. At least I would not be alone with her. I had barely sat down when the clerk reappeared and motioned me over to where she stood in the passageway.

"The judge says you can wait in our conference room, if you like." I thanked her and followed her in. I described Jim and asked if she would bring him in, as well, as I did not want him to think he was in the wrong courtroom.

Then, I surprised myself by asking her for a tissue. It was only when the words were out of my mouth that I realized I was crying. It had been so much easier to pretend that Fran did not frighten me when I had not been face-to-face with her in four years. Finally seeing her, and even more, seeing her see me, I just could not pretend any longer. I was no superspy. I was just a frightened, victimized woman who was about to face her tormentor. And her tormentor's attorney. Could he even get the restraining order itself invalidated so that I would lose what little protection I already had? I remembered that was what Fran had wanted done only a few months ago. Why, oh why, had I sought this further restriction?

I knew I had to pull myself together. I had to think what the attorney's objections might be and what my responses would be to them. As I did, I paced around the empty conference room, as if to work up the energy I needed to get steamed. It didn't take long. An attorney was taking money from a mentally ill woman so that she could stalk me better. How could he sleep at night? I was glad I was getting angry. I knew from experience that I thought much better on anger than on fear. Besides, I did not want Fran or her hired gun to see that she could make me cry.

By the time Jim came in, I was ready, even anxious to begin. When he told me he had recently been in the same court to pay a fine on a misdemeanor charge of urinating in public, that provided all the release of any remaining tension I needed. Jim had been at a party and relieved himself in the backyard. Unfortunately for him, the police had been called due to the noise at the house and had just gotten out of their patrol car while he was in mid-stream.

"I really appreciate your support, but if it's the same judge, you're outta here," I informed him. He did not think it was. At that moment, the judge himself poked his head into the conference room and let us know that Fran's attorney was there. I shot a warning glance at Jim and he shook his head imperceptibly, letting me know he did not recognize his honor, and then followed me into the courtroom.

Fran and her attorney, a man closer to my age than hers, were sitting in the front row of the spectator section. The guard had left and there was no one else in the courtroom. Jim and I sat down across the aisle from them. When the judge came in, Fran and her attorney moved up to the defendant's table and I did the same on the plaintiff's side. There was a lectern between the tables so that I could not see Fran at all, and could only see her attorney when he rose to address the court. So far, I had not looked at her once I entered the courthouse and I was relieved that now I could not see her or she me, even by accident.

The judge stated the name of the attorney for the record and asked me if I was appearing *pro se*. I assumed that meant I was representing myself and answered, "Yes." I had tried to come up with arguments against whatever her attorney might say. Now I began to wonder if I would even understand him.

Her attorney began by offering to stipulate to the motion I had filled out for the court if I was also willing to do so, so that he would not have to put me on the stand.

"Great," I thought. "I'll stipulate to it and then he'll hang me on some legal mumbo-jumbo I didn't even know I put in it."

But I did not want to have to take the stand and allow Fran to look at me unfettered. I did not know what to do. The judge must have had the same notion, because he said to Fran's attorney, "Let's see what you say about it, first." I relaxed a little for the first time that day and listened to her counsel. I could not believe what I heard.

"Your honor," he began. "My client would like the court to know that she is getting a handle on her obsessions. In fact, she saw her psychiatrist only this morning and is starting a new medication. She is truly sorry for the difficulties she has caused Dr. Orion," he asserted.

Did he have any idea how many times I had been told that in the past? He went on, "I do not believe you have jurisdiction for this motion."

"How so?" The judge asked.

"Section 327. . ." he continued.

I could feel myself losing focus. I did not know anything about sections or jurisdictions. I forced myself to listen to the rest of his argument. It seemed to hinge on the fact that to grant a "no contact" order, the judge had to have evidence that I would come to physical harm by the defendant, or that she had made threats against me, or "molested" me. The attorney concluded, "None of that is applicable in this case." The judge asked if he wished to present any more arguments and the attorney said no. I was astonished. I had thought of several he could have used against me and what I would have said in return. I realized in that moment what I should have known all along; that I, of course, knew more about stalking, more about erotomania and more about

Fran than her attorney did. Just the fact that she appeared to contest my motion and hired an attorney to help her do it, proved her intent to continue to stalk me. I felt my nerves calm. Completely.

The judge indicated he was going to render his opinion and, suddenly brimming with confidence, I interrupted, "Your honor. May I respond to counsel?" I hadn't watched every episode of *L.A. Law* for nothing.

The judge looked at me over the top of his reading glasses and said, "I'm going to rule in your favor. Do you still want to respond?"

I couldn't help smiling with relief and gratitude as I said, "No. Go ahead."

Her attorney laughed and I was immediately sorry. I had meant no disrespect. The judge ignored this minor break in protocol and told Fran's attorney he considered me molested by the defendant. Her attorney responded that the section's intent in using that word was to apply to cases of domestic violence. The judge replied he was going to interpret the word, "molest" in the way he saw fit and was granting the "no contact" order. The attorney tried another tack.

"Your honor," he asked, "are you still going to hold that my client maintain a distance of 500 yards from the plaintiff as you did in the original restraining order?"

"That's more than I usually do," the judge conceded, "but I think it's warranted in this case."

"Your honor, that's five football fields. Isn't that a bit excessive?" the attorney asked. It was the wrong thing to say.

"Counsel," he replied, "there have been far too many 'coincidences' in this case up to now. Far too many. Your client needs to understand that if she has any further contact with Dr. Orion, she will go to jail and it's not going to be a light sentence." Her attorney tried a yet different approach.

"Your honor, psychiatrists usually practice in groups. My client will be changing jobs soon and will be changing insurance. She may need to see another psychiatrist. Is she really to check within a five-football-field radius around her new psychiatrist's office to insure that Dr. Orion doesn't practice in the vicinity?" He raised his hands in a helpless gesture and his tone indicated he thought this was entirely unreasonable.

He continued, "Dr. Orion's current office is attached to a hospital. My client is mentally ill and needs periodic hospitalization. On one of her previous violations she had come to that hospital to seek treatment. Is that fair?" he asked, seemingly in all sincerity.

It was too much for me. Instantly, I forgot all my television training on courtroom procedure. I didn't wait for the judge to give me my turn. I just piped in, and I'm afraid my tone was a bit indignant.

"Your honor, the only thing that is unfair in this entire case is the seven-and-a-half years the defendant has stalked me." I told him about the time the judge in Tucson had made an exception to the restraining order, allowing Fran to come to my hospital once a week for a group that she never attended, instead leaving me a weekly letter.

I continued, "When she recently came to the hospital attached to my office, it was for an evaluation, not treatment, and I am sure it was no coincidence that she chose that hospital. She is currently not receiving any treatment there and with the many psychiatric institutions and numerous psychiatrists in this area, there is no reason for her to receive treatment anywhere near me. Given the resourcefulness and cunning the defendant has shown in stalking me all these years, I have no doubt she will be able to ascertain if I practice in a 500-yard radius of any future psychiatrist she sees. Besides, with her many violations of this court's order over the last two-and-a-half years, I think the onus should be on the defendant."

I did not know if the judge was going to censure me for my outburst, or suggest that I go to law school if I wanted to argue with him, but he just looked at the attorney and asked if he had any more to say. He did not and the judge told him, "The onus will be on the defendant."

Then he read the "no contact" order to Fran and her attorney. It was two pages long and basically stated that she was to have no contact whatsoever with me, directly or indirectly through enlisting other people. The order itself instructed the police that she was to be taken to jail for any violation and that the penalty could be up to two years and $5,000.

Whoever originally worded the preprinted statement, must have had experience with erotomania, for it stated that, "If you violate this order thinking that the other party has given you permission to do so, *you are wrong* and can be arrested and prosecuted."

After he read the order, the judge asked Fran if she agreed to its terms. I did not hear her answer. After several long moments in which her attorney could be heard prodding her from the other side of the lectern, Fran mumbled a hesitant, "Yes."

The judge left the courtroom and the clerk had us both sign the order. When she came over for my signature, she said I had to walk down the hall to another office to have the order officially filed. She told me the judge would keep Fran in the courtroom while I did so. I left feeling exhilarated that I had won, tempered by the knowledge that I really hadn't won a thing. I did not look back.

Fran would, of course, be granted yet another court-sanctioned contact with me. Still to be scheduled was the hearing for her probation violation the month before, when she had her drunken friend call to wish me a Merry Christmas on her behalf. But, buoyed by my "victory", I was no longer afraid of Fran or her attorney. Besides, I had something more positive to look forward to.

Three days later, I met with attorneys representing the Division of Criminal Justice and the state's District Attorneys Council. I was pleased to share with them what I felt was the cream of the crop in terms of other states' antistalking laws as well as excerpts from the federal guidelines. I also put them in touch with experts in other states for their advice on what changes to make in the law. The attorneys told me that amending the antistalking law should not be a problem this legislative session. After all, there is no stalkers' lobby clamoring for the rights of perpetrators. I could not have felt more satisfied, even as I continued to wait, in spite of numerous calls to my local district attorney's office, for the hearing on Fran's probation violation to even be scheduled. Two months since she had her drunken friend call me, and it was still not on the docket.

I will be testifying before the legislature on behalf of this amendment to the antistalking law in the next few months. I have also been asked to speak to DAs', victims' and law enforcement groups about the crime of stalking. I feel more hopeful now than I have in years. When Fran contacts me after the new law goes into effect, she will finally be charged with a felony—stalking. The reward I feel in knowing that through legislative changes, lectures and writing this book, I will directly help other stalking victims as well as educate others who work with them, makes me feel as if my erotomanic ordeal has been worth it—almost.

Notes

CHAPTER TWO: WHEN LOVE IS JUST A DELUSION

1. American Psychiatric Association, *Diagnostic Statistical Manual of Mental Disorders (DSM-III-R)*, 3rd ed., rev. (Washington, D.C.: American Psychiatric Association, 1989), 199.

2. R. L. Goldstein, "De Clérambault in Court: A Forensic Romance," *Bulletin of the American Academy of Psychiatry* and *the Law* 6 (1978): 36.

3. J. I. Teoh, "De Clerambault's Syndrome: A Review of 4 Cases," *Singapore Medical Journal* 13 (1972): 230.

4. J. R. Meloy and S. Gothard, "Demographic and Clinical Comparison of Obsessional Followers and Offenders with Mental Disorders," *American Journal of Psychiatry* 152 (1995): 258–63; R. Harmon, R. Rosner, and H. Owens, "Obsessional Harassment and Erotomania in a Criminal Court Population," *Journal of Forensic Sciences* 40 (1995): 191–92.

CHAPTER THREE: WHAT'S LOVE GOT TO DO WITH IT?

1. American Psychiatric Association, *Diagnostic Statistical Manual of Mental Disorders (DSM-III-R)*, 3rd ed., rev. (Washington, D.C.: American Psychiatric Association, 1989), 201.

2. M. Rudden, J. Sweeney, A. Frances, and M. Gilmore, "A Comparison of Delusional Disorders in Women and Men," *American Journal of Psychiatry* 140 (1983): 1575–78.

3. P. Mullen and M. Pathé, "The Pathological Extensions of Love," *British Journal of Psychiatry* 165 (1994): 614–23.

4. *Hard Copy,* 21 November 1994.

5. "Psychiatric and Sociological Aspects of Criminal Violence: An Interview with Park Elliott Dietz, M.D., Ph.D., Part 2," *Currents in Affective Illnesses XI* (May 1992), as reported in L. Gross, *To Have or to Harm* (New York: Warner Books, 1994), 157.

6. D. McNeil, "When Broadway's Lights go Down, Stalkers Appear," *The New York Times,* 23 April 1996, 37.

7. *Ibid.,* 40.

8. "Investigative Reports/Stalkers: Assassins Among Us," *Arts and Entertainment Network,* 29 October 1993.

9. A. A. Brill, *Psychoanalysis* (Philadelphia and London: W. B. Saunders Company, 1914), 189–92.

10. M. Zona, K. Sharma, and J. Lane, "A Comparative Study of Erotomanic and Obsessional Subjects in a Forensic Sample," *Journal of Forensic Sciences, JFSCA* 38 (1993): 894–903.

11. B. Rubenstein, "The Stalker," *Chicago* February 1992.

12. Gross, *To Have,* 158.

13. M. Thorpe, "In the Mind of a Stalker," *U.S. News & World Report,* 17 February 1992, 29.

14. "Profile: Part 1—Stalkers: Killer of Rebecca Schaeffer Interviewed," CBS News, *48 Hours,* 4 March 1996.

15. D. Evans, L. Jeckel, and N. Slott, "Erotomania: A Variant of Pathological Mourning," *Bulletin of the Menninger Clinic* 46 (1982): 507–20.

16. M. Hayes and B. O'Shea, "Erotomania in Schneider-Positive Schizophrenia: A Case Report," *British Journal of Psychiatry* 146 (1985): 661.

17. R. Markman and R. LaBrecque, *Obsessed: The Anatomy of a Stalker* (New York: Avon Books, 1995), 61.

18. Zona, "A Comparative Study," 894–903.

19. M. Zona, telephone interview with author, 28 June 1996.

20. R. Ward, telephone interview with author, 14 September 1996.

21. Zona, "A Comparative Study," 894–903.

22. P. Mullen, "Disorders of Passion," in *Troublesome Disguises: Underdiagnosed Psychiatric Syndromes,* eds. D. Bhugra and A. Munro (Oxford: Blackwell Science, in press).

23. *Ibid.*

24. J. R. Meloy and S. Gothard, "Demographic and Clinical Comparison of Obsessional Followers and Offenders with Mental Disorders," *American Journal of Psychiatry* 152 (1995): 258–63; Zona, "A Comparative Study," 894–903.

25. J. Clarke, *On Being Mad or Merely Angry: John W. Hinckley, Jr. and Other Dangerous People* (Princeton, N.J.: Princeton University Press, 1990), 49, 55.

26. *Ibid.,* 58–59.

27. *Ibid.,* 52.

28. P. McKenna, "Disorders with Overvalued Ideas," *British Journal of Psychiatry* 145 (1984): 579–85.

29. J. R. Meloy, "Unrequited Love and the Wish to Kill," *Bulletin of the Menninger Clinic* 53 (1989): 477–92.

30. J. R. Meloy, "The Psychodynamics of Stalking" (lecture presented at the Fifth Annual Threat Management Unit Conference, Los Angeles, CA, August 1995).

CHAPTER FOUR: *FUROR AMORIS*

1. I. Ray, ed., *A Treatise on the Medical Jurisprudence of Insanity,* 1st ed. (Boston, MA: Charles C. Little & J. Brown, 1838), 192–93.

2. G. Zilboorg, *A History of Medical Psychology* (London and New York: Norton, 1941), 159–60.

3. L. J. Rather, *Mind and Body in Eighteenth Century Medicine* (Berkeley and Los Angeles, CA: University of California Press, 1965), 228–29.

4. *Ibid.,* 151.

5. *Ibid.,* 179.

6. *Ibid.,* 150.

7. M. D. Enoch and W. H. Trethowan, "De Clérambault's Syndrome," in *Uncommon Psychiatric Syndromes,* 2d ed. (Bristol, England: John Wright, 1979), 18.

8. *Ibid.*

9. Zilboorg, *A History,* 81.

10. Enoch, "De Clérambault's," 18.

11. D. H. Tuke, ed., *A Dictionary of Psychological Medicine* (London: Churchill Livingstone, 1892), as cited in P. Bowden, "De Clérambault Syndrome," in *Principles and Practice of Forensic Psychiatry,* eds. R. Bluglass and P. Bowden (London: Churchill Livingstone, 1990), 821.

12. R. Krafft-Ebing, *Text-Book of Insanity,* trans. C. G. Chaddock (Philadelphia, PA: F. A. Davis Company, 1904), 409–11.

13. G. Savage, "Jealousy as a Symptom of Insanity," in *A Dictionary of Psychological Medicine,* ed. D. H. Tuke (London: Churchill Livingstone, 1892), 721–23.

14. *Ibid.,* 721–23.

15. J. Macpherson, *Mental Affections: An Introduction to the Study of Insanity* (London: Macmillan, 1899), 316.

16. L. Bianchi, *A Text-Book of Psychiatry,* trans. J. H. MacDonald (London: Baillière, Tindall and Cox, 1906), 607–13.

17. H. Baruk, "Delusions of Passion," in *Themes and Variations in European Psychiatry: An Anthology,* eds. S. R. Hirsch and M. Shepherd (Charlottesville: University Press of Virginia, 1974), 376.

18. Enoch, "De Clérambault's," 23.

19. T. Reik, *The Need to be Loved* (New York: Noonday Press, 1963), 45.

20. Baruk, "Delusions of Passion," 378–79.

21. S. Freud, *The Standard Edition of the Complete Psychological Works of Sigmund Freud,* vol. 12, *The Case of Schreber: Papers on Technique and Other Works,* trans. J. Strachey (London: Hogarth Press, 1958), 63.

22. Reik, "The Need," 50.

23. J. R. Meloy, "The Psychodynamics of Stalking" (lecture presented at the Fifth Annual Threat Management Unit Conference, Los Angeles, CA, August 1995).

24. J. Bowlby, *Attachment and Loss,* Vol. 1, Attachment (New York: Basic Books, 1969).

25. M. Pearl and B. Hoffmann, "Roberta Flack Stalker Goes Berserk in Court," *New York Post,* 23 November 1995, 7.

26. J. Clarke, *On Being Mad or Merely Angry: John W. Hinckley, Jr. and Other Dangerous People* (Princeton, NJ: Princeton University Press, 1990), 16.

27. R. Menzies, J. Fedoroff, C. Green, and K. Isaacson, "Prediction of Dangerous Behaviour in Male Erotomania," *British Journal of Psychiatry* 166 (1995): 530.

28. A. Pearce, "De Clérambault's Syndrome Associated with Folie à Deux," *British Journal of Psychiatry* 121 (1972): 117.

29. A. Stanley, "Erotomania: A Rare Disorder Runs Riot—In Men's Minds," *New York Times,* 10 November 1991, sec. 4, 2.

30. H. E. Lehman, "Unusual Psychiatric Disorders, Atypical Psychoses, and Brief Reactive Psychoses," in *Comprehensive Textbook of Psychiatry,* 3rd ed., eds. H. I. Kaplan, A. M. Freedman, and B. J. Sadock (Baltimore, MD: William and Wilkins, 1980), 155–56.

31. "Investigative Reports/Stalkers: Assassins Among Us," *Arts and Entertainment Network,* 29 October 1993.

32. H. Chiu, "Case report: Erotomania in the Elderly," *International Journal of Geriatric Psychiatry* 9 (1994): 674.

33. F. K. Rugeiyamu, "De Clérambault's Syndrome (Erotomania) in Tanzania," *British Journal of Psychiatry* 137 (1980): 102.

34. J. Nadarajah, N. Kidderminster, and C. Denman, "Erotomania in an Asian Male," *British Journal of Hospital Medicine* 45 (1991): 172.

35. M. A. Zona, K. K. Sharma, and J. Lane, "A Comparative Study of Erotomanic and Obsessional Subjects in a Forensic Sample," *Journal of Forensic Sciences, JFSCA* 38 (1993): 894–903.

36. J. Meyers and J. R. Meloy, "Discussion of 'A Comparative Study of Erotomanic and Obsessional Subjects in a Forensic Sample,'" *Journal of Forensic Sciences, JFSCA* 39 (1994): 905–7.

37. A. C. Garza-Guerrero, "Culture Shock: Its Mourning and the Vicissitudes of Identity," *Journal of the American Psychoanalytic Association* 22 (1974): 410.

38. Meyers, "Discussion," 906.

38. *Ibid.*

CHAPTER FIVE: RESTRAINT

1. D., P., K., and J. Lennon, *Same Song—Separate Voices: The Collective Memoirs of the Lennon Sisters* (Santa Monica, CA: Roundtable Publishing, 1985), 246.

2. United Press International, "Lennons' Father is Slain on Coast," *The New York Times,* 13 August 1969, 48–49.

3. "9 Wants to Know," KUSA, Denver, 6 O'clock News, 2 May 1995.

4. *Ibid.*

5. S. Lindsay, "Breast Surgery Ended Friendship, Man Says," *Rocky Mountain News,* 17 March 1995, 12A.

6. "9 Wants to Know," KUSA.

7. Lindsay, "Breast Surgery," 12A.

8. "9 Wants to Know," KUSA.

9. *Ibid.*

CHAPTER SIX: NO ORDER IN THE COURT

1. P. Mullen and M. Pathé, "Stalking and the Pathologies of Love," *Australian and New Zealand Journal of Psychiatry* 28 (1994): 475.

2. M. Zona, telephone interview with author, 28 June 1996.

3. M. Zona, K. Sharma, and J. Lane, "A Comparative Study of Erotomanic and Obsessional Subjects in a Forensic Sample," *Journal of Forensic Sciences, JFSCA* 38 (1993): 894–903.

4. M. Pathé and P. Mullen, "A Study of the Impact of Stalkers on their Victims," *British Journal of Psychiatry,* in press.

5. *Ibid.*

6. E. von Heussen-Countryman, personal correspondence with author, 27 August 1996.

7. Zona, interview.

8. B. Hammell, telephone interview with Author, 17 May 1996.

9. M. Puente, "Legislators Tackling the Terror of Stalking," *USA Today,* 21 July 1992, 9A; M. Schaum and K. Parrish, *Stalked: Breaking the Silence on the Crime of Stalking in America* (New York: Pocket Books, 1995), 133–38.

10. A. Simakis, "Why the Stalking Laws Aren't Working," *Glamour,* May 1996, 247.

11. R. Saunders, telephone interview with author, 29 July 1996.

12. Amber W., telephone interview with author, 20 May 1996.

13. Mullen and Pathé, "Stalking and the Pathologies," 475.

14. "Tracking the Star Stalkers," *Geraldo,* 20 March 1990.

15. *Ibid.*

16. R. Goodale, *Immediate Measures if You Are Being Stalked* (Tampa, FL: Survivors of Stalking, 1995).

17. Mullen and Pathé, "Stalking and the Pathologies," 475.

18. Pathé and Mullen, "A Study of the Impact."

19. Anonymous psychiatrist, telephone interview with author, 14 May 1996.

20. "Stalkers, their Victims, and the Law," *Larry King Live,* 12 May 1993.

21. M. Eftimiades, "Leaving Town Alive," *People,* 17 May 1993, 67.

22. Threat Management Unit, *Security Recommendations.*

23. National Victim Center, *Helpful Guide for Stalking Victims* (Arlington, VA.: National Victim Center, 1994), 3–5.

24. Goodale, *Immediate Measures.*

CHAPTER SEVEN: STALKING THE STALKERS

1. M. Thorpe, "In the Mind of a Stalker," *U.S. News & World Report,* 17 February 1992, 28.

2. P. Tjaden and N. Thoennes, "Stalking in America: How Big is The Problem?" (paper presented at the Annual Meeting of the American Society of Criminology, Chicago, IL, November 1996).

3. E. Royce, "Keynote Address," (lecture presented at the Fifth Annual Threat Management Unit Conference, Los Angeles, CA, August 1995).

4. J. Silverman, "A Victim's Perspective on Stalking" (lecture presented at the Fifth Annual Threat Management Conference, Los Angeles, CA, August 1995).

5. D. Raymond, telephone interview with author, 10 June 1996.

6. D. Raymond, "How to Manage a Stalking Case" (lecture presented at the Fifth Annual Threat Management Unit Conference, Los Angeles, CA, August 1995).

7. S. Braun and C. Jones, "Victim, Suspect from Different Worlds: Actress' Bright Success Collided with Obsession," *Los Angeles Times,* 23 July 1989, 1.

8. Raymond, interview.

9. M. Zona, K. Sharma, and J. Lane, "A Comparative Study of Erotomanic and Obsessional Subjects in a Forensic Sample," *Journal of Forensic Sciences, JFSCA* 38 (1993): 894–903.

10. D. Ellis, "Nowhere To Hide," *People,* 17 May 1993, 63; R. Harmon, R. Rosner and H. Owens, "Obsessional Harassment and Erotomania in a Criminal Court Population," *Journal of Forensic Sciences* 40 (1995): 188–96.

11. Raymond, interview.

12. *Ibid.*

13. R. Saunders, telephone interview with author, 29 July 1996.

14. W. De Cuir, telephone interview with author, 27 June 1996.

15. E. von Heussen-Countryman, personal correspondence with author, 24 June 1996.

16. E. von Heussen-Countryman, interview with author, Los Angeles, CA, 24 August 1995.

17. Von Heussen-Countryman, correspondence.

18. L. Margie., telephone interview with author, 10 July 1996 and personal correspondence with author, 27 June 1996.

CHAPTER EIGHT: NOWHERE TO HIDE

1. "Investigative Reports/Stalkers: Assassins Among Us," *Arts and Entertainment Network,* 29 October 1993.

2. J. Monahan, *The Clinical Prediction of Violent Behavior,* softcover ed. (Northvale, NJ: Jason Aronson, Inc., 1995), 60.

3. J. Clarke, *On Being Mad or Merely Angry: John W. Hinkley, Jr. and Other Dangerous People* (Princeton, NJ: Princeton University Press, 1990), 108.

4. *Ibid.,* 103. Samuel Byck, Sara Jane Moore, Lee Harvey Oswald, Lynette "Squeaky" Fromme and John Hinckley, Jr.

5. Department of Justice, National Institute of Justice, *Secret Service Exceptional Case Study Project* by R. Fein, and B. Vossekuil (Washington, DC: National Institute of Justice, in press).

6. Clarke, *On Being Mad,* 105.

7. R. Menzies, J. Fedoroff, C. Green, and K. Isaacson, "Prediction of Dangerous Behaviour in Male Erotomania," *British Journal of Psychiatry* 166 (1995): 529-36.

8. R. Fein, telephone interview with author, 10 October 1996.

9. Department of Justice, National Institute of Justice, *Domestic Violence, Stalking, and Antistalking Legislation: An Annual Report to Congress Under the Violence Against Women Act* (Washington, DC: U.S. Department of Justice, April, 1996), 5.

10. Fein, interview.

11. S. Braun and C. Jones, "Victims, Suspect from Different Worlds: Actress' Bright Success Collided with Obsession," *Los Angeles Times,* 23 July 1989, 38.

12. R.L. Goldstein, "More Forensic Romances: De Clérambault's Syndrome in Men," *Bulletin of the American Academy of Psychiatry and the Law* 15 (1987): 271.

13. Braun, "Victim, Suspect," 1.

14. R. Markman and R. LaBrecque, *Obsessed: The Anatomy of a Stalker* (New York: Avon Books, 1995), 203.

15. J.R. Meloy, "Unrequited Love and the Wish to Kill," *Bulletin of the Menniger Clinic* 53 (1989): 484.

16. M. Brenner, "Erotomania," *Vanity Fair,* September 1991, 188-265.

17. P. Dietz, "Threats and Attacks Against Public Figures" (paper presented at the annual Meeting of the American Academy of Psychiatry and the Law, San Francisco, CA, October 1988), as reported in Meloy, *Unrequited Love,* 479.

18. M. Zona, telephone interview with the author, 28 June 1996.

19. S. Hays, "Stalking Fame," *Los Angeles Times,* 17 October 1990, E2.

20. R. Saunders, telephone interview with author, 29 July 1996.

21. P. Mullen and M. Pathé, "Stalking and the Pathologies of Love," *Australian and New Zealand Journal of Psychiatry* 28 (1994): 469-77.

22. *Ibid.*

23. *Ibid.*

24. J.R. Meloy, telephone interview with the author, 21 June 1996.

25. *Tarasoff v. Board of Regents* (1976).

26. R.L. Goldstein, "De Clérambault in Court: A Forensic Romance," *Bulletin of the American Academy of Psychiatry and the Law* 6 (1978): 36-40.

27. Meloy, interview.

28. J.R. Meloy, *Violent Attachments* (Northvale, NJ: Jason Aronson Inc., 1992) 324.

29. P. Taylor, B. Mahendra, and J. Gunn, "Erotomania in Males," *Psychological Medicine* 13 (1983): 645-50.

30. Menzies, "Prediction of Dangerous Behavior."

31. R. Saunders, "Criminal Justice Management of Stalking Cases," (presented at the Fifth Annual Threat Management Unit Conference, Los Angeles, CA, August 1995).

32. Mullen, "Stalking."

33. L. Kok, M. Cheang and K. Chee, "De Clérambault Syndrome and Medical Practitioners: Medico Legal Implications," *Singapore Medical Journal,* 35 (1994): 487-8.

34. Department of Justice, National Institute of Justice, *Threat Assessment: An Approach to Prevent Targeted Violence,* by R. Fein, B. Vossekuil and G. Holden (Washington, DC: National Institute of Justice, September, 1995), 2.

35. J. McDonald, *Homicidal Threats* (Springfield, IL: Charles C. Thomas, 1968).

36. D. Bacon, "When Fans Turn into Fanatics, Nervous Celebs Call for Help from Security Expert Gavin de Becker," *People,* 12 February 1990, 103.

37. P. Dietz, D. Matthews, C. Van Duyne, D. Martell, C. Parry, T. Stewart, J. Warren and J. Crowder, "Threatening and Otherwise Inappropriate Letters to Hollywood

Celebrities," *Journal of Forensic Science* 36 (1991): 185–209; P. Dietz, D. Matthews, D. Martell, T. Stewart, D. Hrouda, and J. Warren, "Threatening and Otherwise Inappropriate Letters to Members of the United States Congress," *Journal of Forensic Science,* 36 (1991): 1445–68.

38. V. Geberth, "Stalkers," *Law and Order,* October (1992), 143.

39. J. R. Meloy, personal correspondence, 15 January, 1997.

40. J. R. Meloy, "Stalking (Obsessional Following): A Review of Some Preliminary Studies," *Agression and Violent Behavior* 1 (1996): 158, 160.

41. R. Harmon, R. Rosner, and H. Owens, "Obsessional Harassment and Erotomania in a Criminal Court Population," *Journal of Forensic Sciences* 40 (1995): 188-196.

42. Geberth, "Stalkers,", 138.

43. K. McAnaney, L. Curliss and C. Abeyta-Price, "From Imprudence to Crime: Anti-Stalking Laws," *Notre Dame Law Review* 68 (1993): 876.

44. Fein, interview.

45. B. Trebilcock, "I Love You To Death," *Redbook,* March 1992, 113.

46. Meloy, interview.

47. G. de Becker, correspondence with author, 17 June 1996.

48. Anonymous security expert, personal correspondence with author, 10 June 1996.

49. Anonymous security expert, personal correspondence with author, 25 May 1996.

50. Anonymous security expert, personal correspondence with author, 24 June 1996.

51. Anonymous security expert, personal correspondence with author, 18 May 1996.

CHAPTER NINE: THE EVOLUTION OF
ANTISTALKING LEGISLATION

1. B. Trebilcock, "I Love You To Death," *Redbook,* March 1992.

2. M. Schaum and K. Parrish, *Stalked: Breaking the Silence on the Crime of Stalking in America,* (New York: Pocket Books, 1995), 92-3.

3. M. Corwin, "When the Law Can't Protect," *Los Angeles Times,* 8 May 1993, 1.

4. E. Royce, telephone interview with author, 15 July 1996.

5. California Legislature, *Stalking Law, 1990: Hearings on SB 2184 Before the Assembly Committee on Public Safety* (Sacramento, 3 July 1990), 2.

6. Royce, interview.

7. S. O'Malley, "Nowhere to Hide: Why the New Stalking Laws Still Don't Protect Women," *Redbook,* November 1996, 138.

8. "Investigative Reports/Stalkers: Assassins Among Us," *Arts and Entertainment Network,* 29 October 1993.

9. U. S. Department of Justice, Bureau of Justice Assistance, *Regional Seminar Series on Developing and Implementing Antistalking Codes* (Washington, DC: U.S. Department of Justice, June 1996), 11.

10. U. S. Department of Justice, National Institute of Justice, *Domestic Violence, Stalking, and Antistalking Legislation: An Annual Report to Congress Under the Violence Against Women Act* (Washington, DC: U.S. Department of Justice, April 1996).

11. D. Raymond, telephone interview with author, 10 June 1996.

12. R. Saunders, telephone interview with author, 29 July 1996.

13. U. S. Department of Justice, National Criminal Justice Association, *Project to Develop a Model Anti-Stalking Code for States* (Washington, DC: U.S. Department of Justice, October 1993), 43-5.

14. R. Fein, telephone interview with author, 10 October 1996.

15. Department of Justice, Bureau of Justice Assistance, *Regional Seminar Series,* 11.

16. Press conference of Kathleen Gallagher Baty (Washington, DC: Office of Congressman Ed Royce, 7 May 1996).

17. Royce, interview.

18. M. Beck, et al., "Murderous Obsession," *Newsweek,* 13 July 1992, 60.

CHAPTER TEN: FOREVER EROTOMANIC

1. M. Lait, "Skater Confronts Her Alleged Tormentor," *Los Angeles Times,* 12 March 1992, A3.

2. M. Brenner, "Erotomania," *Vanity Fair,* September, 1991.

3. J. R. Meloy, telephone interview with author, 14 June 1996.

4. S. Dougherty, L. Stambler, J. Schnaufer, and B. Donahue, "Material Witness," *People,* 15 January 1996, 48-49.

5. Meloy, interview.

6. J. R. Meloy, personal correspondence with author, 21 November 1996.

7. R. Menzies, J. Fedoroff, C. Green and K. Isaacson, "Prediction of Dangerous Behaviour in Male Erotomania," *British Journal of Psychiatry* 166 (1995): 530.

8. U.S. Department of Justice, Bureau of Justice Assistance, *Regional Seminar Series on Developing and Implementing Antistalking Codes* (Washington, DC: U.S. Department of Justice, June 1996), 5.

9. R. Fein, telephone interview with author, 10 October 1996.

10. P. Mullen, "Disorders of Passion," in *Troublesome Disguises: Underdiagnosed Psychiatric Syndromes,* eds. D. Bhugra and A. Munro (Oxford: Blackwell Science, in press).

11. R. Saunders, telephone interview with author, 29 July 1996.

12. R. Ward, telephone interview with author, 14 September 1996.

13. Fein, interview.

14. P. Davis, "New Stalking Law Flushing the Crime into the Open in Virginia," *Washington Post,* 24 January 1993, B1.

15. Anonymous Rabbi, telephone interview with author, 29 April 1996.

16. Saunders, interview.

17. D. Raymond, "How to Manage a Stalking Case" (lecture presented at the Fifth Annual Threat Management Unit Conference, Los Angeles, CA, August 1995).

18. Associated Press, "9-Year-Old Accused of Stalking Schoolmate," *The New York Times,* 8 March 1996, 21.

19. R. Harmon, R. Rosner and H. Owens, "Obsessional Harassment and Erotomania in a Criminal Court Population," *Journal of Forensic Sciences* 40 (1995): 188-96.

20. O'Malley, "Nowhere," 122.

21. M. Zona, K. Sharma and J. Lane, "A Comparative Study of Erotomanic and Obsessional Subjects in a Forensic Sample," *Journal of Forensic Sciences, JFSCA* 38 (1993): 894-903.

Bibliography

BOOKS

American Psychiatric Association. *Diagnostic Statistical Manual of Mental Disorders (DSM-IV)*. 4th ed. Washington, DC: American Psychiatric Association, 1994.

Arieti, S., ed. *American Handbook of Psychiatry*. Vol. 1. New York: Basic Books, 1959.

Baruk, H. "Delusions of Passion." In *Themes and Variations in European Psychiatry: An Anthology*, edited by S. R. Hirsch and M. Shepherd. Charlottesville, VA: University Press of Virginia, 1974.

Bianchi, L. *A Text-Book of Psychiatry*. Translated by J. H. MacDonald. London: Baillière, Tindall and Cox, 1906.

Blackstone, Sir William. *Commentaries on the Laws of England*. Vol. 2, 2nd ed., rev. Chicago, IL: Callaghan and Company, 1873.

Bowden, P. "de Clérambault Syndrome." In *Principles and Practice of Forensic Psychiatry*, edited by R. Bluglass and P. Bowden. London: Churchill Livingstone, 1990.

Bowlby J. *Attachment and Loss*. Vol. 1, *Attachment*. New York: Basic Books, 1969.

Brill, A. A. *Psychoanalysis*. Philadelphia and London: W. B. Saunders Company, 1914.

Clarke, J. *On Being Mad or Merely Angry: John W. Hinckley, Jr. and Other Dangerous People*. Princeton, NJ: Princeton University Press, 1990.

De Clérambault, C. G. "Les Psychoses Passionelles." In *Oeuvres Psychiatriques*, edited by J. Fretet. Paris: Presses Universitaires de France, 1942.

Enoch, M. D. and Trethowan, W. H. "De Clérambault's Syndrome." In *Uncommon Psychiatric Syndromes*, edited by M. D. Enoch and W. H. Trethowan. 2d ed. Bristol, England: John Wright and Sons, 1979.

Freud, S. *The Standard Edition of the Complete Psychological Works of Sigmund Freud*. Vol. 12, *The Case of Schreber: Papers on Technique and Other Works*. Translated by J. Strachey. London: Hogarth Press, 1958.

Gross, L. *To Have or To Harm*. New York: Warner Books, 1994.

Hunter R. and Macalpine, I. *Three Hundred Years of Psychiatry*. London: Oxford University Press, 1963.

Krafft-Ebing, R. *Text-Book of Insanity.* Translated by C. G. Chaddock. Philadelphia, PA: F. A. Davis Company, 1904.

Kretschmer, E. "The Sensitive Delusion of Reference." In *Themes and Variations in European Psychiatry: An Anthology,* edited by S. R. Hirsch and M. Shepherd. Charlottesville, VA: University Press of Virginia, 1974.

Lehman, H. E. "Unusual Psychiatric Disorders, Atypical Psychoses, and Brief Reactive Psychoses." In *Comprehensive Textbook of Psychiatry,* edited by H. I. Kaplan, A. M. Freedman, and B. J. Sadock. 3rd ed. Baltimore, MD: William and Wilkins, 1980.

Lennon, D., P., K. and J. *Same Song—Separate Voices: The Collective Memoirs of the Lennon Sisters.* Santa Monica, CA: Roundtable Publishing, Inc., 1985.

Low, P. L., Jeffries, J.C.L., and Bonnie, R. *The Trial of John W. Hinckley, Jr.: A Case Study in the Insanity Defense.* Westbury, NY: Foundation Press, 1986.

Macpherson, J. *Mental Affections: An Introduction to the Study of Insanity.* London: Macmillan, 1899.

Markman, R. and LaBrecque, R. *Obsessed: The Anatomy of a Stalker.* New York: Avon Books, 1995.

McDonald, J. *Homicidal Threats.* Springfield, IL: Charles C. Thomas, 1986.

Meloy, J. R. *Violent Attachments.* Northvale, NJ: Jason Aronson, Inc., 1992.

Monahan, J. *The Clinical Prediction of Violent Behavior.* Softcover ed. Northvale, NJ: Jason Aronson, Inc., 1995.

Mullen, P. "Disorders of Passion." In *Troublesome Disguises: Underdiagnosed Psychiatric Syndromes,* edited by D. Bhugra and A. Munro. Oxford: Blackwell Science, in press.

Rather, L. J. *Mind and Body in Eighteenth Century Medicine.* Berkeley and Los Angeles, CA: University of California Press, 1965.

Ray, I., ed. *A Treatise on the Medical Jurisprudence of Insanity.* 1st ed. Boston, MA: Charles C. Little & J. Brown, 1838.

Reik, T. *The Need to be Loved.* New York: Noonday Press, 1963.

Savage, G. "Jealousy as a Symptom of Insanity." In *A Dictionary of Psychological Medicine,* edited by D. H. Tuke. London: Churchill Livingstone, 1892.

Schaum, M. and Parrish, K. *Stalked: Breaking the Silence on the Crime of Stalking in America.* New York: Pocket Books, 1995.

Scheler, M. *The Nature of Sympathy.* Translated by P. Heath. London, England: Routledge & Kegan Paul, 1954.

Tuke, D. H., ed. *A Dictionary of Psychological Medicine.* London: Churchill Livingstone, 1892. As reported in P. Bowden, "De Clérambault Syndrome." In *Principles and Practice of Forensic Psychiatry,* edited by R. Bluglass and P. Bowden London: Churchill Livingstone, 1990.

Zilboorg, G. *A History of Medical Psychology.* London and New York: Norton, 1941.

JOURNAL ARTICLES

Apter, A., Plutchik, R., Sevy, S. Korn, M., Brown, S., and van Praag, H. "Defense Mechanisms in Risk of Suicide and Risk of Violence." *American Journal of Psychiatry* 146 (1989): 1027–31.

Chiu, H. "Case Report: Erotomania in the Elderly." *International Journal of Geriatric Psychiatry* 9 (1994): 673–74.

Dietz, P. "Threats and Attacks Against Public Figures." Paper presented at the Annual Meeting of the American Academy of Psychiatry and the Law, San Francisco, CA, October 1988. Reported in J. R. Meloy, "Unrequited Love and the Wish to Kill." *Bulletin of the Menninger Clinic* 53 (1989): 479.

Dietz, P., Matthews, D., Martell, D., Stewart, T., Hrouda, D., and Warren, J. "Threatening and Otherwise Inappropriate Letters to Members of the United States Congress." *Journal of Forensic Science* 36 (1991): 1445–68.

Dietz, P., Matthews, D., Van Duyne, C., Martell, D., Parry C., Stewart, T., Warren, J., and Crowder, J. "Threatening and Otherwise Inappropriate Letters to Hollywood Celebrities." *Journal of Forensic Science* 36 (1991): 185–209.

Dunlop, J. "Does Erotomania Exist Between Women?" *British Journal of Psychiatry* 153 (1988): 830–33.

El-Assra, A. "Erotomania in a Saudi Woman." *British Journal of Psychiatry* 155 (1989): 553–55.

Evans, D., Jeckel, L., and Slott, N. "Erotomania: A Variant of Pathological Mourning." *Bulletin of the Menninger Clinic* 46 (1982): 507–20.

Feder, S. "Clérambault in the Ghetto: Pure Erotomania Reconsidered." *International Journal of Psychoanalytic Psychotherapy* 2 (1973):240–47.

Gagné, P. and Desparois, L. "L'érotomanie mâle: Un type de harcèlement sexual dangereux" (Male erotomania: A form of dangerous sexual harassment). *Canadian Journal of Psychiatry* 40 (1995): 136–41.

Garza-Guerrero, A. C. "Culture Shock: Its Mourning and the Vicissitudes of Identity." *Journal of the American Psychoanalytic Association* 22 (1974): 408–29.

Geberth, V. "Stalkers." *Law and Order*, October 1992, 138–43.

Goldstein, R. L. "De Clérambault in Court: A Forensic Romance." *Bulletin of the American Academy of Psychiatry and the Law* 6 (1978): 36–40.

Goldstein, R. L., "More Forensic Romances: De Clérambault's Syndrome in Men." *Bulletin of the American Academy of Psychiatry and the Law* 15 (1987): 267–74.

Harmon, R., Rosner, R., and Owens, H. "Obsessional Harassment and Erotomania in a Criminal Court Population." *Journal of Forensic Sciences* 40 (1995): 188–96.

Hayes, M. and O'Shea, B. "Erotomania in Schneider-Positive Schizophrenia: A Case Report." *British Journal of Psychiatry* 146 (1985): 661–63.

Kok, L., Cheang, M., and Chee, K. "De Clérambault Syndrome and Medical Practitioners: Medico Legal Implications." *Singapore Medical Journal* 35 (1994): 486–89.

McAnaney, K., Curliss, L., and Abeyta-Price, C. "From Imprudence to Crime: Anti-Stalking Laws." *Notre Dame Law Review* 68 (1993): 819–900.

McKenna, P. "Disorders with Overvalued Ideas." *British Journal of Psychiatry* 145 (1984): 579–85.

Meloy, J. R. "Stalking (Obsessional Following): A Review of Some Preliminary Studies." *Aggression and Violent Behavior* 1 (1996): 147–62.

Meloy, J. R. "Unrequited Love and the Wish to Kill." *Bulletin of the Menninger Clinic* 53 (1989): 477–92.

Meloy, J. R. and Gothard, S. "Demographic and Clincial Comparison of Obsessional Followers and Offenders with Mental Disorders." *American Journal of Psychiatry* 152 (1995): 258–63.

Menzies, R., Fedoroff, J., Green, C. , and Isaacson, K. "Prediction of Dangerous Behavior in Male Erotomania." *British Journal of Psychiatry* 166 (1995): 529–36.

Meyers, J. and Meloy, J. R. "Discussion of 'A Comparative Study of Erotomanic and Obsessional Subjects in a Forensic Sample.'" *Journal of Forensic Sciences , JFSCA* 39 (1994): 905–7.

Mullen, P. and Pathé, M. "Stalking and the Pathologies of Love." *Australian and New Zealand Journal of Psychiatry* 28 (1994): 469–77.

Mullen, P and Pathé, M. "The Pathological Extensions of Love." *British Journal of Psychiatry* 165 (1994): 614–23.

Nadarajah, J., Kidderminster, N., and Denman, C. "Erotomania in an Asian Male." *British Journal of Hospital Medicine* 45 (1991): 172.

Noone, J. A. and Cockhill, L. "Erotomania: The Delusion of Being Loved." *American Journal of Forensic Psychiatry* 8 (1987): 23–31.

Pathé, M. and Mullen, P. "A Study of the Impact of Stalkers on their Victims." *British Journal of Psychiatry*, in press.

Pearce, A. "De Clérambault's Syndrome Associated with Folie à Deux." *British Journal of Psychiatry* 121 (1972): 116–17.

Raskin, D. E., and Sullivan, K. E. "Erotomania." *American Journal of Psychiatry* 131 (1974): 1033–35.

Retterstol, N. and Opjordsmoen, S. "Erotomania—Erotic Self-Reference Psychosis in Old Maids." *Psychopathology* 24 (1991): 388–97.

Rudden, M., Sweeney, J., Frances, A., and Gilmore, M. "A Comparison of Delusional Disorders in Women and Men." *American Journal of Psychiatry* 140 (1983): 1575–78.

Rugeiyamu, F. K. "De Clérambault's Syndrome (Erotomania) in Tanzania." *British Journal of Psychiatry* 137 (1980): 102.

Salame, L. "A National Survey of Stalking Laws: A Legislative Trend Comes to the Aid of Domestic Violence Victims and Others." *Suffolk University Law Review* 27 (1993): 67–111.

Schachter, M. "Erotomanie ou conviction delirante d'être aime. Contribution a la psychopathologie de le vie amoureuse" (Erotomania or the delusional conviction of being loved. A contribution to psychopathology). *Annales Mèdico-Psychologiques* 1 (1977): 729–47.

Segal, J. "Erotomania Revisited: From Kraepelin to *DSM–III-R.*" *American Journal of Psychiatry* 146 (1989): 1261–66.

Taylor, P., Mahendra, B,. and Gunn, J. "Erotomania in Males." *Psychological Medicine* 13 (1983): 645–50.

Teoh, J. I. "De Clérambault's Syndrome: A Review of 4 Cases. *Singapore Medical Journal* 13 (1972): 227–34.

Signer, S. F. " 'Les Psychosis Passionelles': A Review of de Clérambault's cases and Syndrome with Respect to Mood Disorders." *Journal of Psychiatry and Neuroscience* 16 (1991): 81–90.

Signer, S. F. "de Clérambault's Concept of Erotomania and its Place in His Thought." *History of Psychiatry* 2 (1991): 409–417.

Zona, M., Sharma, K. , and Lane, J. "A Comparative Study of Erotomanic and Obsessional Subjects in a Forensic Sample." *Journal of Forensic Sciences, JFSCA* 38 (1993): 894–903.

NEWSPAPER AND MAGAZINE ARTICLES

Anderson, J. "Virginia Targets Stalkers." *Washington Post,* 10 February 1992, D5.

Associated Press. "Women Winning Legal Help Against Stalkers." *Chicago Tribune,* 16 April 1992, 30.

Associated Press. "9-Year-Old Accused of Stalking Schoolmate." *The New York Times,* 8 March 1996, 21.

Bacon, D. "When Fans Turn into Fanatics, Nervous Celebs Call for Help from Security Expert Gavin de Becker." *People,* 12 February 1990.

Beck, M., et.al. "Murderous Obsession." *Newsweek,* 13 July 1992.

Braun, S. and Jones, C. "Victim, Suspect from Different Worlds: Actress' Bright Success Collided with Obsession." *Los Angeles Times,* 23 July 1989, 1.

Brenner, M. "Erotomania." *Vanity Fair,* September 1991.

Corwin, M. "When the Law Can't Protect." *Los Angeles Times,* 8 May 1993, l.

Davis, P. "New Stalking Law Flushing the Crime into the Open in Virginia." *Washington Post,* 24 January 1993, B1.

Dougherty, S., Stambler, L., Schnaufer, J., and Donahue, B. "Material Witness." *People*, 15 January 1996, B1.

Eftimiades, M. "Leaving Town Alive." *People*, 17 May 1993.

Ellis, D. "Nowhere To Hide." *People*, 17 May 1993.

Goleman, D. "Dangerous Delusions: When Fans are a Threat." *The New York Times*, 31 October 1989, C6.

Gorman, J. "After Losing Case, Waller Calls for New Attention to Stalk Law." *Chicago Tribune*, 3 December 1992, 5.

Hays, S. "Stalking Fame." *Los Angeles Times*, 17 October 1990, E1.

Lait, M. "Skater Confronts Her Alleged Tormentor." *Los Angeles Times*, 12 March 1992, A3.

Lindsay, S. "Breast Surgery Ended Friendship, Man Says." *Rocky Mountain News*, 17 March 1995, 12A.

McNeil, D. "When Broadway's Lights go Down, Stalkers Appear." *The New York Times*, 23 April 1995, 37.

Miller, B. "Thou Shalt Not Stalk." *Chicago Tribune Magazine*, 18 April 1993.

O'Malley, S. "Nowhere To Hide: Why the New Stalking Laws Still Don't Protect Women." *Redbook*, November 1996.

Pearl, M. and Hoffmann, B. "Roberta Flack Stalker Goes Berserk in Court." *New York Post*, 23 November 1995, 7.

Puente, M. "Legislators Tackling the Terror of Stalking." *USA Today*, 21 July 1992, 9A.

Ratliff, R. "Computer Misuse Puts Snoopers into Private Lives." *Detroit Free Press*, 30 August 1992, 9.

Riley, J. "Wachtler Case: Is Insanity a Crazy Idea?" *Newsday*, 11 February 1993, 8.

Rubenstein, B. "The Stalker." *Chicago*, February 1992.

Simakis, A. "Why the Stalking Laws Aren't Working." *Glamour*, May 1996.

Staimer, M. "Low-Tech Problem Hits PC Networks." *USA Today*, 6 August 1993, B1.

Stanley, A. "Erotomania: A Rare Disorder Runs Riot—In Men's Minds." *New York Times*, 10 November 1991, sec. 4, 2.

Taylor, S. "Hinckley Hails 'Historical' Shooting to Win Love." *New York Times*, 9 July 1982, A10.

Thorpe, M. "In the Mind of a Stalker." *U.S. News & World Report*, 17 February 1992, 28.

Trebilcock, B. "I Love You to Death." *Redbook*, March 1992.

United Press International. "Lennons' Father is Slain on Coast." *The New York Times*, 13 August 1969, 48.

Weddle, A. "When Obsession Leads to Stalking." *Kansas City Star*, 11 April 1995, Teen Star, 4.

Resources for Victims

UNITED STATES

ATLANTA STALKING VICITIM ASSISTANCE
Director: Robyne Chastaine
P.O. Box 675251
Marietta, GA 30006
Provides information to victims on how to start their own community education or support group.

NATIONAL CRIMINAL JUSTICE
REFERENCE SERVICE
(800) 851-3420
P.O. Box 6000
Rockville, MD 20849-6000
Sponsored by the National Institute of Justice. Victims and others can order papers reporting various studies done under grants by the Institute on stalking, violence and domestic abuse.

NATIONAL DOMESTIC VIOLENCE
HOTLINE
(800) 799-7233
3616 Far West Blvd., Suite 101-297
Austin, TX 78731
A free, 24-hour hotline that provides victims with referrals to agencies in their own areas.

NATIONAL ORGANIZATION FOR VICTIM
ASSISTANCE (NOVA)
(800) 879-6682 or (202) 232-6682
P.O. Box 11000
Washington, DC 20009
A free, 24-hour hotline that provides information and referral for victims to resources in their own states.

NATIONAL VICTIM CENTER
(703) 276-2880
2111 Wilson Blvd., Suite 300
Arlington, VA 22201
Through Infolink, (800) FYI-CALL or (817) 877-3355. Victims and others may obtain information and referral on victim and crime-related issues. Open M-F: 9-5:30 ET.

SURVIVORS OF STALKING (SOS)
(813) 889-0767
P.O. Box 20762
Tampa, FL 33622
Web site: www.soshelp.org.
Gives workshops on stalking. Victims and others can order cassettes of these workshops that include information on stalking, laws, threat assessment, safety, and workplace violence. Keeps list of support groups for victims in various states and provides information, support, and referral for victims who call.

THREAT MANAGEMENT UNIT (TMU)
(213) 893-8339
Los Angeles Police Department
150 N. Los Angeles Street
Los Angeles, CA 90012

CANADA

BARBRA SCHILFER COMMEMORATIVE
CLINIC
(416) 323-9149
489 College Street,
Suite 503
Toronto, Ontario M6G 1A5
   Provides free legal, counseling, cultural
interpretation, and information and
referral services to women who are
survivors of violence.

CANADIAN RESOURCE CENTER FOR
VICTIMS OF CRIME
(613) 233-7614
141 Catherine Street, Suite 100
Ottawa, Ontario K2P 1C3
   Acts as a resource center for victims
of crime and assists victims and their
families in dealing with sentence
administration, parole authorities, and
securing legal counsel.

CAVEAT (CANADIANS AGAINST
VIOLENCE EVERYWHERE ADVOCATING
ITS TERMINATION)
(905) 632-1733
3350 Fairview Street, Suite 3-164
Burlington, Ontario L7N 3L5

CAVEAT B.C.
(604) 530-5829
21102-83rd Avenue
Langley, British Columbia V3A 6Y3

CAVEAT ALBERTA
(403) 464-9935
5642-33rd Avenue
Suite 300
Edmonton, Alberta T6L 6N2

LONDON FAMILY COURT CLINIC
(519) 679-7250
254 Pall Mall Street,
Suite 200
London, Ontario N6A 5P6
   A mental health clinic specializing in
the needs of children and families
involved in the justice system. Advocacy
includes assessment, counseling and
prevention services, research, and
training.

VICTIMS FOR JUSTICE
(519) 972-0836
P.O. Box 22023
3079 Forestglade Drive
Windsor, Ontario N8R 2H5
   An organization that provides a
research library of stalking incidents in
Canada as well as handouts on "How
to Survive a Stalker" and "How to
Safeguard Yourself."

UNITED KINGDOM

NATIONAL ANTI-STALKING AND
HARASSMENT CAMPAIGN AND
SUPPORT ASSOCIATION
Tel: 011-44-1926-850089
Fax: 011-44-1926-850089.
Director: Evonne von Heussen-
Countryman
Bath Place Community Venture,
Bath Place,
Leamington Spa,
CV31 3AQ, England.

index

erotomanics, 15, 19–20
  anger toward third parties, 203–5
  defenses against, 23, 35, 59, 61, 99–120
  delusions of, 33, 34, 36, 46–48, 52–53,
      54, 58, 64–67, 69, 71–74, 76, 112,
      126–27, 145–48, 202, 207–8
  and distortion of truth, 71
  and drug use, 199–200
  effects of media on, 93
  effects on victims, 22–23, 24, 31, 32,
      35–37, 38, 39, 54, 58, 65, 70, 75,
      101–103, 112–14, 115, 117–18,
      129, 133–39, 144, 174–78, 237–38,
      244, 250–52, 275, 281–88
  families of, 42–45, 67–68, 125–26, 146,
      148, 187, 190, 195, 196, 250,
      258–62
  incompleteness, feelings of, 66
  intervention with, 216–18
  intimacy and, 50–51, 54, 70
  legal system and, 125–55, 160–192,
      216–20, 249–76, 277–88
  letters from, 35–38, 53, 57, 75, 76,
      99–100, 102, 112, 175, 210–11, 220
  literature on, 81–96, 132, 135, 136,
      270–71
  media treatment of, 273–74
  objects of, 63–66, 75, 124
  persistence of, 115, 125, 135, 141, 161,
      174–177, 197, 200, 220, 254–55,
      267–68
  phone calls from, 57, 103, 112, 125,
      159, 161, 173, 175, 249
  police response to, 107, 111–12,
      123–25, 142, 149, 160–192, 214,
      218, 249, 252
  progression of obsession, 205–6
  and rape, 209–10
  sex of, 72
  surveillance by, 117–18
  threats from, 20, 37, 57, 120, 141, 168,
      173, 201
  violence and, 20–21, 28–29, 60, 61, 72,
      99, 105–7, 127, 129, 141, 142, 144,
      164, 165, 174, 177, 198–99,
      201–223, 266
Esquirol, Jean Etienne, 83
Evans, Andrea, 150, 151

F
Farley, Richard (stalker), 229, 230, 233
Fein, Dr. Robert, 200–01, 210, 213,
      241, 269
Ferrand, Jacques, 81–82
Flack, Roberta, 90
Freud, Sigmund, 89
furor amoris, 81–96
furor uterinus, 82

G
Gaub, Jerome, 82–83
Gifford, Kathie Lee, 60, 63, 74
Gless, Sharon, 60, 61
Goodale, Renee, 143, 154

H
Hammell, Dr. Bonita, 137–38
harassment, legal definition of, 105
Hill, Anita, 60
Hinckley, John, Jr. (stalker), 67, 72, 90,
      198, 216
Hoskins, Robert (stalker), 205, 264, 265

I
*I Can Make You Love Me: The Stalking
      of Laura Black,* 230
intermittent reinforcement, 143

J
Jackson, Arthur (stalker), 69, 203, 216, 268

K
Kübler-Ross, Elisabeth, 133, 134

L
la belle indifférence, 146–47
Lane, Lt. John, 196